IT STARTED AT
THE SAVOY

A memoir about family, celebrities and the highlights from a

52-year career in hotel management

by

Bill Pullen

The information in this book is accurate to the best of my knowledge.

It was written from memory and from what records I had available to me. The conversations all come from my recollections, though they are not written to represent word-for-word transcripts. Rather, I have retold them in a way that evokes the feeling and meaning of what was said and in all instances, the essence of the dialogue is accurate.

Cover design by Bob Hurley
Interior design and layout by Linda Hurley
Author's jacket portrait by Maria Barry

ISBN 9781542992060

Available for purchase on Amazon.com

A portion of the profit from the sale of this book will be donated to the Joseph Neary Memorial Foundation (see Chapter 16).

I dedicate this book to my dear wife, Anita, who was my wonderful companion and friend for 50 years, two months and three weeks. She is so largely responsible for the warm and loving family she left behind. How she put up with a hotel man in this crazy, time-consuming business, I'll never know. Thank you so much, my love. May we meet again and may you rest in peace.

Contents

Foreword

What do you mean, you want to be a hotel manager?

The Goring, a 5-star luxury hotel located just behind Buckingham Palace, is one of London's finest but lesser known exclusive establishments. It has remained a family-run business, now under the management of the fourth generation of the Gorings. O. G. Goring, son of the original developer, wrote a book in 1960 titled "50 Years of Service"; commemorating the hotel's first 50 years. In the foreword, he quoted Sinclair Lewis' "Work of Art" (published in 1934), which explores service and being helpful to others through the eyes of a hotel manager. I do not think there could be any better description of a hotel manager's responsibilities.

"You will have to learn manners, learn to be poker-faced with people that would take advantage of you. You will have to know all about china and silver, glass, linen, brocades and the best woods for flooring and furniture.

A hotel manager has to be a combination of a hausfrau; a chef; a bar-room bouncer; a doctor for emergencies; a wet-nurse; a lawyer that knows more about the rights and wrongs of guests and how far he dare go than old man Supreme Court himself; an upholsterer; a walking directory that knows off-hand without looking it up just where the Hardshell Baptist Church is, what time the marriage license bureau opens, and what time the local starts for Hick Junction.

He's got to be a certified accountant; a professor of languages; a quick-action laundry man; a plumber; a heating engineer; a carpenter; a swell speech-maker; an authority on the importance of every tinhorn state Senator or one-night-stand lecturer that blows in and expects to have the red carpet already hauled out for him; a fly cop that can tell from looking at a girl's ears whether she's married to the guy or not; a money-lender, only he doesn't get any interest or have any security.

He's got to be dressed better than a Twenty-Third Street actor, even if he has nothing in his pocket. He's got to be able, just from hearing a cow's moo, to tell whether she will make good steaks.

He's got to know more about wine and cigars than the fellas that make them. They can fool around and try experiments, but he's got to sell them.

All the time he's got to be a diplomat that would make Thomas Beyard look like John L. Sullivan on a spree. He's got to set a table like a Vanderbilt, yet watch the pennies like an Arab pedlar.

If you can do all this, you'll have a good time. Go to it."

Enjoy!

Note: Sinclair Lewis was awarded the 1930 Nobel Prize for Literature for his vigorous and graphic art of description and his ability to create, with wit and humor, new types of characters.

Acknowledgments

This book was written primarily for the benefit of my immediate family and their heirs. However, I am also mindful that young people considering a career in the hotel business might find this interesting from the standpoint of someone who has been there, and to compare this with their expectations.

As with any project like this, it could not be completed without help, guidance and encouragement from many people and I would like to thank the following.

The late **S. Joseph Tankoos, Jr.**, to whom I am indebted for almost this entire book. Had we not met in Paris in 1959, my life would never have included these priceless experiences. I will be eternally grateful to him for the faith and confidence he had in me (see Chapter 2).

Kathy and Jerry Vanderhoof, dear friends who first suggested that I should do this and who essentially started me off on this journey.

Mary Ann Revell, a retired English professor and instructor for the *"Write Your Life"* and *"Publishing Options"* classes at The Villages Lifelong Learning College and the Lake Sumter State College in Leesburg who went out of her way to help and encourage me. Her detailed grading of my manuscript could not have been any better had it been part of my finals! (That single '!' is for her.)

Linda Hurley, for her professional editing and detailed research without whom I could not have completed this project. Her help and guidance far exceeded my expectations.

Bob Hurley, for his artistic cover design and restoration of photographs throughout the book.

Maria Barry, for her friendship and her great gift of my portrait on the back cover. She has amazing artistic skills and so deserves all her wonderful successes. (see www.mariabarryart.com)

Asli Tasci, Ph.D., Assistant Professor at the Rosen College of Hospitality Management for her suggestion to include 'teaching moments' in the book. These have been incorporated at the beginning of each chapter as 'Keys to Success'.

My brother **Jim**, who instead of laughing at me for doing this, treated it with interest and respect.

My daughters **Wendy (Richter)** and **Diana (Harvey)** for their critical and helpful insight and for not just saying "Oh, Papa, this is great." In fact, I think Wendy was the most thorough reader of my early drafts and gave me excellent suggestions and changes. This forced me to learn many frustrating computer editing tools. (Maybe now I wish she <u>had</u> just said "Oh, Papa, this is great.")

Margaret Larkin, who co-ordinates the activities of the Westminster College Hotel School Old Students Association, for referring my manuscript to Ron Kinton for his critical review.

Ron Kinton for volunteering to take the time to read the draft manuscript and to give me his comments. Ron, like me, is an "old" Old Student.

O. G. Goring for giving me his newly published book *"50 Years of Service"* in 1960 when I was working at The Bull Hotel in Wrotham. I would not have known otherwise of Sinclair Lewis' priceless description of a hotel manager's responsibilities, which I have also used in this Foreword.

Walter and Ed Smyth who came to School House from America when their father worked for the U.S. military in England. They sent me the photographs of our temporary 'prison' at No. 1, Warwick Avenue in Bedford and the indoor 'plumbing' of 'B' Dorm.

Millard Johnson and the Writers of the Villages group for their help and guidance. They kindly educated me in some of the basic skills of writing and taught me that once you have a 'final' manuscript, you can literally spend the rest of your life editing it.

And, finally, to my dear friend, the late **David Ward**, with whom I shared so many happy memories for over 50 years, going back to our training days at The Savoy. Many of these occasions occurred at various venues around the world including London, Paris, New York, Jerusalem, Venice, Arizona, the Bahamas and others, some of which are included in this book. Had he written a book about his fabulous and unique career, it would have dwarfed this one. Rest in peace my friend. Thank you for all the laughs and happy times we shared. You enriched my life.

This book is the first project of its kind that I have undertaken and I am reminded of a saying attributed to my hero, Winston Churchill.

"Writing a book is an adventure. To begin with it is a toy and an amusement. Then it becomes a mistress, then it becomes a master, then it becomes a tyrant. The last phase is that just as you are about to be reconciled to your servitude, you kill the monster and fling him to the public."

Sir Winston Churchill

I can now relate to that.

Key to Success #1

Inquire: *Be honest. If you don't know, ask. Don't try to fake it; it will show.*

1. The Early Years (1936-1957)

I was born in the early morning hours of September 11, 1936 to my parents Len and Dorothy Pullen. I was their second son, my brother Jim being five years older. Our family lived above Woollens, the shop we owned in Hayes near West Wickham, Kent, just south of London. My Uncle Bill, my father's elder brother, had three unrelated shops selling ladies' wear called *Four Price Store*, literally meaning everything was priced one of four prices. One of these shops was in High Wycombe and my father subsequently moved us there to go into this business, initially with my Uncle Bill. We lived at 155 London Road near the cricket ground and the tennis club east of the town center.

The Second World War started in 1939 and at the time of the German blitz on London, for safety reasons, children were evacuated to homes in more rural areas of the country. My paternal grandparents also lived in High Wycombe (Buckinghamshire) about 30 miles west of London and, rather than both families having to take children into our homes, our family moved in with them at 166 West Wycombe Road just a little west of the main town. My Aunt Gladys, who had never married, lived there also. My father then ran the shop in High Wycombe, which was located on the corner of White Hart Street and Pauls Row, across from Guildhall. My father was, eventually,

My mother in front of Woollens

Me (left) with my mother, father, brother Jim and our
boxer Punch on the beach at Middleton on the south coast

called up by the Royal Air Force (RAF) as a fitter armorer; working primarily on the Browning gun, which was mounted on our planes. My mother ran the shop during the war years.

Jim went off to Westbury Manor, a boarding school near Brackley, and in 1941, I went to Crown House Preparatory School in High Wycombe where I have some of my earliest memories. I especially remember Mrs. Cubbage. the head mistress, and a Miss Taylor, a much younger teacher. My first 'crush' was on a girl named Beryl Clark. One of my favorite memories was when we accidentally took each other's raincoats home. She and her mother came to our home to sort them out. I didn't do it on purpose, but had I thought about it, I would have.

In those rather grim years, we had food rationing, and I remember a distribution of chocolate powder for making hot chocolate drinks from the people of Canada that was given to all school children. It was a special treat. The school was in a small, almost industrial area between Newlands car park and the gas works. Since there was not much need for car parks in those days, as few people could use cars, the local authorities built numerous small air raid shelters all over it.

During breaks from school, I would go up nearby Tom Burts Hill to play. It was behind the school and gas works and past Loakes Park, the Wycombe Wanderers football (soccer) field. The field had a great home team advantage as it had a renowned side-to-side slope.

It was during these times I smoked my first cigarette, probably a Woodbines. It was just a 'puff and blow' ritual and I am glad now I never took it up as a habit. My dad smoked quite heavily, which ultimately was a factor in his early death at the age of 56. My mother smoked a little during the war years but never kept it up.

Living in a relatively rural area of England, even though we were only 30 miles from London, I was not fully aware of the gravity of what was going on around us. This was brought home to me when we visited my maternal grandparents in Croydon, just south of London. Croydon had a large aerodrome and during the Battle of Britain, there was a lot going on in the skies above their house at 19 Ridgemount Avenue. My Grandpa Faulkner, a veteran of World War I, and Little Granny, as we lovingly called her, had an air raid shelter under their kitchen table and I remember being there when the siren sounded. Instead of using the shelter, my grandfather got a lawn chair out and sat in his garden. He said that if he was going to be killed by a bomb, he would rather "see it coming".

After moving in with my paternal grandparents and Aunt Gladys, we lived there during the rest of the war years. It was quite a big semi-detached house. I remember the air raid warnings and the coarse grinding sound of the German V1 rockets, we called 'doodle bugs.' Being away from London, we did not get many of these but I remember one Saturday night when the engines cut out on one and we hunkered down waiting for the explosion. One never knew if they would drop like a stone or perhaps glide on for several more miles. This one glided on for some minutes before we heard the explosion. The following day we went to see where it had landed in a wooded area near Downley, a nearby village. The trees had been progressively stripped of their branches then there were just stumps, and finally a big crater. Thankfully, no one had been hurt.

Then there was the nighttime fire, caused by an incendiary bomb, that gutted Hands Furniture factory on Desborough Road. Our house was slightly uphill from the location and, looking down out of my bedroom window, I was in a perfect position to see it when the roof fell in. Sparks shot up into the night sky like a huge firework display.

In those days, my Aunt Gladys was practically my surrogate mother, while my mother was busy taking care of the shop. She would often take me on long walks, sometimes to the nearby park where I would fish for tadpoles and minnows. I used to put the tadpoles in a large old crock pot and I could never understand what happened to them after they grew up to be frogs. We would travel by bus into High Wycombe where we would go to the Rye, a large flat sports park with a children's playground. It was located on a beautiful part of the River Wye where one could take out a punt or a rowing boat. Those were happy times even though we were in a major war.

A factory in High Wycombe, Broom and Wade, was converted to manufacture military equipment. The need for metal was so great, iron railings that were on walls outside people's homes and front gardens were removed and replaced with a curved cement top. Even today, you can still see some of these the way they were left.

One winter's morning a double-decker bus on its way to High Wycombe pulled up to the bus stop just outside our house and skidded on the icy road. It slid across to the other side, hit the curb and nearly toppled over. Fortunately, it righted itself but the passengers on board must have been scared out of their wits.

Grandpa Pullen had a Humber car in the garage at 166. Because petrol was so scarce during the war it was never used, but I recall the wonderful smell of it. I don't know if it was the petrol or the leather but I knew it smelled good. We had a large productive garden with a green house and Grandpa Pullen was an enthusiastic gardener. There were apple, plum, damson and cherry trees and all kinds of vegetables (potatoes, cabbages, Brussels sprouts, carrots, beetroot, peas and string beans) with tomatoes and cucumbers in the greenhouse. I can still see him standing looking out of his shed on a rainy day, puffing on his favorite pipe and anxiously watching his bonfire in the fire pit. One minute it looked like the fire was out and the next a flame shot out of nowhere and things were going along just fine! At the top of the garden was a beautiful tennis lawn with a summerhouse, used for storage, built into the earthen bank which separated the property from the railway lines.

The lawn was not set up for tennis but a part of it was set aside for a chicken coop and run so that we could have fresh eggs during the war years. One time, when my father was home on leave, he asked me to go with him to Speen, a small village outside High Wycombe, to pick up some Rhode Island Reds from a farm. On our way home, we had to take two busses, one from Speen into High Wycombe and then another to go home to 166. We had the chickens in a big sack and it was quite an adventure carrying them on the two-bus journey. My dad had a difficult time trying to control them as they struggled to get free. Once we got them home, he put them in the new hen house and hoped they would start doing what they were supposed to do. Between the fruit and vegetable production from our garden and the chickens, my family did a lot to help feed ourselves during the war. We would lay the freshly picked apples on newspapers on the floor of the attic so that they were not touching each other. They seemed to last well like this, particularly during the cold winter months, and we could enjoy them all winter.

After the war, we moved quite a few times, first to 292 Rutland Avenue in Booker, then to 50 Rectory Avenue in High Wycombe off Amersham Hill, then "Woodlawn", Fennels Way in Flackwell

Heath and finally to "Greenacres" on Links Road, also in Flackwell Heath. This house looked out onto the Flackwell Heath golf course. When my father passed away in 1958, my mother moved to a smaller house, "Winthorpe," on Sedgmore Road, also in Flackwell Heath and subsequently to 1 Haw Lane in Bledlow Ridge so that she could be closer to my brother Jim and his wife, Anne. Prior to her passing away on January 27, 1986 from a heart attack, she had moved to a cute little upstairs apartment in Princes Risborough close to our shop Pullens Ladies' Wear, which Jim was running.

****

In the summer of 1946, a few months before I turned 10, I went away to Bedford Modern School as a boarder in School House at No. 1, Warwick Avenue in Bedford. It is worth mentioning that one of the first significant events that happened was when we were all presented with a letter, dated 8 June 1946, signed by King George VI, with the royal crest in color, celebrating the Allied victory. It read:

"Today, as we celebrate victory, I send this personal message to you and all other boys and girls at school. For you have shared in the hardships and dangers of a total war and you have shared no less in the triumph of the Allied Nations.

I know you will always feel proud to belong to a country, which was capable of such supreme effort; proud, too, of parents and elder brothers and sisters who by their courage, endurance and enterprise brought victory. May these qualities be yours as you grow up and join in the common effort to establish among the nations of the world unity and peace."

This went to every schoolboy and schoolgirl in the country. I am sure I appreciate it even more today than I did at the time and it still hangs proudly on a wall in my home.

School House was under the care and direction of one of the school's primary math teachers, Billy Belcher and his wife. Jim was already there, as a more senior boy, and it was nice for me to have his support. At that age, it was quite a challenge to be away from home and, while I did have some home sickness it was not nearly as bad as it would have been had he not been there.

I started out in Junior Dorm, a room with six other boys. Things settled down after I had survived the normal rite of passage of being locked in what we called "the oracle" for the night. This was just a small space at the bottom of a free-standing cupboard used for hanging our clothes with a bottom section under a shelf for shoes. Obviously, being the new boy, I was quite nervous. Luckily, I found out that the shelf was loose, sitting on supports on each side. Once I was sure the others had gone to sleep, I pushed it up, and with the aid of a wire coat hanger, I slipped the simple latch to open the door and crept back into bed. They had all gone through this routine previously, so I don't think they were surprised to see me sleeping soundly in my bed in the morning.

One of the more adventurous activities was the 'midnight dorm feast'. We all had 'tuck boxes' in which we kept the goodies sent from home, plus anything else we bought with our meager weekly, one shilling pocket money. The idea was to sneak these items up to the dormitory, where food was not allowed, and take turns staying awake to stand guard. Then, around midnight, we would be aroused by the one 'on duty' and start gorging ourselves. Unfortunately, the house matron's room was next to the dorm, and one evening our commotion and loud voices woke her up. She came storming in to see our room in utter shambles and angrily declared, "I am going to call Mr. Belcher. Don't touch a thing!"

Bedford Modern School

B Dorm

*School House
1 Warwick Avenue,
the roof of our escapade is
in the center, far left*

We looked around and figured we could just clean up a little bit. So, by the time he showed up in his dressing gown, it really didn't look too bad. She was standing behind him, just fuming, especially when he said something to the effect, "Well matron, I have seen things worse than this. Now go back to bed boys and be quiet. Good night!" I don't think she ever forgave us.

At the start of the following school year, we got *promoted* to 'C' Dorm. Mr. Belcher was not quite so understanding when, early one sunny, summer, Sunday morning during his stroll up Warwick Avenue, he happened to glance up at the three-story house. There he saw some of the boys in his charge, still clad in their pajamas, straddling a peaked roof protruding from the double windows of the dorm. He just did not seem to understand that to be a true 'C' Dormer one had to straddle the peak of this loose tiled A-framed roof, ease oneself out carefully to the end, touch the brick chimney, then turn around (a bit tricky this) and retreat to the room. I really can't say that I remember exactly what he said but I do remember how mad he was. I am not sure if this tradition was ever continued.

Looking back now, what we endured during those days seems like something from the Victorian days. We were assigned two 15-minute baths a week, whether we needed them or not, and our daily morning washing routine was from a jug of cold water sitting in a chipped enamel bowl on a small chest of drawers. During the winter months, it was not unusual to have a thin film of ice on top of the water in the jug waiting to attack us and wake us up!

At the end of each school year, we would have a carefully scripted parade of boys going out into the garden of the house to shake our blankets. Two boys, each holding one end of the blanket, would put their hands together over their heads and pull down and out several times. Who knows if they were *ever* cleaned properly.

Meal times were also interesting. We had "big" table for the senior boys, "end" table for the junior boys, "side" table for the boys who were at the "end" table last year and "middle" table for those hoping to graduate to "big" table next year. Mr. Belcher always sat at the head of "big" table. Someone was always assigned to say grace. One time, after many of us chipped in our pennies, we bribed a boy to slightly alter the required "For what we *are about* to receive, may the Lord make us truly thankful" to "For what we *would like* to receive, may the Lord make us truly thankful." I think at first, he wondered whether it was worth his punishment but afterwards he was "chuffed" to have the extra funds, which went along with his elevated status in the community.

The punishment we received would be considered abuse today and the perpetrator would be subject to jail time. Certain senior boys, both in the main school and in the boarding house, were given disciplinary responsibility as "monitors" and had broad discretionary powers. Punishment consisted of caning on the behind from a minimum of two strokes for minor offenses, up to a maximum of six. The head of our house and the next two most senior boys occupied a study appropriately named The Bridge. If one was summoned to The Bridge, nine times out of ten, a very sore bottom was the outcome. Protective padding, such as a writing pad, thin book, extra underwear or something similar, always resulted in two more strokes above the assigned punishment. One of the canes had been wrapped with insulated electrical tape, which left its signature behind to jog one's memory before any future misbehaving. It was not unusual for the caning to draw blood.

Our school days always started with a full assembly in the impressive main hall with the head master, the Rev. J. E. Taylor, conducting a brief morning prayer service and making general announcements. This required total silence. One such morning, the boy sitting to my left uttered something under his breath and as I turned toward him to hear what he was saying, a booming voice from the stage yelled "Stand up, boy." The headmaster was looking in our direction and everyone around us glanced at one another, still sitting, until I finally looked at the headmaster with a question, "Me?" "Yes, you boy. Come and see me afterwards". Why me? I hadn't uttered a word. I forget now how many strokes of the cane I was given but I was thrilled to actually see his office. Returning to my class, I was the center of attention and a mini hero. Regrettably my newly acquired status was only fleeting.

The school comprised six Houses; North, South, East, West, County and United Boarders (there were three separate boarding houses) and there were many intramural competitions both in sports and other activities. In the United Boarders House, we were always encouraged to participate in everything. One reason was because we were away from home and the activities would be interesting and time consuming. The other reason was because our numbers were smaller than the other houses and we needed more participation to be competitive. Every year there was a school play competition and I am sure I was signed up for it whether I wanted to take part or not. In December 1951, United Boarders made the finals; one of three. It was a play by Lord Dunsany called "The Golden Doom" and the action took place outside the King's great door some time before the fall of Babylon. I was given the role of second spy, which, thankfully, was not a speaking part. I only had a few minutes on stage and I was completely covered in a dark robe or cape. My big moment came when I entered stage right in a crouched position with my right arm bent over my forehead exactly as any good second spy would do. Everything had gone perfectly during rehearsals, and there was no reason to think this would be any different. I was beginning to think about Broadway and the West End being a part of my future. All I had to do was go across the stage in an elaborate spy-like manner, as I had been directed. However, about center stage I realized I was doing such a good job in my crouching that I was walking up the inside of my cape. It got better and better and I got bent lower and lower until I finally fell over completely and made an inauspicious exit stage left. I can't remember the results but I'm pretty sure we didn't win.

I graduated from Bedford Modern (High) School in the summer of 1953 after seven years and, having selected a potential career path, entered Westminster College in London to study at their renowned hotel school. I had entertained the idea of being a sports journalist but was dissuaded by my father after he had done some research and felt so few reach the top in that field. The notion of a career in the hotel industry came after a recommendation from John Boon, a good friend of his in our hometown.

Boon had an interesting background. He had served in the RAF and during an air raid over Germany, his plane was shot down and he was captured. He was interned in Stalag-Luft III prisoner-of-war camp which became well known for "The Wooden Horse" escape. Later this became a bestselling book by Eric Williams and then a popular movie.

Boon served on the prisoner's escape committee. The plan involved a wooden vaulting horse, which would be carried out onto the main open recreation area in the compound and used by the prisoners for exercise. Inside the vaulting horse were two of the prisoners who, little by little, dug a tunnel from which three of the internees ultimately escaped. Boon, being on the committee, was not permitted to try to get out but the event prompted a complete shake up of the camp.

He was sent off to another prison camp from which he did manage to break out. He found his way to Switzerland where he joined the Swiss underground for the duration of the war, assisting in the repatriation of other escapees. During this time, he met a Monsieur Hans Bonn and, because of the similarity of their names, they bonded. Bonn was a prominent hotelier in Switzerland and, after the war, became general manager of the Suvretta House Hotel in St. Moritz, one of the premier resorts in the country. He offered John Boon a position, which gave him experience in a first-class hotel operation.

It was John who recommended that, if the hotel business was going to be my chosen profession, I should go for the top by seeking an entry-level position at The Savoy Hotel in London. This was considered the finest hotel in the country. Following his advice, my father wrote to the general manager, W.A. 'Willy' Hofflin, to see if this might be possible. Hofflin responded promptly and explained that the hotel did not have a trainee program but, if I was serious about following this career path, I should go to a prominent hotel school first. He recommended The Westminster Technical College in Vincent Square, near Victoria Street.

In those days, England still had National Service, or the draft, which required two years of mandatory military service following high school graduation. One could apply for deferment if doing advanced studies and this is what I did. Thus, in September 1953, I entered the Hotel Operations course at Westminster Technical College, a two-year program in comprehensive hotel administration, which included housekeeping, maintenance,

French, and restaurant and kitchen operations. The college had an excellent public restaurant, open during the times classes were in session, where, for the grand sum of three shillings and six pence (about 52 cents), you could sample some excellent classic French cuisine. The meals were prepared by second year students under the watchful eye of M. Jean Vincent, the head chef instructor, along with a cadre of other highly qualified instructors. The servers were also second year students assisted by first year students like my class.

In January 1954, I started my second term, and our class was assigned to food preparation. It was here that events helped determine my future career path. Our job was to prepare the daily meals for the student cafeteria and our instructor was Chef Spreadbury. He was a rather serious little man, and it didn't take long for me to figure out *why* he was so serious. I don't think teaching freshman students was his first choice!

My assignment that first day was *Cabillaud Dugléré,* French for poached cod with a white wine sauce. He started me out with directions on how to make a *fumet de poisson* (fish stock) in which to poach the cod. Taking a huge copper pot, he had me put in a pile of fish bones, whole onions with cloves stuck in them and other ingredients. I then added a lot of water, put it on the stove and brought it to a boil. In the meantime, he was parading around assisting my sixteen classmates with their various tasks. After a while he returned to me, peered into the pot, and said "Okay, son. Now strain that off." As he headed off to check on the others, I glanced over the range where a few kitchen utensils hung, including something that looked like it would do the job. I soon learned it was a conical strainer. Taking the heavy pot in my right hand and putting the end of the handle under my right arm for support, I headed over to the nearest sink and proceeded to do as he had directed, namely to strain it off. Having achieved this and not knowing what to do with the bones and other ingredients in the strainer, I dumped them back into the now empty pot. I then returned happily to my station thinking I had followed his orders to the letter. I soon found out that assumption was in error. He returned to me and said, "Okay, son. Now where is your *fumet*?"

"I strained it off, chef", I proudly replied.

"Yes son, I know, but *where* is it?"

"Down the sink!" was apparently not the answer he wanted to hear. The memory of the rest of that morning is conveniently vague at this point and I do not remember if the cafeteria ever saw any *Cabillaud Duglére* that day or not. As you might imagine, along with tackling issues caused by the rest of our freshman class that first day, Chef Spreadbury was not a happy man.

That incident was not the only 'success' I had that term. Our pastry instruction always took place in the afternoons under a talented pastry chef, Emile Lefebvre. I felt this aspect of cooking was a little easier, as everything required specific measurements, and it was much easier to avoid making a mistake. Well, I soon found out, that was not necessarily true. My assignment that day was cream horns. After preparing the pastry per the recipe, I rolled it out, cut it into strips and folded them around small, metal, ice cream cone-shaped molds. I then put them neatly onto baking trays, basted them with egg wash, and put the trays in the oven. What could go wrong? After the required baking time, Chef Lefebvre had me remove them from the oven and put the trays on metal triangles to allow the pastry to cool so the molds could be gently removed.

I thought, *maybe I am suited for this job after all* and I think I probably had a satisfied smirk on my face. This seemed to be confirmed when he looked at my array of cream horns, called out to the rest of the class to come over to my prep table and to bring their notebooks! *Finally, I have found my niche!* Unfortunately, that was not the case. He had everyone open their notebooks and said, "Now I am going to give you the recipe for cake crumbs". He took both hands, ran them through the cream horns and, rubbing his hands together, created a pile of cake crumbs in the middle of each baking tray. At this point we were close to recess and, as if this wasn't humiliating enough, I had to stay behind and do it all over again. The worst thing about it was that I *still* don't know what I did wrong! I think my instructors probably concluded Pullen was more suited for front of the house assignments.

Despite my tongue-in-cheek descriptions above, I really enjoyed all the classes in which we were enrolled. I found it fascinating learning about wines, proper restaurant service, correct and efficient housekeeping procedures, essential mechanical and maintenance requirements along with my three-month internships at both the Metropole Hotel in Brighton, on the south coast of England, and at The Savoy Hotel in London.

Despite some of my early blunders in the kitchen, upon graduating, Doug Lee, the principal, wrote on my class report "No. 1 at last." At the end of each term, I had usually been one of those in the top tier, but only in the end, did I finally make it to the top of my class. I was now clear in my vision for my future.

I wanted to be in the hotel business.

****

It was about this time that I had my one and only brush with the law. Going to London by train every day to attend my hotel operations classes, I got to know all the gate personnel both at Marylebone Station and on the London Underground. When my annual pass reached its expiration date, I failed to renew it and just continued to flash it as I went past the attendants. One day, coming out of the Underground at the St. James Park station near the college, there were different attendants on duty and, after flying past the gate, I heard "Come back here, sonny." Of course, when they looked at my pass, I was in trouble. A few weeks passed and I received a notice to appear at Bow Street Magistrates Court in London for a hearing. This is a most intimidating venue, even for seasoned adults, and I was more apprehensive about the impending proceedings when I recognized the London Transport station attendants, who had stopped me, at the opposite end of the courtroom. My father, although quite mad at me, attended the hearing at which the judge, after reviewing my infraction, assigned a fine. When asked, "Can you pay now, son?" my dad forked over the cash. We caught the train back home barely talking to one another. I can still feel the pain in my stomach as I recall this part of my youth. The Bow Street Magistrates Court was often featured in high profile cases and if there was any good news in all of this, it was the opportunity to see the inside of this legendary courtroom.

Boys will be boys.

****

When we were living at Woodlawn on Fennels Way, during the time I was in hotel school, my parents took a holiday on the island of Majorca in the Mediterranean. My father had asthma and had been in poor health for several years. He had great difficulty in walking due to shortness of breath. They decided to come home early and had sent us a telegram to pick them up upon their arrival at London's Heathrow Airport. However, we did not receive the telegram before they left Majorca so, when they arrived, Jim and I were at a tiny pub not far from home. Assuming we knew of their return, they were afraid we might have had an accident or that we had some other problem. We returned to the house and retired for the evening, totally unaware that they were waiting for us at the airport, where my poor mother was totally stressed due to my dad not being well and worrying and wondering what could have happened to us. Around two o'clock in the morning, we were awakened by them coming into the house, after a long taxi ride from Heathrow. There were many tears as we each explained our side of what had happened. The telegram finally came the next day. It was all quite traumatic.

****

In September 1955, when I had just turned 19, I began my mandatory two years of National Service. The first step was to report to a recruiting location and choose my preferred branch of service. As both my father and my brother had served in the RAF, this was my first choice. However, when I asked if I could get an assignment in the food service area, so that at least I could get experience in my chosen profession, I was advised that my level of education was too advanced for that. They would put me in a department for which they thought I was better suited; such as radar. And this was without them even knowing about my food prep skills at college!

I then chose to see what the Army would offer. Here I was met with a more positive reaction to my request; other than to be warned that when the recruiters met with candidates who could barely read or write, they put them into the Army Catering Corps. Notwithstanding that warning, I signed up.

Anyone who has served in any branch of the military, either in the U.S. or in the U.K., knows full well that basic training is not fun. My introduction to military life was no different. It took place in the town of Aldershot, south of London where there were many barracks representing several regiments. At that time, new recruits came in to Aldershot for basic training every two weeks. There used to be a joke saying, "I escaped three times during the war!" to which one would invariably get the question "Where from?" The answer would be "Aldershot."

After the obligatory ten-second haircut, new members of our squad were marched off to Ramillies Barracks to get set up around our assigned bunks. We were introduced to the sergeant and corporal who would be "taking care of us". Sergeant Bill Gregory evidently wanted to make a strong first impression – which he did! He was a little chap with a thin waist but what he lacked in size, he more than made up for with his voice, which was coarse, loud and high pitched. One could literally hear him a mile away across many parade grounds. I won't bore you with the gory details of basic training other than to say that, despite the rigors, there developed a squad and sergeant bonding after a while. I could imitate him pretty well and one day I walked in to the building and shouted, ***"Stand by your beds"*** in his voice. Everyone jumped up and stood to attention. I have never been received in this manner since. As the weeks went by and we suffered through all the marching, drilling, cleaning, weapons instruction and so forth, we came to the time when we would be moving on to whatever assignments we were given. I wrote a poem entitled "Ode to Greg" in honor of Sergeant Gregory, focusing on several of his characteristics, idiosyncrasies, and his oft-barked commands. (I have included this in Appendix II just for posterity.). I am sure the reader will conclude from this remarkable piece of original poetry, it was just as well I did not go into sports journalism.

After basic training, we were now ready for our assignments. Our squad was fortunate in that we were not one of the alternate squads being shipped off to the Christmas Islands in the Pacific where the Army was doing nuclear testing. We were given assignments in the U.K. I was assigned to the Officers Mess at Ranby Camp in Nottinghamshire, which was a Royal Army Service Corps (RASC) tank transporter unit. I and another fellow, Corporal Wood, were the two cooks responsible for taking care of the kitchen.

This was at a time when the British military were involved with issues in the Suez Canal Zone. Often, sand-colored military transport vehicles, carrying tanks and other equipment to be shipped to the Canal Zone, passed through on their way to the London docks. I well remember one quiet Sunday morning when I answered the telephone in the mess, as there was no one else around. It was an NCO from our camp calling for our commanding officer to advise him that a tank had slipped its chains while being loaded on to a ship and was now sitting partially submerged in the River Thames. I called Major Wilton to the phone and it was fascinating listening to only his half of the conversation. Naturally, he seemed a little concerned, but when I heard him exclaim "What do you mean man – *only* one?" it was obvious the person on the other end didn't have quite the same perspective on the problem. The following day a photograph of the tank was published in one of the national newspapers.

I had not been there long when Major Wilton's daughter caught my eye. She was rather cute and I got up the courage to ask her out on a date. To my amazement, she agreed and we arranged to meet in town outside a well-known national chain store called the Fifty Shilling Tailors. Ranby Camp was situated in a rather bleak moor-like area almost half way between the two nearest towns, Retford and Worksop. Busses frequently ran between the two with a stop at the camp. Being quite excited about a possible impending romance, I arrived in Worksop in plenty of time and I waited – and I waited – and I waited until I finally gave up and hopped on a bus back to the camp. Just my luck. Upon seeing her pass by the mess the following day, I ran out to ask what had happened only to find out that she had the same experience, only she was outside the Fifty Shilling Tailors in Retford while I was in Worksop. Needless to say, that was as far as the romance went.

Working this job at the camp had its rewards. We were never required for any special drills or workouts and, other than going over to the commissary for food and supplies, we never had to be on the main base at all. One day we had some visiting 'brass' come to the mess among whom was Major General Ralph Younger of the Younger's Scotch Ales family, a well-known family-owned Edinburgh, Scotland brewery. General Younger was the officer commanding the North Midland District based in Nottingham. He and his family lived in the village of Cuckney, half way between Worksop and Mansfield. This was a beautiful little village surrounded by the Duke of Portland's property with nothing to offer but a simple crossroads intersection, a co-op general store and the local pub, the Greendale Oak. Not even a traffic light.

The general needed a new chef for his residence since the one he had was being discharged at the end of his two years' service. It was quite fortunate for me that he never got sick from anything he ate at the mess, and perhaps not knowing any suitable alternative, he tapped me to take this fellow's place. I was transferred to his residence, Cuckney House, where I spent pretty much the entire second year of my service. For all intents and purposes, this was about as close to a civilian job as one could get and still be in the Army. Cuckney House was a big country mansion, the largest and most impressive building in the village, and my room was up under the eaves on the third floor. The property had a huge garden, which required two full-time gardeners, Mr. Thorn and Mr. Stark, who never seemed to get along with each other. As they both had specific areas of the garden under their control, they rarely even spoke. Thorn was a warm and friendly fellow, while Stark was stern and brittle. Mr. Stark had the responsibility for the vinery, a glass enclosed building producing rather nice grapes. We were told never to go in there but I gradually befriended him and took a great interest in his vine-tending expertise. He showed me, with some pride, the correct way to cut the grapes off the vine so that the cut bunch had a 'T' at the top of the stem holding the grapes. In the past, he had always complained loudly if anyone had ventured inside and stolen any grapes. If we needed any we were supposed to only ask him. Now that he had shared with me some of his proudly held prowess, I could harvest at will without getting in trouble.

The house was situated alongside the road that ran from Cuckney, Nottinghamshire, to Chesterfield, Derbyshire. Across from the house was the village cricket field, on property belonging to the Duke of Portland. He allowed the village to use it as such while he maintained grazing rights. During the summer cricketing months, it was quite common for sheep, cattle or other animals to be grazing in the field so the area would require some cleaning up before our weekend games. As I was so close to the field, and often had time on my hands, I volunteered to help. I never changed clothes to do this and was often sighted over on the cricket pitch with a bucket and shovel, still in my chef's uniform. This led to some interesting village gossip about what the Younger family may be dining on that evening.

At the start of the cricket season, I had offered to paint the sightscreen, a very large flat-sided, wooden wall on wheels. The farm animals du jour were young bulls and, at that time, I being more of a city boy, wasn't quite sure what they were. When several of them congregated around the bottom of the ladder, I painted as far to the right as my arms and balance would allow and repeated the same on the left. I was not sure if it was safe to climb down. They did not look friendly and I was essentially stuck. I was stranded there longer than was comfortable when I finally saw the general's batman, Pat Bryan, across the street and my yelling for help brought him to my rescue. Incidentally, after one of our weekend matches, I made the newspaper with my score of 14 runs not out, despite this being a very modest performance. I think this was when I peaked as far as my cricketing days were concerned.

Cuckney House

One of the village cricketers, who brought fame to Cuckney, was a batsman by the name of Norman Hill. He was playing first class county cricket for Nottinghamshire, which played their home games at a well-known venue known as Trent Bridge in Nottingham. This would be on the same level as going to a New York Yankees game here in the states. The general was quite a cricket fan and, occasionally, he would come back to the kitchen and say "Pullen, I'm going to Trent Bridge today, would you care to come along?" He would drive himself with me alongside. The first time he did this, he dropped me off at the general admission entrance and then drove around to the VIP section in the main pavilion. I then called Norman in the player's area, and he got me a special pass to the same VIP section. That afternoon, when play took a break, I was in the tea line in the pavilion when I heard this booming, familiar voice behind me saying "Pullen? What are *you* doing in here?" I explained that it was Hill who had kindly made the arrangements for me. He wasn't impressed.

As far as my culinary expertise was concerned, most of the family's meals were simple. However, the general did entertain periodically at which time the numbers to be fed got up into the teens. And then there were the times when the post office would deliver pheasant and other game and fish sent from his family members in Scotland. This presented some challenges which had not been addressed in my college curriculum. They had a large, flag-stoned larder, which stayed cold regardless of the weather. He would have me hang the birds by their feet so that blood would drip on the floor for several days as they aged. They would even get white blow fly maggots under the wings. He would come into the kitchen regularly to inspect them. He would take a close look at them, lift the wings and turn to me and say, "Two more days, Pullen!" and walk out. When they finally passed his inspection, he advised me they would have them for dinner that night. I would then take the birds into the scullery where we had two big sinks under the window. Opening the window and placing a bottle of Airwick on the ledge, I would pluck the birds and, closing my eyes, finally remove the innards – not my favorite thing to do. I must admit, that once cleaned, seasoned and wrapped in bacon for roasting, they were indeed more appealing.

Side note: Sometime after I left the Army, the national, two-year, mandatory military service for graduating high school seniors was discontinued. This gave rise to a nasty rumor that it might have been due to my culinary skills being considered more dangerous than the enemy! I don't know who started this, so I never had an opportunity to confront my accuser.

It Started at The Savoy

Key to Success #2

Commit: *Work hard. Try to be the first to report to work and the last to leave. Faster progress will be the result. Give before you get.*

2. The Real Start to My Career (1957-1961)

September 1957 finally came along and, with an exceptionally complimentary report from the general on my discharge papers, I returned to civilian life. I think he was happy he had survived my time with him without food poisoning. In fact, he told me the Army had sent his first report back to him because he had used the word "exemplary" and this was not an expression they accepted. It was probably because they didn't know what it meant.

During the two years I was at the hotel school, I had the good fortune of gaining some practical experience at The Savoy Hotel in London and the Metropole Hotel on the seafront in Brighton on the south coast. The school year was split up into three terms and in each year one of the terms was to be spent working in a hotel as an unpaid intern. During this time, I had to maintain a daily record of duties and complete two project reports on some aspect of hotel operations. I spent my weeks at The Savoy in both the audit and billing offices and developed some good relationships. I was told that I would be welcome to return if I applied for a job after completing my National Service. My father gave me much advice over the years but the one I will never forget as I entered the work force was the following: "I don't care if your job is just peeling potatoes, you are to be the first one to report for work, the last one to leave and when the fellow next to you gets sick and tired of peeling his potatoes, you pick up his potato peeler and do his as well. You will be the first one to be picked to stop peeling potatoes and move on to a better job." Work ethic! I have never forgotten these motivational words and have tried to apply this example all my life.

Taking advantage of this opportunity, I applied to The Savoy using the favorable references I had earned during my 12 weeks of internship. I was offered a position as a barman (bartender to us) and was assigned to work in the Grill Dispense Bar, a behind-the-scenes service bar, which served the waiters working in The Savoy Grill Room. The Grill Room at The Savoy was probably one of the most well-known and respected restaurants in London at the time, many of its guests being VIPs. High ranking politicians, stars of stage and screen and famous people in all walks of life were among its regular clientele. (Here I must confess, one time I made a drink for Lady Churchill and put my finger in it just so I could say, "I stuck my finger in Lady Churchill's Pimms No 1."). My pay was five guineas a week, at that time equivalent to about $16.50. Our head barman was an older Irish fellow named Mick Nelligan and the other barmen were Phillip Marks (a real crazy South African), Mike Dias (a Jewish fellow often the subject of leg pulling), Chris Evans (a regular English lad), Jean Coulon (a Frenchman) and Bill McEvoy (another Irishman) who was always saying "Oim gettin' owt any day now." Quite a mixture.

Incidentally, my questionable poetic skills were not abandoned once I left military service as, during this phase of my career, I penned another masterpiece related to the above-mentioned staff of the Grill Dispense Bar and their various characteristics. This is also included in Appendix II.

The eclectic makeup of our group led to many memorable moments. A couple of these involved Phillip who, when Mick

Nelligan went on his two-week vacation, adjusted our schedules so that we had four days off a week instead of just two. In today's world, computers would have handled this in the blink of an eye. Back then what he created on paper was a masterpiece. All employees were required to punch in and out of work using time cards. What Phillip put together was a schedule whereby we all spent much of our workday running down to the employee entrance to punch various members of our group in and out according to the plan. Up in the payroll department, everything on our time cards appeared normal. What genius!

One time, Phillip, preparing for his day off, ran downstairs to see John, the chef in the staff kitchen, to get a little rice to prepare a meal for himself at home. What John gave him was close to 10 pounds of white rice in a brown paper bag with the top folded over, marginally secured by a rubber band. Returning to the bar, Phillip lamented that there was no way he could get past security at the employee entrance with such a large bag and asked me if I would drop it to him out of the window of the bar. The Savoy is built on a slope by the River Thames going uphill from Victoria Embankment to the elevated level of the Strand. Our bar overlooked the employee entrance about half way up the slope, three floors above the sidewalk. On the surface, it seemed to be a plausible idea until we realized the windows had not been opened in decades. In fact, from the inside, you would not have realized there were even windows there at all. Adding to the challenge, shelves had been built across the windows on which we kept the various sizes of carafes used for decanted wines and below the shelves were two old zinc sinks, one full of chopped ice and the other used for washing the carafes.

To do what Phillip was asking was no simple task. I had to first remove all the carafes, which would not have been too difficult other than the fact that space in the bar was very limited and there was nowhere to put them. We accomplished this using any flat area, including the floor. We then tried to remove the shelves to get access to the window, but the maintenance staff of old had done such a thorough job of installation that we would need to employ major mechanical equipment. So now we had to open the window, working between the shelves. Accomplishing this, and standing astride the sinks and squeezing my head between the shelves, I could indeed look outside. At this point, Phillip was ready to punch out and leave.

It was the evening shift, so it was cold and dark outside. He punched out, emerged from the staff entrance, positioned himself below the window and indicated that he was ready for me to drop the bag. Squeezing between the wretched, immovable shelves and holding the bag, while balancing myself on the sides of the sinks, I then loyally fulfilled my portion of the operation. Calling out, "Now," I dropped the bag to Phillip below who was patiently holding out both hands in preparation for catching tomorrow's dinner. Well, what happened next was not something we had planned for. The bag of rice passed through his hands, hit the road, and after a pregnant pause, exploded so that the rice spread all over the road as if we had just had a recent snowfall. Phillip, luckily was wearing a long raincoat and I last saw him scurrying away to the bus stop having scooped up a few handfuls of the rice which he put in his large pockets. At this point I almost fell off the sink in hysterics. Later, I followed a trail of white rice all the way to the bus stop. I have no idea who might have cleaned it up, but we never heard a word.

While at The Savoy, I was working the evening of Sunday, April 13, 1958 when a special reception was held in honor of Agatha Christie to celebrate the record for the longest running show in the history of the British theater for her fabulous mystery, *The Mousetrap*. The show originally opened in 1952 and, believe it or not, the show is still running; now in its 64th year. Does that make me feel old or what? She had originally estimated it would run for eight months. Up until recently, I still had a copy of the menu of that evening's event. A few years ago, I sent it to Susan Scott, the archivist for The Savoy. They did not have a copy and she was happy to have it. It is probably not true today but the big joke used to be that you could never find anyone who had actually seen the production in spite of its long-running success.

In those days, I lived in a room at 50 Upper Berkeley Street about two blocks from Oxford Street and one block from the Edgeware Road near Marble Arch. My father was not at all well, and when he made what was to be his last buying trip to London in the autumn of 1957, he came to see where I was living. Shortly after that he was basically bed ridden until his final days. As time went by and his health continued to decline, my mother would stay up with him all night, even if Jim and I would take turns when we could. If she did go to bed, she didn't sleep. I don't know how she did it. She was not a big woman, in fact she was quite slight, but I was always in awe of her tremendous inner strength and courage as she nursed him day and night. I suppose when we need that kind of courage and commitment, our good Lord gives it to us. She was nothing short of amazing during his last six or seven months.

Still, as serious and as devastating as this time was, it was not devoid of a little humor. Dad's doctor was Dr. Low, and in those days in England making house calls was routine. My dad was an asthmatic, and had cancer, probably from his smoking. This was further aggravated by phlebitis and at one point his body became filled with fluid from his chest to his ankles. It was important for him to pass water to get rid of some of this fluid. We would often try to stimulate him to do this by pouring cold water from one jug into another. One day, the doctor was doing this for quite some time and just when my dad thought he was going to be successful, Dr. Low put the jugs down on the dresser. My dad told him that he thought they were making progress and not to stop, whereupon Dr. Low said, "Mr. Pullen this may not be working for you but it is for me. I'll be back in a minute."

My father died on June 17, 1958, the start of a terrible year for my poor mother. We had a beautiful boxer dog named Punch and shortly after my father passed away, we found he had a growth in his neck which grew to the size of a golf ball. We took him to our vet who removed it but poor Punch was not a good patient and split the wound open by shaking his head, as boxers do. My mother had to have him put down, as the wound was not healing. Punch would not cooperate with his doctor's orders. I was living and working in London and one week I came home and Punch was not there to give me his normal boisterous welcome. I was devastated. He was MY dog! I loved him as much as a brother and it took quite a while for me to get over it. I knew it was the right thing for Punch but the pain was awful. The second loss.

That summer Jim became engaged to Anne Grace, a lovely girl from a wonderful family. Her father owned and ran a chemist's shop, Lansdale's Chemists, just around the corner from Pullens. The wedding, planned for September 3rd, was an occasion with some mixed feelings due to my father's recent death. Despite that, it was a grand event held at the little village church on top of the hill on Bledlow Ridge. The reception took place under a big tent in the front garden of Anne's parents' home, Crendon House, not far away. I was best man and had the duty of saying a few words to the gathered guests. I remember saying that some people said that Jim was marrying Anne because she had a 'little' money. I told them that was not true. "He would have married her anyway – even if she had a lot of money!" Maybe that's just British humor.

Jim leaves home – the third loss.

That summer I was called to meet with Olive Barnett, who worked for Sir Hugh Wontner, chairman of The Savoy Hotel Company. She asked if I would be interested in being an exchange trainee for a French fellow from the Plaza Athénée Hotel in Paris. He was requesting a chance to work at The Savoy and to accommodate this request, there had to be an exchange of people on a one-year permit. This seemed to be an opportunity few people were fortunate enough to be given, and I enthusiastically accepted. After all the necessary paperwork was completed I took my first airplane ride and landed in Paris the first week of December 1958. Since I was a barman, and the fellow coming to replace me had been working in the prestigious Bar Anglais in the Plaza Athénée, I had anticipated that is where I would be working. Wrong! Upon reporting to the hotel, I found I was just going to be a *commis débarrasseur,* which is French for the lowest form of life in the hotel and restaurant business. It was a great sounding title to put on a business card but in fact it was French for a busboy without a station. So be it!

But for my mother, it was a fourth loss. She had gone from a family of five – counting Punch – to being alone. I don't remember thinking of it in those terms at the time, but it must have been terribly difficult for her to adjust. She sold the house "Greenacres" on Links Road adjacent to the Flackwell Heath golf course and she moved into a much smaller house called "Winthorpe" on Sedgemore Road, still in Flackwell Heath.

The Plaza Athénée was one of the finest hotels in Paris and definitely on the same level as The Savoy. It had a first-class restaurant plus Le Relais Plaza, an exclusive, high level but more casual restaurant with its own street entrance on the Avenue Montaigne. It was Le Relais to which I was assigned as a busboy. I started out working behind a counter that was open to the restaurant where we opened oysters and clams and made up the orders for *steak tartare* and other cold items on the menu. I quickly learned to speak French as, when the restaurant closed, I needed assistance in taking out the heavy trash cans. *"Voulez vous m'aidez a porter la poubelle, s'il vous plâit"* ("Want to help me carry the trash, please?") seemed to work alright.

I was not alone on the bottom rung of the hotel career ladder and one of my fellow commis waiters was a nice French fellow named Pireau. His father was a retired high ranking military officer who lived permanently in the hotel. The Relais Plaza was situated close to the theater district as well as several exclusive fashion houses and the general pattern of our business in the evening was a busy pre-theater period, then a bit of a lull and then busy again later when the theater patrons got out. Pireau and I would often get a little something to eat during the quiet period in the cramped storage area behind the counter where we worked and, as is the French custom, he would always wish me *"Bon appetit!"* to which I would answer the same. One day however, he said to me *"Bill, comment on dit bon appetit en Anglais?"* (How do you say 'bon appetit' in English?) In my limited French, I told him we did not have an expression quite like that in English but if we did say anything, it would be "I hope it fucking chokes you!" After that it would be *"Bon appetit, Pireau"* and he would politely answer *"I 'ope it fucking chokes you, eh Bill?"*

Yes, it was funny for a while but as time went by the humor

somehow got lost and the greetings became routine. That was until several weeks later, when I was leaving the dining room with a tray of dirty dishes. Pireau was coming in the opposite direction with an order from the kitchen for one of his tables. As we passed, he said to me, *"Bill, j'ai un table Anglais là bas – I 'ope it fucking chokes you, eh."* At this point, I was getting a little more comfortable with my French and I quickly understood that he was telling me he was taking a food order in for a table of English people and he was about to proudly show off his proficiency in his English. I immediately put down my tray of dishes in the middle of the hallway and ran after him at which point my French left me completely. How do you say, "I was joking!" in French? I thought the French word for joke was *plaisanterie* but my mind was completely frozen. All I could do was stand between him and the guests seated at the table and in a loud whisper say, *"Pireau, non, non, non, non!"* Somehow it worked and he didn't say anything but he did demand an explanation from me later!

As I said, Le Relais had many famous people from the theater and from various fashion design houses come in, especially later in the evening. I had not been there long when Lauren Bacall, the movie actress, came in for dinner. She looked fabulous. I was walking by her table and she motioned for me to come over. (No, she wasn't after my body) *"Oui, madame?"* I asked. (OK, so far!) *"Un verre d'eau fraiche, s'il vous plâit"*, *"Oui, madame"* I answered. (see, I'm fitting right in). One small problem! What does she want? What the hell is "un verdeau"? I immediately ran all over the restaurant trying to find somebody, just anybody, who would tell me what a *verdeau* was; many of my fellow staff members, like Pireau, couldn't speak English. I was getting frantic. Finally, I found someone who thought they knew and told me she probably wanted a glass of water! At this point she was probably on the floor dying of thirst but that is what I got for her. I don't know how *fraiche* it was, but it seemed to do the trick. It's probably just as well they didn't put me in the bar.

After a few months in Le Relais, I was transferred to the main restaurant, which provided great experience, as well as the opportunity to meet some famous people. One day Alfred Hitchcock, the Hollywood movie director and producer, and his wife came in for lunch and were seated in my station. Another time, there was an amusing incident when Sir Anthony Eden, a former prime minister of the United Kingdom, came in with a small group of people. They were not on my station but he had ordered an expensive bottle of champagne and after tasting it, asked the sommelier if we had any more of it, to which he got the proud reply, "Mais oui, monsieur, we 'ave plenty more." "Then throw it away," he replied, "It's terrible!"

Working in this restaurant was exciting for a number of reasons, not the least of which was my exposure to the finest table service imaginable. Time and again I watched as the professionals performed their artistry tableside. I well remember the first time it was my responsibility to filet a Dover sole on the table-side gueridon. I had, by now, seen this done so many times that I thought I knew exactly what to do. Think again. It was quite different when I picked up the two forks and did it myself in front of these discriminating guests. Instead of ending up with four perfectly formed filets, less the center bone, I think my first one probably looked more like mashed potatoes!

This happened again when a guest asked for a beautiful *doyenne du comice* dessert pear and asked me to peel it in front of him. This is usually done with great fanfare using a fork to hold the pear in the air and, after cutting off the base and reversing it so that it resembles a shield, peeling it dramatically with an extremely sharp knife. I was shaking so much, I had to put it down on a plate and massacre it the best I possibly could!

Living and working in Paris was a priceless experience. After a few weeks of living in a tiny room at the Hotel du Gros Caillou on the street of the same name, a small group of us English lads, all basically doing the same thing, decided to move in together at the Hotel de la Gare at 87 Rue Truffaut, a little hotel owned by M. et Mme. Pierre Sevat. This probably did not help us in acquiring knowledge of French as quickly as otherwise we might have but we were a great support group for each other. One day, while standing in the crowded Metro subway car, the lightbulb went on in my head. I suddenly realized I could understand the conversations going on around me. After that, my French improved dramatically, and I began dreaming in the language.

For obvious reasons, we were not supposed to cook in our rooms, but we often did. Once I was creating an imitation of *Poulet Chasseur* out of chicken and mushroom soup when M. Sevat caught me walking up the stairs to take it to the others. *"Ah, Monsieur Pullen, vous êtes le chef, huh?"* ("Ah, Mr. Pullen, so you're the chef, eh?), so I guess it was not the big secret we thought it was. At least he was smart enough not to want to join us.

Getting around Paris was always a challenge, so not long after I arrived, I purchased a Velo Solex from one of the hotel employees for 10,000 francs, then equivalent to about $25. This bicycle had a large front tire with a small two-stroke motor that made it run like a moped. I started out by cycling and then, using a lever, lowered the motor on to the wheel and the motor took over. Thinking about it now scares me to death, given the chaotic Parisian traffic, but I don't remember it bothering me then. One night, rather late, I was riding home after my shift carrying a large (restaurant size) empty tomato juice can. My mother, as all mothers tend to be, was concerned for me while I was away and had asked me to boil my dirty handkerchiefs. I thought the empty can would work just fine, as I did have a small electric burner in my room. There was not much traffic around and when I was about half way back to my hotel, I heard a police siren behind me. I did not think much about this at first, as it was a familiar sound in the streets of the city. However, the vehicle overtook me, stopped and the officer approached me to ask what I was carrying. Maybe he thought it was a bomb or something. Even though there was nothing particularly threatening about an empty tin can; I was a bit uncomfortable trying to explain in French that it was only a substitute utensil for boiling my dirty handkerchiefs. *"Qu'est ce que c'est?"* ("What is that?), he demanded in a rather unfriendly tone. Once again, my French let me down. I managed to sputter out something about boiling my dirty handkerchiefs, adding hand gestures for illustration. He soon realized I had nothing dangerous. I think he was as relieved as I was. I think he muttered something uncomplimentary about the British as he walked back to his car.

****

Our small cadre of English trainees, or *la petite colonie Anglaise*, as we were sometimes referred to, often tried to get the same day off work so that we could do some day trips. These were all great fun. One time we headed out to the Loire Valley, well known for its exquisite *Pouilly Fumé*, and visited the famous French chateaux of Chenonceau and Chambord. Another time we went down to Orléans and visited an art colony in the Forêt de Fontainebleau. The best and most memorable trip was when, M. Boudet, our restaurant manager, arranged for three of us to visit the champagne region of Rheims and Epernay, with an introduction to the house of Moët et Chandon. We were, after all, very low on the totem pole as far as hotel employees were concerned, albeit we had all attended hotel schools, so this introduction was most helpful.

We rented a car, and I volunteered to pick it up the night before so that we could get an early start the following morning. The car rental location was on one of the grand boulevards leading down from the magnificent Arc de Triomphe. I went in, fulfilled the documentation requirements, they gave me the keys and showed me where the car was parked on one of the small parallel feeder roads that ran beside the boulevard. The car was a small Renault Dauphine and it was parked at a bend in the curb so that whether I pulled forward or went backward it would have to go over it. Parking in Paris is no different than in most major cities of the world, and the car was narrowly wedged in between two other cars. There was no way I could pull forward, so reversing was my only option. I was a little apprehensive, as the Parisian traffic is notorious and this car was totally unfamiliar to me. How do I put this thing into reverse? I tried everything. No matter what I did, the stupid car moved forward so that it was bumper to bumper with the car in front. It surely *must* have a reverse, doesn't it? It must! Why can't the French even build a car right? I was out there trying to get it into reverse for what had to be well over half an hour. Even if I went in to ask for help, what is French for *reverse*? How can I ask? Finally, I had no option other than to do exactly that, and I went back into the office. They expressed their surprise that I was *still* there and somehow, I managed to get across the problem I was having, and they showed me how to find reverse. In French reverse is translated as *go backwards*, so the good news was that I learned *"marche arriére"*!

I finally got out of there and had my first experience driving around Paris in the rush hour in a totally strange car. Once you get in the circle going around the Arc de Triomphe, you could literally spend the rest of your life there or at least until you run out of gas. It was a nightmare, but I am here today as proof positive that I must have accomplished it somehow, but I have no recollection at all how I did it. Sometimes, fear can be a wonderful thing! Once on the Champs-Elysée, everything else was a breeze.

At Moët et Chandon, we were treated like royalty. We were met by René Sabbe, the secretaire general, who escorted us through their magnificent operation and gave us firsthand information about the famous monk Dom Pérignon and how he discovered the miracle of the second fermentation in the bottle producing the magnificent drink we now know as champagne. The walk through their cellars was a very special treat for us. Following our tour and a special champagne tasting in their VIP lounge, he took us to lunch at a fine nearby restaurant where we enjoyed a fabulous *Soufflé au Fromage* with, of course, more champagne. It was indeed a magical day for us. Imagine being a busboy one day and treated the way we were by Sabbe, the next!

Then, there was the time when our lunch was not quite so grand. It was another day off with my friends Peter Silvester and David Ward. We decided to go out for lunch to a restaurant that had been recommended to Peter and which, supposedly, was reasonably priced - meaning cheap. We had very meager discretionary funds in those days so we were always careful how we spent our resources. He thought it was called *"La Truite"* and that it was within walking distance of our hotel. He said it had outside seating with planter hedges around the tables, as many Parisian restaurants have. We found it all right and got there around noon, a bit early by local standards. The first hint that things might not be what we had expected was that the headwaiter and, it seemed, all the rest of the wait staff, were in tuxedos. Nonetheless, that did not stop us and we were politely seated. I think we were the only ones in there at that time and everyone seemed to be hovering over us.

We were given menus and it only took a matter of seconds to realize that we had made a mistake. As we perused the menus we quickly found that the only thing we would be able to afford was a *demi pamplemousse* (a half grapefruit). We held the oversized menus up high so that we could talk to one another from behind them; it would seem to the casual observer that we were discussing our options. This, in fact, was true but it wasn't menu options. We were talking about how the devil we could get out of there with some British dignity. Finally, Peter and I elected David to extricate us. His French was better than ours and we certainly couldn't stay there. With great flair, he summoned our waiter. "*Oui, monsieur?*" the waiter asked, whereupon David expressed his desire to see the maître d'hôtel. "*Oui, monsieur, certainement.*" and off he went to get him. Now, in truth, David spoke French rather well, but in this case, he put on a very British accent with accentuated pronunciation. When the head waiter arrived, David spoke up.

"*Monsieur, eel foe dear la veritay. Noo noo sommes trompay du restaurant. Noo sommes presque forshay, monsieur, eh votre menu eh trow share poor noo.*" It was truly an academy award moment. (For those of you who can't decipher the above, he basically said, "Sir, to tell you the truth, we have made a mistake. We are at the wrong restaurant. We are almost broke and your menu is too expensive for us.)

Once again, we were unwittingly responsible for bringing humiliation on the entire population of the United Kingdom as we got up and waved goodbye to all and sundry and literally backed out of *La Truite*. At least it gave the staff something to talk about until the real customers came in.

Thank you, Peter!

As we walked into the place where we eventually ate, we felt right at home. I clearly remember seeing a fellow drinking out of his soup bowl!

****

I knew the day would come when I, and my beloved Velo Solex, would have to part company, and before I returned to England in December 1959, I sold it for the same amount I had paid for it. It was a valuable asset I had for most of my time in Paris and I came out even – and still alive!

There was one small incident that took place right before I left Paris where my Velo Solex was involved in some minor criminal activity for its last hurrah. On my commute from my first home in Paris at the Hotel du Gros Caillou to the Plaza Athénée, I traveled down the Avenue Bosquet and crossed the Pont de l'Alma at the point near where dear Princess Diana met her unfortunate death many years later. I had noticed, and commented many times, that the small street sign for Avenue Bosquet was only being supported by the bottom two retainers which kept it attached to the adjacent building. The top two had come loose and for the whole year I was in Paris the poor sign just hung there pathetically, probably in anguish. A day or two before my departure, having celebrated the end of my year's stay with many friends, while simultaneously contributing to the French wine economy, it was time to act. It was early morning by this time and I felt it was my civic duty to put the poor sign out of its misery.

Recognizing the wisdom of "safety in numbers", we traveled over

Me and my Velo Solex

to where the sign hung and found the sign was just a little higher than I could reach. However, my trusted Velo Solex came up with the idea that if I would stand on its upper parts, I could probably reach it. Oh boy, that was right on. My friends kindly supported my Velo Solex as I climbed up and rescued the poor sign from its perilous predicament and pulled the remaining supports out of the wall. It was bigger than it seemed from street level, and a lot heavier too. I felt a warm glow at this charitable feat, even at the expense of some car rental tourists not knowing where the devil they were. That was the easy part; now I had to get it home.

Because of its size and weight, I placed 'Avenue Bosquet' on the bottom of the metal trunk I had purchased for my trip to Paris the year before. I laid it on some soft material and packed around it. The U.K. customs official that I was fortunate to be assigned, took a great deal of interest in this newly bi-lingual native returning after a questionable year-long stay in a foreign country. He *must* be dealing in something. Maybe he was right. Only in my case it was signs.

Being the good son and friend of several that I was, I had appropriately purchased several small gifts as souvenirs. Among these gifts were quite a few wooden plaques portraying various beautiful scenes of the City of Light. These were on angular pieces of wood cut from their original places of birth and were both attractive and, what was even better, inexpensive. As the customs officer was carefully unwrapping my dirty underwear, which had cushioned them from any potential damage, he kept asking, "What is this?" to which I would reply, "That is just a souvenir plaque from Paris that I am bringing back as a gift."

Well, it was going to happen, wasn't it? He finally reached down to the bottom of my trunk and ran his finger slowly around the edge of poor old 'Avenue Bosquet', which was covered with some of my clothes. Oh dear. The game was up. At least at Wormwood Scrubbs Prison I would be in England.

"And what is this?" he asked.

I was about to come clean. "Well, "I started, "That's a plaque that I..."

He interrupted. "Oh, that's another plaque?"

"Yes." And, believe it or not, that was it.

I know I have already had a few "phews" (sorry about that!) in this narrative and, believe me, this was another one. Of course, I have no idea if they would have done anything about it but I had such a guilty conscience I thought we might end up with another war with the French or something more serious. Regardless, I finally got home and 'Avenue Bosquet' became a British prisoner.

****

In November 1959, just before the end of my one-year *stagiaire* experience, something happened which directed my life in a totally different and marvelous direction. It was my final week at the Hotel Plaza Athénée. I had been promoted during the year to *demi-chef de rang*, which meant on certain days I worked as a *chef de rang,* providing full table-side service, and on other days I was a *commis de rang* (busboy) again. This had given me additional and important experience. One Tuesday evening the restaurant was moved temporarily to one of our banquet rooms so that a large private party could be accommodated in the more elaborate surroundings of our beautiful restaurant dining room. We were not particularly busy and I became engaged in conversation with a single American gentleman at one of my tables.

"You're not French?" he said.

"No, sir, I'm English," I replied.

"What the hell are you doing here?"

"Sir, I'm here on an exchange program to learn the language and the business. My year is just about up and I will be returning to the U.K. shortly."

He introduced himself as Joseph Tankoos, Jr. and told me he had just purchased the Colony Hotel in Palm Beach, Florida where he already had the Duke and Duchess of Windsor as guests in one of the top floor suites.

He said, "I'm leaving Thursday. If you want to come back with me, I'll give you a job."

While I was not able to accept his enticing offer, he gave me a book of matches from his New York-based company imprinted with his address and phone number (which I still have today). Even though I did not have a written agreement with The Savoy, I appreciated the fact they had given me the opportunity of working in such a magnificent hotel. I felt it was incumbent upon me to return to London and accept another assignment with them. As it turned out, this was to be as assistant reception manager at the Berkeley Hotel in Piccadilly, opposite The Ritz. While I relished the challenges of this new assignment, the amazing, unexpected offer from Tankoos, was never far from my consciousness. Every now and then I would stumble across his matchbook and wonder what might have been. The thought of going to America was indeed exciting, and it was something to dream about, but the story doesn't end here.

At the Berkeley, my position came with live-in quarters, shared with two other employees, off the old courtyard above what had been the stables in a bygone era. The uniform was a formal frock coat with tails, striped black trousers, highly polished shoes, shirts with detachable, stiff starched collars and the obligatory grey tie. I looked like I was going to Ascot for the Derby and all for six and a half guineas a week; in U.S. terms, about $20. It did include room and board, and was a higher profile position which would give me some great new experience. All and all, I was happy.

About three months into this new position, my boss, Peter Hornsby, the reception manager, got married, went on his honeymoon and was seriously injured in a motorcycle accident. This left him off work for an indefinite period. As his assistant, I took on his responsibilities, which went on much longer than had been anticipated. I felt comfortable in this role, and thought I was doing a pretty good job.

However, things can go wrong on occasion. One evening an American lady checked into the hotel. As she registered, she advised me that her husband would be arriving on an overnight flight from New York early the next morning. I assured her I would take care of everything and escorted her to one of our better suites.

The following day I was back on duty at 7:00 am, when the woman's husband arrived about half an hour later. As I had been advised to expect him, I did not bother to have him register and instead offered to take him straight up. I felt he would appreciate this little extra service after his long flight. With me leading the way, we took the lift, walked down the corridor and I opened the suite door with my passkey. As I let him in, I whispered my best wishes for an enjoyable visit. I also offered my services should they need anything during their stay. I closed the door, taking great care to be as quiet as possible, and proceeded back to the lift. It was then that the guest came charging down the corridor yelling at me at the top of his voice.

"What on earth is going on? Who are those people in there? Is that our suite or not?"

"Sir, I'm so sorry. I have no idea!" Then it hit me. I was on the wrong floor! A simple error, as the guest room configuration was the same on every level. I had been so confident that I knew which suite his wife was in, I had failed to double-check before escorting him upstairs. Apparently, upon entering the suite, he had quietly entered the bedroom and was astonished (maybe that's the wrong word) to see two bodies in the bed, whereupon he leapt to a rather shattering conclusion. Turning on a light, the two bodies wakened and it did not ease the situation when he realized the woman was not his wife. No doubt the couple in the bed were equally distressed to have a stranger walk in on them at 7.30 in the morning.

"Sir, I'm so terribly sorry. This is the fourth floor and your suite is on the fifth. I don't know how I could have made such an awful mistake. I should have checked before bringing you up. I'm *so* sorry."

He was in no mood to listen to my explanation. He was still muttering to himself when I ushered him into the correct suite.

Not the best way to start the day – for either of us! I think my job was only saved when Hornsby returned to work shortly afterwards to take over his managerial duties again.

My misadventures did not end there. On a quiet Saturday morning, I stood in the middle of the lobby talking to our two hall porters, Stanley and Isherwood. I was feeling quite Savoy-like, with my legs slightly apart and both hands clasped behind my back under my tails. Evidently, I was cheekily pulling their legs in some fashion; we were always playing jokes on one another. As I said, it was quiet and there was no guest activity at all. Well, they quickly bundled me into the lift, set it to go to the top floor and started to tickle me around the ribs. I was on the floor by this time. Upon reaching the lift's destination, they reset it to return to the lobby, still attacking me in a hearty, good-natured way. In the melee, my stiff collar pulled out of its studs and stuck out of the top of my formal frock coat. My key chain, attached to a suspenders button got pulled somehow and ripped my beautiful striped trousers down to my thigh. Of course, my hair, so carefully coifed earlier, was now a complete mess. The lift arrived back at the lobby level, and Stanley and Isherwood opened the door and quickly departed leaving me to sweep myself up off the floor in the corner of the lift. Looking up from my position, I was surprised to see the hotel wasn't quite as quiet as it had been. Yes, that's right - there were several guests standing at the lift door. I quickly exited and went to my room for some repairs before returning to my desk. Somehow my once promising career kept being punctuated by situations I should have avoided.

****

One of my closest friends, with whom I stayed in touch right up to the time he unexpectedly passed away in November 2014, was David Ward. We met during our training days at The Savoy and we worked in Paris at the same time where he had a position on the reception desk at the prestigious George V Hotel. Upon his return to The Savoy, he was given a position at reception there, so he and I were working in similar situations at two of the company's finest hotels. As I related above, there are often interesting situations connected with the exposure we both had in these roles and he had several that he related to me. Two of these concerned established celebrities of the day, movie heart throb Errol Flynn and singer Bing Crosby.

One day while Errol Flynn was checking in to The Savoy with his party, they were discussing the favorable reaction to his latest film, and Flynn was telling them about a fan letter he had recently received. The writer had raved about him, his acting, and all things related to his films and then signed with a P.S. which said, "Please excuse me writing this letter with a paint brush, but where I am at present they won't let me have anything sharp!" An indication of the mental state of his fan base or perhaps just one of his stories?

In the incident with Bing Crosby, he had flown in to Heathrow Airport and had been met by some of his London hosts. He was there to make a Bing Crosby Christmas special for the BBC. On the way in from the airport, they had been discussing the production and had decided, because of his international celebrity status, that he did not need any special introduction. Upon their arrival at The Savoy, he was greeted by a polite, young Swiss receptionist who asked for the name on the reservation. When he replied, "Bing Crosby," the young man said, "Thank you, sir. Is that with a 'y' or an 'ie'?" He did have a full introduction for his Christmas special.

When Peter returned and I went back to my regular duties, I became restless. I had learned about all I could in this position and, given the conservative nature of The Savoy, they would not likely move me to a different department so soon. I started looking at other opportunities and, after interviewing with Philip Churchman, general manager of the Compleat Angler, a beautiful Thames riverside hotel in nearby Marlow, I accepted a position there as assistant manager. When I went to see Charles Fornara, our general manager at the Berkeley, to give him my notice, he talked me out of it. I was then in the rather uncomfortable position of having to go back to Churchman and withdraw my acceptance. Still, I was restless, and I followed up on an advertised position at the Ship Hotel in Shepperton on the River Thames, not far west of London.

On a Saturday morning, I drove down to meet with the manager, but we both felt the position was not a good match. I was about to leave and drive back to London when he asked if I would mind giving a lift to one of his guests. One of the things Shepperton is known for is its movie studios and my passenger was a delightful American fellow who was there, in some way, related to the movie industry. It was truly fascinating listening to him on our drive back into London, as he was there filming a Jules Verne story called "Mysterious Island." In this movie, they had to fight off giant crabs, chickens and all kinds of other oversized beasts and he was telling me how they filmed the actors' parts and then married that footage with the animated parts. It occurred to me that I might have someone in my little Morris Minor that I should know and before we arrived in Hammersmith, where he wanted to be dropped off, I finally had the courage to say, *"Who are you?"* Well, it turned out he was Gary Merrill, a prominent movie actor of the day, and even though he had many movie credits to his name, he was perhaps best known for being married to that movie icon, Bette Davis.

We arrived in Hammersmith and he invited me to have a drink with him at a nearby pub. I gladly accepted and we joined a small number of people sitting at a long, rather unattractive bar. I was sitting to his left and the gentleman sitting several seats away on his right kept staring as if he recognized him. Merrill had grown a rather large beard for his part in the movie and, not being clean shaven, he probably looked a little different from his promotional photographs. Anyway, this poor fellow could finally stand it no longer and came up to us and said, "You're Gary Merrill, aren't you?" When Merrill answered that indeed he was, his fan went on, "Goor! Oi've seen all your pictures" in his strong London accent. He then went on to recount Merrill's entire movie career. I felt embarrassed that I hadn't even known who Gary Merrill was.

****

The Shepperton position was not for me but seeing an opening advertised at the Bull Hotel in Wrotham in Kent, a small inn about 25 miles south of London, I decided to try again. I was interviewed by the owners, accepted the job, and resigned from the Berkeley. The Bull was a well-known, highly respected, country inn with eight rooms and an excellent restaurant. As it was small, I had the opportunity of experiencing a complete operation.

It was while I was there that I met one of the most unforgettable characters in my life. He was retired Lt. Colonel Alfred Daniel Wintle of the 1st the Royal Dragoons. He wore a monocle, due to a war injury, and was the stereotypical highly disciplined British army officer. During the Second World War, he had been captured and imprisoned by the Vichy French, a group sympathetic to the Nazis. He took great exception to the unkempt appearance of his guards. He insisted that, if they were going to keep him captive, they should at least clean themselves up, be professional and wear their uniforms. His amazingly strong will ultimately prevailed over his slovenly captors and it became his badge of honor.

He and his adoring wife, Dora, lived locally and he was one of our regulars at The Bull, frequently occupying *his* seat at the bar where our lovable, stocky and jovial blond barmaid, Paddy Byrne, took pains to take great care of him. He drove an old and rather decrepit black Austin with a colorful child's rubber ring on the driver's seat. Meeting him provided many of our diners with a memorable and unexpected bonus.

He was quite a celebrity in England, as he had made legal history having won a civil lawsuit taken all the way to the House of Lords (the English equivalent to the Supreme Court) over an 11-year effort. He had finally resorted to representing himself, having depleted all his financial resources during the process. This lawsuit came about when his second cousin, Kitty Wells, had passed away, and her estate had, in part, mysteriously passed on to her solicitor. Colonel Wintle knew that had to have been rigged, as his sister Marjorie had been Kitty's caregiver for many years and there had been an understanding that she would ultimately inherit from Kitty's estate. He made several efforts to bring the solicitor, Frederick Harry Nye, to court but without success. In an excerpt from his autobiography, "The Last Englishman", he records:

"I tried to flush him into the open by writing him extremely libelous letters and sending copies to his neighbours, to the Law Society, newspapers, MPs (Members of Parliament) and the police. 'My God,' said a solicitor when he read it. 'He's got to prosecute you for criminal libel. Otherwise he's a crook.' Nye did not prosecute."

Finally, totally frustrated and desperate for some way to move his mission forward, Wintle devised an unusual and audacious plan. Using a friend's flat in Hove, a town near Brighton where Nye had his practice, the colonel set about trapping Nye there. He and Nye had a mutual acquaintance, the Earl of Norbury, known to his friends as Reggie. Impersonating Reggie, even assuming the earl's 'fruity' accents (his words), Wintle invited Nye to meet him there on the pretext of discussing a shady business deal. When Nye arrived, the colonel had him remove his trousers, placed a paper dunce's hat on his head and then took photographs of Nye from the front and

Lt. Col. Alfred Wintle

A return visit to the Bull Hotel, 1992

rear. He then turned him out into the street in his long underwear. Wintle then took a train back to London with Nye's trousers still over his arm and proudly showed them off in the trophy room of his club. He then called the police, the press and Nye's partner to confess and went home to enjoy a large whisky.

A little after midnight, the police arrived at his home with an arrest warrant for common assault. At last, the colonel was going to get Nye into a courtroom. However, it did not turn out as he had hoped, since the judge hearing the case did not allow the will issue to be discussed. He sentenced the colonel to six months, which he served partially in the notorious Wormwood Scrubbs prison in London. At this point he was becoming quite well known and one of Kitty Wells' cousins came forward and assigned his small interest in her estate to Colonel Wintle. This provided him the tools he needed to contest the estate. It was a long drawn out case and at the end, assisted by one of his loyal staff from their military days, Trooper Cedric Mays, he prevailed.

He was subsequently honored on the popular BBC television show, *"This is Your Life"* with host Eamonn Andrews. It was on this occasion that he again met the former commandant of the Vichy French facilities where he had been held captive during the war. Wintle was delighted to hear that, largely due to his disciplined example, the commandant and over two hundred of his soldiers had returned to fight with the French National Army.

It was during my time at The Bull that Colonel Wintle wrote a fictional book called *The Club*, which was about a terribly British and exclusive all male London club. He used to say that it was *so* exclusive that you had to have your application in several years before you were born, and it was just too bad if you turned out to be a girl! He had a special event scheduled to launch the book at the military club in Piccadilly to which he belonged and on which he had based his book. He had many close friends in Wrotham but he only invited one person to this fascinating event and that was the young 24-year-old me. I still have no idea why. I always had great admiration for him, and I felt we had a warm and respectful relationship but this was a totally unexpected honor. I certainly felt a little out of place but being his guest was most assuring.

****

As assistant manager, I did anything and everything. One morning I was behind the bar getting things set up before we opened for lunch when a liquor salesman representing Gilbey's Gin walked in and gave me his pitch for their brand. As he finished, I reached up and proudly pulled down one of their

Anita at The Moat, 1992

bottles to show that we were already using it. We had further conversation and as he was about to leave, he turned and said, "Oh, by the way, we stopped using those frosted bottles about five years ago." Thank goodness, he didn't hang around long enough to see the stupid look on my face.

After a few months of showing what I could do, the owners, Charles Dixon and his former wife (Mrs. Dixon had re-married and was now Mrs. Vernon Hay-Bolton) made me the manager of their other small property nearby, The Moat Hotel, an historic 14th century inn. It was a marvelous little hotel converted from an old farmhouse and located on the Pilgrims Way, which 600 years earlier had been the road the pilgrims had taken to visit the shrine of the former Archbishop of Canterbury, Thomas a'Becket, who had been famously slain on the altar of the cathedral in the reign of King Henry II in 1170. The pilgrims' trek was beautifully recorded in Geoffrey Chaucer's classic, *The Canterbury Tales*.

Just before I moved to The Moat, I took a day off and went to London to visit my friends on reception at the Berkeley. They had a direct line to the reception desk at The Savoy, and I asked if I could use it to call David, as we had planned to meet after his shift. When David answered and I told him I was on the direct line from the Berkeley, he said "Oh, good. Can you hold on a minute?" He came back on the line saying, "We're oversold here, do you know if they have a twin with a bath for several nights? I have a very nice American couple here and I need to find them something." Hornsby was away from the desk at that moment so I looked at their reservations chart, that I had worked on myself for several months, and saw that indeed they could accommodate the request. I looked at my two former co-workers and said, "It seems you do have available what he needs, do you think it would be OK for me to tell him?"

They said, "Well, you are more familiar with that than we are, so we think it would be fine."

I got back on the line with David and said, "Yes, they have a twin with a bath available for that length of stay."

"Great", he said, "That gets us out of a tight spot. Hold on, I'll give you their names." He came back on the line and gave me the names of the couple and said, "They were very happy we could take care of them. The doorman is just getting them a taxi. They should be there in the next 15 to 20 minutes."

I said, "David, there's one thing I should tell you. I am not really at the Berkeley, I'm calling from a pay phone at Victoria Station."

There was a moment of silence during which time he realized that he had just sent off two guests to the Berkeley and that when they got there no one would know anything about it. What then? I don't remember exactly what he said, but I was sure our close relationship was severely and permanently damaged. David was overheard by the highly esteemed and long-standing Reception Manager, Mr. St. John (pronounced 'sin-gin') Brooks who snatched the phone out of David's hand. The next thing I heard was his loud and impressive voice, almost yelling. "Pullen, what on earth are you doing?"

I had not expected this turn of events; I had anticipated saying, "It's OK David, I'm only kidding."

Instead, I stuttered, "It's alright Mr. Brooks, I really *am* here at the Berkeley. There's no problem, really."

I quietly put the phone down, said goodbye to my friends and left the hotel.

Just another self-inflicted wound. Why can't these people take a joke?

****

The Moat Hotel also had an excellent restaurant, which operated in an adjacent building that had previously been an old tithe barn. The huge, interior, dark, uneven beams were magnificent and several of the characters from The Canterbury Tales were painted on the inside of the high-pitched roof. There was also a minstrel gallery and a huge walk-in fireplace giving it a warm and cozy atmosphere. The chairs were miniature thrones covered in a brocade material made exclusively for Maples of London, the design of which was taken from one of King Henry VIII's hunting outfits. To get to some of the tables, patrons had to double over to get under the beams. A restaurant reviewer, Samuel Cobb, gave the restaurant a glowing report and ended his critique with some of the famous lines from Geoffrey Chaucer this way:

"As we bade farewell...and went out of the well-lit inn into the starlit night, we felt well fed, very content. As we drove back home to London along the Canterbury road I thought of the lines in the Canterbury Tales:

> *"Great cheer made our host us every one*
> *And to the supper set he us anon*
> *And served us with victuals as he could*
> *Strong was the wine and well we drunken would."*

****

In those days, being young, enthusiastic, energetic and hardworking, I worked from early morning, opening up and cooking breakfast, until turning out the lights last thing at night. The closest thing to a day off was driving my little Morris Minor to the local garage, just a mile up the road, to fill it with petrol. One example of my enthusiasm was when a couple, who had been vacationing in Europe, came in for dinner. They had driven up from Dover that afternoon and on the way, had passed numerous roadside stands where the new crop of raspberries was being sold. They asked if we had them on our menu and we did not, as it was the very start of the season. I said nothing specific, something like, "Let me see" and immediately got in my car and drove south, the way they had come so that I could buy some for them and for other guests. It was now early evening and many of the stands had already been taken in. I don't know how long it was or how far I drove but it seemed to be forever; so long that I thought they would probably be gone by the time I got back. Finally, yes finally, I came across a stand, bought a few baskets and headed back to the inn as fast as I could. Running into the kitchen, I asked if the guests were still there and thankfully, they were. I put one of the containers on a silver tray with a doily underneath and calmly walked into the restaurant presenting the tray just as their main course was being cleared. Just in time. Little did they know the effort to which we would go to please our guests.

Before my arrival, the owners put in a big swimming pool. During the construction of the pool, the workers came across several old coins, most of which I was told were taken by them. We still had two, which were sent to the British Museum for identification and dating. These were returned to us mounted on a solid walnut board, which hung on a wall at the entrance to the inn. The oldest of these was dated between AD 96–110 and the other was more recent, 1623 from the reign of King James I. The board just hung on a single hook. If it were like that today, I'm afraid it wouldn't have lasted there 24 hours!

Of historical note, the age of the building came to light when Mr. Dixon ordered decorative glass installed behind the bar off the main lobby. The installer had previously come in to measure and trace the uneven sides of the vertical beams so that the mirrored glass would fit exactly. Nothing was prepped until they were ready for installation. They started by removing the existing plaster which exposed what was believed to be the original construction of the farmhouse. The wall consisted of hard packed mud with traces of grass held in place by horizontal strips of wood about ten inches apart. I told Dixon that if we had known that, we could have just put up a piece of plain glass so that our guests could see it. It would have been quite an attraction.

It was here at The Moat, that I met another memorable gentleman. And I *do* mean gentleman. His name was Geoffrey Treadway, the owner of the Pilgrim Cleaners, a dry-cleaning shop in Maidstone, a delightful town about seven miles south of us. He was soft-spoken and had a warm and infectious laugh. I have never forgotten the incident he related concerning his business dealings. It was another learning moment for me and it was something I have unapologetically plagiarized over the years.

He had a confrontation of some kind with someone associated with his business and that person had sent him a strong and rather vulgar letter to which he had drafted a reply in a similar tone. This was not his true personality and, as he was not comfortable in sending it, he had taken it to his friendly local banker to get his opinion. The banker suggested that he think about it some more before responding. Treadway took his banker's advice and re-drafted his reply. I have never forgotten it and its magnificent simplicity. It said:

"Dear Mr._____,

I acknowledge the receipt of your letter dated_____ and I only hope the satisfaction that you gained from writing it equally compensated you for your loss of dignity.

Yours truly, Geoffrey Treadway"

How priceless was that!

Key to Success #3

Be Sincere: *Say "I'm sorry" and mean it. These words may be difficult to express sometimes but can be powerful and healing in resolving a situation.*

3. America, Here I Come (1961-1963)

A good friend of mine, Peter Silvester, whom I first met in the Army during my days of basic training in Aldershot, was a 2nd Lieutenant. It was he whom I saluted to receive my first pay packet. It was cash in an envelope in those days. We stayed in touch after being discharged, worked in Paris at the same time, and both lived at the Hotel de la Gare. A year or so after we returned from our Paris experience, we were talking and I told him about my conversation with Joe Tankoos. Peter had been looking for work in the United States so I wrote Tankoos a "You may not remember me but..." letter telling him about my friend's interest. He replied that he remembered me well, and that we should meet when he was in London the following month. In the meantime, Peter accepted an offer to manage the Ikeja Arms Hotel at the Lagos Airport in Nigeria. I met Tankoos in his suite at the Dorchester and told him what had taken place. Then he said, "What about you? Do you think you are ready now?" At the time, I was managing The Moat Hotel in Wrotham, but I was far more flexible in making my future plans than I had been two years earlier, so I told him I would be interested.

Over the next several weeks, even months, I spent a great deal of time doing the required paperwork, to include getting police clearance from the local government agencies where I had lived in Paris. Eventually, I was called to the American Embassy in

London and was issued a 'green card' to become a legal resident alien of the United States. Now I could make my travel plans. Not knowing how long I would be gone, I packed ample clothing and personal belongings. After considering my travel options, I finally selected the new *S.S. United States*, which was recognized in 1952 with the Blue Riband for being the fastest ship to cross the Atlantic Ocean westbound between England and America. The media had interviewed Bob Hope after he arrived in England on its inaugural crossing. One of the reporters asked him, "What's all this we hear about you and Jayne Mansfield?" (a voluptuous Hollywood movie star). Bob Hope, known for his quick one-liners replied, "It's just a rumor – but keep spreading it!"

These were exciting, and yet somewhat apprehensive, times. Going to Paris had given me the same nervousness but this was definitely a bigger step. My idea at this stage was to get two or three years' experience and then return to England. As we now know, that didn't happen.

My mother and Jim came to see me off at Southampton on November 16, 1961. There were sad "goodbyes," "take good care of yourself," "please write as often as you can," and similar affectionate and caring last minute familial well-intentioned expressions. The one thing I clearly remember my mother saying was, "Bill dear, please don't come back with an American girl." I don't remember if I answered that or not, but, as you can see, I never forgot it.

Being on a big ocean-going liner was exciting and there was so much to explore. My tiny cabin was loaded with all my stuff, which included a sizeable trunk and some suitcases, so I did not have much extra space to move around. The first-class section was somewhat isolated from the tourist-class, where I was, but I discovered that it could be accessed by going through the swimming pool area. I also found the first-class movie theater, which I later went to and was then disappointed to find out that the films I had seen there during the first half of the trip were switched over to the tourist class section for the second half. I had already seen them all.

On a cold November morning, I went up on deck and sat in one of the many deck chairs, covered by a warm blanket. I was the only one there. Did the other passengers know something I didn't? I was determined to stay there, until I noticed the horizon coming into view more and more above the railing as the ship rolled to one side and then the other. After a while, this became more pronounced and, discretion being the better part of valor, I decided to head back to my cabin. I found going down the stairs was a challenge. One moment I reached for the next step, which did not seem to be there, and the next moment I was almost running down the stairs as they came up to meet me. Finally, I arrived at my cabin and that was the end of my wandering for the next 24 hours. My knees were sore from spending so much time looking into the toilet, if you know what I mean. I missed dinner, breakfast, and lunch but did finally emerge for dinner that next evening. Evidently, I had not suffered alone. There were many similar stories going around the dining room, not that it was a good time to talk about such things.

The well-known saying, 'America and England are two countries separated by a common language' was brought home to me as my journey across the northern Atlantic progressed. I had been assigned to a dining table for 10, among them was a small group of Canadian nurses from Toronto. I received a real education from them during the next several days. I learned that 'a lift' was an elevator, the 'boot' of a car was the trunk, the 'bonnet' was a hood

The SS United States

and many, many others. When one of them told me that she had received a wakeup call at 6 a.m. and had gone down to the pool, I casually replied, "If anyone had knocked me up at that time of the morning, I'd be furious." Well, I knew from their reactions that I must have said something wrong. Thankfully, one of them was kind enough to quietly translate what I had said. That was one mistake I never made again.

It was a thrilling trip all around, but nothing compared to the morning of Tuesday, November 21st, when I peered out of my cabin porthole and saw lights on the horizon. I washed, got dressed, and spent the next several chilly hours on deck transfixed on the land ahead. It was not long before we went under the new Verrazano Bridge, still under construction, and sailed past the iconic Statue of Liberty. Little did I know that two years later I would be working for Restaurant Associates, the company which catered a huge event there for the bridge's opening celebration.

New York! What a sight! Now I was seeing the fabulous skyscrapers for myself. I was so excited. We docked mid-morning and the natural tendency was to want to disembark immediately. Because the tourist-class passengers were subjected to health and immigration clearances, it seemed ages before we were allowed off the ship. Finally, I identified all my belongings and, with the help of a porter, wound my way toward a taxi which would take me to the Knickerbocker Hotel on 45th Street, not far from the dock. Not knowing what to tip the porter, I decided the dollar equivalent of five shillings would be fine. I don't think it was, especially with the trunk, the suitcases and other small stuff. He certainly did not seem too thrilled. The cab took me to the hotel, we unloaded, I checked in and I was officially in New York.

The Knickerbocker Hotel was located right next to a bar called the Peppermint Lounge where some fellow by the name of Chubby Checker was packing the place every night, doing something called the Twist. It was all the rage, and the club was always busy. In the evenings, I would look down from my room and see four or five police cars parked along our side of the street. The hotel had a direct entrance to the lounge from the lobby but I never picked up enough courage to go in there.

I was also less than a block from Times Square, which meant Broadway was there, too. "The Sound of Music" was playing at a theater close by so I booked the cheapest seat I could get and went to the show. I cannot adequately explain the thrill of sitting in that theater on Broadway in New York. It wouldn't be such a big deal today but in the early sixties, for a young fellow like me, it really was beyond exciting – and of course, it was and still is, a fabulous show.

On Thursday morning, November 23rd, I walked over to Times Square where I encountered massive and enthusiastic crowds. I could not imagine what was going on, but on looking up I saw these huge balloons of different cartoon characters and other objects. My God, do they do this every day? It seemed quite odd to me, until I went to a nearby Howard Johnson's for lunch and was told it was Thanksgiving. This was not a holiday with which I was familiar, but I did partake of the roast turkey dinner on their menu. It made me realize I was going to have to adjust to traditional American holidays and customs.

My five days in the city went by far too quickly and at the weekend, I took a National Airlines flight to Palm Beach. The sub-tropical weather was idyllic and such a vast contrast to the cold, bleak, gray and white November weather back home. The Colony Hotel had sent a car to meet me, a Chevrolet Impala station wagon. It was driven by a very nice fellow by the name of

Paul Howard, superintendent of service for the hotel. He was so short that he could barely see over the steering wheel and from the outside, it must have seemed like the car was driving itself. I cannot adequately express the emotion of being there among the swaying palm trees, the beaches, and the massive, ocean-side homes. I was in heaven.

I was greeted at reception by Jim Ponce, who became a very good friend and with whom I maintained contact until he passed away at the age of 98 in December 2015. He was an amazing person, a direct descendant of Ponce de Leon, the explorer who discovered Florida in the 15th century around St. Augustine. Jim was widely known for his historical knowledge of Florida and for several years did walking tours of Palm Beach and the Breakers Hotel (where he worked for many years). He received numerous accolades and was known as "The Island's Only Two-legged Historical Landmark". I was assigned room 218 on the second floor, probably the worst room in the hotel overlooking the huge dumpsters at the rear of the property, and I settled in. I am not sure what Tankoos had told the general manager, Ledyard Gardner, about me but I sensed that Gardner did not think he needed an assistant manager. Perhaps he initially saw me as a threat to his position. After a time, though, he and his dear wife, Bobbie, treated me like family, and as my career later took off, we maintained contact for many years.

The Colony was, and still is, a relatively small, upscale hotel. It is situated just one block from the beach and had three magnificent suites on the top floor overlooking Worth Avenue and the Everglades Golf Course. It's Pool Room Restaurant and Lounge was one of Palm Beach's hot spots featuring the Colony Cubans, a fabulous Cuban band led by Floreal Anaya. It was quite common to see the 'who's who' of the Palm Beach social scene dining and dancing there. Incidentally, the Duke and Duchess of Windsor had left a long time ago but a copy of one of their checks is in a framed display in the lobby, as a reminder of their visit. There was no office space for me, so a desk and chair, along with my nameplate, were placed in the lobby adjacent to the front desk. It was a great vantage point from which to greet many of our incoming guests, including celebrities such as Victor Borge and Robert Goulet, fresh from his big hit "Camelot" on Broadway. They were both appearing locally at the Royal Poinciana Playhouse in separate engagements.

I developed some great relationships with several of the staff members and, in fact, one of the restaurant captains, Norman Krohn, was to be the best man at my wedding three years later. He had an acting background, having performed in theater, and a wonderful tableside manner. He was known for creating flaming entrées, putting the various ingredients together seemingly off the cuff. Once, when we had a major push on wine sales, I was having lunch near an elderly couple, and I overheard Norman taking their order. The gentleman ordered a glass of milk, which stopped Norman in his tracks. He said, "Milk, sir? Milk? With wine?" The man sheepishly said, "But I didn't order any wine," to which Norman said, "That's right, you didn't did you?" and immediately presented the guest with the wine list and 'sold' him a half bottle of wine that I'm sure he didn't want. That is salesmanship! And *that* was Norman.

Our chef, Camille Desmaison, was excellent and this was confirmed when he was later hired by the White House as one of their key culinary staff members.

During the early days of 1962, I encountered an attempt by a local union to organize restaurant employees in the Palm Beach area. Gardner, and several owners and operators of area restaurants, had put together a list of contact information so that if any one property was hit with a walkout, they would know who to contact for support. Just as the busy winter season was getting under way, a walkout of servers was called at the Royal Poinciana Playhouse during a black tie opening night event. Their manager, Nick Garra, began making his calls for help, progressing through the list, one-by-one. As soon as Gardner was called, he asked me to get over to the theater as quickly as I could to see how I could help. When I arrived, I was given a station of a few tables and went to work in a totally strange environment. The formally dressed guests were most understanding and appreciative and, despite some inconvenience, seemed to enjoy the effort to take care of them. At some point that evening, Garra handed me the keys to his Ford Thunderbird and asked me to go and get something they needed. I well remember getting into his car and being confronted by an instrument panel the like of which I could only imagine being in a commercial airplane. How do I start this thing, let alone drive it? It reminded me of the predicament I had in Paris with the rental car. My Morris Minor had the minimum of buttons and things to push to get it going so this car was totally confusing to me. I must have spent a long time trying to find out what to do because, when I finally gave up and ran inside to ask him for help, he asked me if I was back with what he needed. He was not particularly thrilled to learn I had not even left yet. All in all, it was an interesting evening and I came out of it having collected a few generous tips from the tables I served.

****

At night, The Colony restaurant hummed with activity, and on weekends we would have a long line at the door. I was commissioned by the headwaiter, a marvelous professional from Monte Carlo named Jacques Casanova (who was previously the maître d'hôtel of the prestigious Four Seasons in New York), to man the rope and only let guests in when he advised their table was ready. Sometimes it was hard to keep total control, and once a gentleman got by me and led his party of six to a dirty table that had just been vacated. It was our policy to never seat anyone until the table had been cleaned and properly reset. Jacques went over and asked them to please be patient and wait by the door until the area was cleaned. Regrettably, the man reacted unfavorably to this and insisted that they would stay where they were. The scene became most unpleasant. Ultimately, Jacques had his way and the people left but on the way out, the man said to me, "I want his name – his full name." Finding a slip of paper, I wrote, "Jacques Honoré Archibald Isidore Napoléon Casanova." The man then got mad at me because he thought I was making fun of him but this *was* Jacques' full name, having been named after all his uncles. I never saw this guest again.

****

I have indeed been fortunate in my life to have met many fascinating people. One of these was Igor Pantuhoff, a Russian painter. His was an amazing talent and in early 1962, many of his works were featured prominently by the Findlay Galleries on Worth Avenue, and in the lobby of The Colony. He had even done a portrait of Princess Grace of Monaco at a live sitting. He was *that* good. I got to know him well and once, while in his studio, I saw one of his smaller paintings, which caught my eye. It was of the beautiful face of a young Hawaiian girl. The eyes sparkled, the mouth had the trace of the beginning of a smile and I *really* liked it and I told him so.

He said, "You like it that much?"

"Yes, I do Igor. It's just beautiful."

"Then it's yours." He replied.

Ruth and Joe Tankoos

The Colony

At my desk in the lobby of The Colony

"No, Igor. I can't just take it. Tell me what you would sell it for and if I can afford it, I'll buy it."

"No, I insist. It's yours. I want you to have it." I protested. I did not want him to think I was angling for it, but he was insistent. Of course, I still have it and it is one of my personal treasures. It has been hanging prominently in my home ever since.

During this same visit to his studio, he had a much larger painting on his easel on which he was still working. It was in the final touch-up phase and this too was gorgeous. I told him how much I loved it and I asked what he was planning on asking for it. He promised me that when it was done, he would give me first refusal to see if I could afford it.

Igor was true to his Russian roots and the reputation Russians have of being serious drinkers. He spent a great deal of time circulating around the various premier nightspots around Palm Beach and The Colony was on his route. He would frequently approach a table uninvited and introduce himself with, *"Good evening. My name is Igor, I am a painter."* in his strongly accentuated Russian accent. I often had to rescue the poor guests and guide him out the door; but he was just a teddy bear with no malice of any kind. I think it was probably this tendency that caused him to forget his promise to me concerning the painting I had admired.

Sometime later, just by chance, I read in the Miami Herald that his paintings were being featured at an art gallery on the Lincoln Mall on Miami Beach. I drove down to see if that painting was one he was showing. To my pleasant surprise, it was and it had a price tag of $300. Igor was there and I reminded him of the promise he had made to me. I told him I would give him $300 for it and he took it down and put it in the back seat of my

Corvair. As we were doing this, the woman who owned the gallery came out yelling at Igor and asked him what on earth he was doing. Apparently, she did not want him selling his own paintings directly from her showing. I explained how I had seen it several weeks earlier when Igor had promised to give me first refusal. She did settle down but she was still not happy about it. This one also has been hanging in our home ever since.

My wife, Anita, and her sister Barbara, had their formal portraits painted while their father was serving in the Army in Frankfurt, Germany and the girls were attending the American High School. The one of Anita, age 16, is hanging in the most prominent place in our living room, often getting admiring glances from our guests. Igor's painting is of a beautiful young girl, maybe just subtly sexy. When guests remarked on Igor's, I always said, "And this is the one who got away!" Anita's response was always the same. "You're not funny!"

I had an English girlfriend for a while in Palm Beach, named Peta Rimington, and one evening we were invited to go to Miami with the most senior black police officer in Florida at that time. His name was Lt. Boone Darden and Peta was a friend of he and his wife, Rose. He had been transferred from Miami to Palm Beach, and in later years, was appointed as the chief of police for Riviera Beach. (He was the first black police chief of a major Florida city). It was an amazing night and we went to several locations that Peta and I would *never* have gone to on our own. We started out at a motel on the west side of Miami (I guess there isn't an east side!) where the well-known black entertainer, Earl Grant, was appearing with his band. Peta and I were the only white people there, but they all seemed to know Boone, so we were in good hands. Not only did we stand out that way, but we were not dressed for the occasion, as everyone else was dressed in evening clothes. Evidently, it was quite a big occasion. From there we went to a few other clubs and lounges where Boone was known, and arrived back in Palm Beach the next morning. At that point, I must have looked a complete wreck and, as I lived in the hotel, there was no way I could creep back to my room unnoticed.

****

Since the off-season hotel business was quiet, I made arrangements for my mother to come over for a visit in the summer of 1962. I was given permission to take off for several weeks and we planned to use the time to tour the country by car. Shortly after arriving in Palm Beach, I had purchased a second-hand gray 1960 Chevrolet Corvair with a white roof from a dealership recommended by my boss. At that time 'purchased' was probably the wrong word as, after showing me the various other models available and I had picked this one out, Gardner's contact just said, "Take it, we can do the paperwork later" and I drove back to the hotel in my 'new' car. I don't think that would have happened in England. Of course, I did have to pay for it eventually. Even though this was considered a small car, it seemed double the size of my nice blue Morris Minor back home.

This trip was one of a lifetime and in all, we drove 12,378 miles. We started in Key West and drove north through the Florida panhandle to New Orleans; then through Texas with a stop in Juarez, Mexico to see a bull fight (which mother hated); on to the Carlsbad Caverns in New Mexico; then to Los Angeles, and San Francisco; back through Las Vegas, the badlands in South Dakota, Chicago, Detroit, Toronto, Niagara Falls and back down the east coast where my mother flew home from Washington, D.C.

Overall, everything went smoothly but we did have a brush with the law, the chief of police, no less, in Winslow, Arizona. We were on the famous Route 66, heading into Winslow, where we had planned to spend the night. When selecting our accommodations, we routinely used the AAA guide and picked the least expensive motel with their rating. It was after sundown and, after driving across the rather barren Arizona desert landscape, we transitioned from total darkness, pierced only by car headlights, to be faced with lights, lights and more lights. Neon signs advertising businesses of all kinds, some even with moving arrows and such, made identifying our selected destination or, for that matter, distinguishing traffic lights, very difficult. Through part of the town, the two east and west bound routes were split by a wide median on which were many motels and restaurants giving them access to traffic passing in both directions. On our first run through, we must have missed our selected motel, so I did a U-turn at the west end of town and headed back in the direction from which we had come. The flashing signs were confusing, and the situation was further complicated by the siren of a police car with its lights flashing behind us. There was a lot of traffic and, as I was familiar with the law of having to ease over to the right and stop, I accomplished this without hitting anyone. As anticipated, the police car passed us by, but then, to our surprise, it stopped just ahead and an officer in a big western hat got out and approached us. He introduced himself as the chief of police.

"Excuse me, sir. May I see your driver's license and insurance card, please?"

I did have a Florida driver's license but I also had my English license and it was this that I gave him. "I'm sorry to have to trouble you" said the chief, "but you went straight through a red light back there. Are you aware of that?"

"No, I'm afraid I wasn't. We are visitors from England and we're just looking for our motel. After coming out of the desert, all the bright lights are very confusing."

He squatted down and looked over at my mother.

"Officer, this is my mother." I offered.

He politely tipped his hat. "Good evening, ma'am. I'm sure sorry to do this, but what your son just did happens quite frequently around here, often resulting in a nasty accident, some even requiring funerals."

"We're only intending to stay here for the night but, thank you for making us aware that we need to be more careful." my mother replied. "We're actually touring all around the country so this is all new to us."

"Well, I won't spoil your visit with a ticket, but please pay attention and be more careful. Can I help you find your motel?"

He was most courteous, and after he gave us directions, we arrived without any further incidents. I wrote a 'thank you' to him after I returned to Palm Beach telling him how much we appreciated the way he had handled the situation and saying that, in fact, it had more of an impact on us than if he had given us a ticket.

There were, of course, many memorable moments during this trip and one was in Las Vegas at the Desert Inn casino. Neither of us had ever seen the inside of a casino before. Before we left Palm Beach, my boss had given me $10 to bet for him at the roulette table. He drew a sketch of how to do it, namely with two dollars on 17, which is the number right in the middle of the board, and then two dollars each on the four corners of 17 so that all the numbers from 13 to 21 had a bet. My mother and I stood at one of these tables for a long time trying to figure out what was going on. Finally, striking up enough courage to get into things, I ceremoniously took the envelope containing his wager and his sketch out of my pocket, slit open the envelope and gave the croupier the $10. He was a balding fellow who looked at me over his thin-rimmed glasses and pushed ten silver dollars towards me. This was confusing because everyone else at the table was playing with colored plastic discs. I stood there for several turns of the wheel and he finally motioned to me to put the money on the numbers I wanted to play. I said, "Yes, I do want to play but..." looking at the table where there were no other silver dollars being bet. "You can play with those," he seemed to snarl at me. After a few more turns of the wheel, and checking the sketch, I placed the silver dollars on the table exactly as depicted. It seemed like the ball would never stop going around and around and around but finally it did and what do you know, it had nestled itself in a little hole right next to 17. "What happens now?", I asked. "You've won $136," he snarled again and then gave me a handful of colored plastic discs. "You can play with these or see the cashier."

It was then that I learned the little plastic discs were called "chips". Still a bit confused and rather overwhelmed with the whole outcome, my mother and I moved away from the table to regroup. We had been there longer than this seemingly simple transaction really required, so we left and went over to the cashier to collect our $136, which I asked for all in silver dollars. They were quite heavy and felt *really* good! I only regretted that they were not mine. We then went over to the gift shop, found a small blue drawstring bag with a big dollar sign on it with the words "Loot from Las Vegas" and, after playing a few turns of the wheel ourselves, we left. On my return to Palm Beach, I went in to see Gardner, plopped the bag on his desk and said, "Sorry, I couldn't do any better than that." He sat in complete amazement.

He just couldn't believe it – but he didn't offer to send me back to try to do it again.

One of the planned stops on this amazing tour was in San Francisco to see Phillip Marks, my old friend from our Savoy Hotel days, and his wife Shirley. He was now manager of the prestigious St. Francis Yacht Club on the marina. One evening we all went to dinner at Ondines, a wonderful waterfront restaurant across the bay in Sausalito. The headwaiter in our section was obviously English and told us, in rather bragging terms, he used to work at The Savoy Hotel. Little did he know to whom he was speaking. It did not take long for him to figure out that he had been caught out after we asked him when he had been there, where he worked and asked him to identify some of the people with whom he worked. We didn't do this on purpose, as we were interested to compare notes with him, but once he realized we knew he was not telling us the truth, he seemed to disappear. We never saw him again all evening!

Another evening Phillip asked if I would like to go with him to the Monterey Jazz Festival. Several well-known performers were appearing including Dave Brubeck and his group and, of course, I said, "Yes." He neglected to tell me it was over 100 miles to the south. It was a great evening, and we had a grand old time but I think it's the only time I have driven nearly 250 miles for an evening out. But it was worth it.

My mother and I experienced a little hiccup on our way back east in the Colorado Rocky Mountains. It was late in the day but still light and we were headed towards Denver. We planned to spend the night in the little town of Frisco. Right before Frisco we needed to traverse the Vail Pass at an altitude of 10,666 feet. It was an excellent highway and the views, as we climbed the winding road, were spectacular. However, it seemed the car was having some difficulty with the climb and despite putting the accelerator all the way to the floor, the poor little Corvair was gradually slowing down until it stopped completely just about 100 yards from the top of the pass. I am not mechanically inclined, and had absolutely no idea what the problem could be. We had not run out of gas and that was about as far as my analysis could go. There were no cell phones then and we were well and truly stuck on a mountain in the middle of nowhere. There was not much traffic at that time of day and having mother in the car only compounded my concern. As we sat there pondering our predicament, a vehicle sped past us and then did a U-turn and came back to see if we needed any assistance. As it turned out, they were young healthy lads who were involved in mining in the area and after we explained our situation, they agreed to get behind us and push us over the top of the pass. Then we could free wheel down the east side the rest of the way into Frisco. This we did and as we got closer to town, I tried to turn over the engine and, to my surprise, it started and we got to the motel where we spent the night.

"Phew," is right.

Of course, I still had concerns, as our challenge the next day would be getting over the Loveland Pass at an elevation of 11,990 feet. This could present the same problem, and it did. We managed a few miles up the side of the mountain but then the same thing happened again. By drifting backwards a little, I was able to turn around and head back into Frisco to find help. I stopped at the first gas station we came to and described our problem, whereupon the service attendant went to the back of the car (where the engine was in the Corvair), opened the hood and unscrewed the top of the air filter and gave it to me saying, "That should do it." I was doubtful and I told him that I was sure

I would be seeing him again in a few minutes. "I don't think so," he said, and I pulled back out into the road heading east. He was right, it seems that due to the high altitude, the air filter was not allowing sufficient air into the engine for proper combustion. We sailed up to the summit of Loveland Pass with relative ease and stopped to take in the incredible views. It was quite cold and there was still some snow on the ground. I picked some of it up to take back to Palm Beach to show my friends but someone must have stolen it out of my car, because when I got back to Florida, it was gone!

Next stop, Denver, then we headed up north to Rapid City to see Mount Rushmore, drove through the Badlands National Park, and traveled east on to Chicago and Detroit. We then crossed into Canada with a planned stop in Toronto to meet up with some of the nurses I had met on the *S.S. United States*. We had a wonderful visit at the phenomenal Niagara Falls and then proceeded on to New York and Washington, D.C. where mother took a flight back to England.

From there I drove back to Florida, stopping for a couple of nights at the famed Greenbriar Resort in White Sulphur Springs, West Virginia, where one of The Colony's former restaurant captains, Paul Baud, was a banquet captain and had made the arrangements there for me. I reached Florida in early November, having been gone for about three months. The average price for an overnight stay in a AAA rated motel in those days was around $8.00. One of the motels we stayed at in Ocala, when we visited Silver Springs, is still there today and still looks good, the Silver Princess Motel on the corner of Route 441/27 and SE 31st Street.

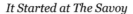

Key to Success #4

Mentor: *If confronted with a problem brought to you by an associate, listen attentively and ask the person to also offer a practical solution.*

4. I Meet Anita (1963-1964)

Now it was back to work, and the 1962/63 season was just beginning to get under way with The Colony once again being in the limelight with many high-profile guests. After the season was over, Joe Tankoos evaluated the quiet summer months to come and decided to close the hotel in May and reopen again in the fall. He had recently purchased the Delmonico Hotel in New York City on the corner of Park Avenue and 59th Street and offered me an assistant reception manager's position, which I gladly accepted. This would provide me wider experience and allow me to see more of New York. The general manager, Alexander Polich, was an impressive gentleman who had been a member of the Yugoslav Davis Cup tennis team. After a few weeks though I felt it was not quite up to the level of The Savoy, Plaza Athénée or even The Colony, and I was seriously considering ending my American adventure.

A friend of my father's, Fred Robinson, was in the restaurant business in Manchester back in the U.K. and he had become a mentor to me, taking an extreme interest in my progress. The Bel and The Dragon, a picturesque country inn in the charming village of Cookham, near Maidenhead on the River Thames, was on the market for around 75,000 pounds. There was some interest, on both our parts, in his purchasing it. I would manage it and have an option to gradually earn an equity position towards eventual complete ownership. It had a London West End quality restaurant but with a local country pub atmosphere with old beams, a big cozy open fireplace and low ceilings. As it turned out, a surprise telephone call ended our plans.

The call was from Stu Levin, restaurant director at The Four Seasons, one of New York's finest restaurants, located in the Seagram Building on Park Avenue. He invited me over there for an interview, following a recommendation from Jacques Casanova, our headwaiter at The Colony. The parent company had several fine restaurants in their portfolio, one of which was the English-styled Mermaid Tavern in Stratford, Connecticut. They were looking for an English person to manage it. What could be more perfect? The town had an open-air theater-in-the-round, which hosted an annual summer Shakespeare Festival. The tavern followed the Shakespearian theme and was part of the same property on which was situated the five-building three-story Stratford Motor Inn built on a picturesque hillside overlooking the Housatonic River and the Sikorsky plant (known for the production of helicopters). The restaurant employees were all dressed in Shakespearean era costumes, the menus were written in Olde English, and beer was often served in traditional yards of ale. The open beamed ceiling and big open fireplace in the lounge continued the same attractive theme.

It was similar to the property I had considered in England, but there would be no chance for an equity position. Levin suggested I take a look at it and get back to them. On my next day off, I drove up there with Judy Benham, a delightful girl with whom I had worked in Palm Beach where she had handled public relations for The Colony Hotel. What I saw, I liked and I accepted the offer to become general manager of The Mermaid Tavern...and guess what happened next! I met Anita.

It was now the summer of 1963, the Shakespeare Festival was on and both the inn and tavern were going full throttle. I quickly found a small, unfurnished studio apartment in nearby New Haven, bought myself a second-hand sofa bed and assumed my new responsibilities. Anita was already working there as banquet manager and it did not take long for me to be attracted to her and her ever cheerful attitude. She had a wonderful personality. We were all so busy that I think we only went out on one date but, of course, we saw each other every day. That one date was to a rather up-market restaurant called Donats where I made a bit of a fool of myself. What's new?

We ordered our food from an elaborate menu and when the wine waiter approached our table and offered a comprehensive wine list, I selected a mid-priced popular wine of the day, a Lancers Crackling Rose from Portugal. It came in a pinkish colored earthenware crock and he presented it to me correctly with the label facing me. He then removed the cork and poured a little into my glass to taste. Following the wine tasting protocol I had learned in hotel school, I lifted my glass to the light to approve the color, stuck my nose through the opening at the top of the glass to smell the bouquet, then swilled it around in my mouth to savor the flavor. With pure gamesmanship, I thought for a moment to keep him in suspense, then, with a bit of a frown, I nodded my approval, whereupon he poured some into Anita's glass. That's when *it* happened. Some foreign object that had been sequestered inside the crock since bottling was finally freed and plopped out into her glass. The wine waiter quickly grasped a clean glass off a neighboring table, poured some of the offending wine into it, tasted it and, as if I were not already dying, pronounced, "That's no good, I'll get you another bottle!" And you know what, she married me anyway! We had reason to recall that incident many times over our 50 years together.

The property had numerous regular guests and two of them, young traveling salesmen types, became our good friends. They were always full of mischief. One time, a group of us left the lounge around closing time, along with some of the bar's inventory, and adjourned to the pool area. This was situated on the hillside in the middle of the property so that it was possible to see all five three-story buildings surrounding it. We had all had a few drinks, but were not wildly drunk, and one of these fellows suggested we play 'tic-tac-toe'. There was a telephone at the pool used for room service, emergency reasons or to call a guest room by dialing '7' and then the room number. It was late and, being the general manager of the restaurant, I really should not have been doing this. The idea was to dial a room number at random and, if answered, ask the guest to turn their light on. If they did, a big cheer went up from the pool area. This went on for a while trying desperately to get three lights in a row either down or across. By the time the game ended everyone was in hysterics and the night auditor had a more interesting evening than normal keeping up with all the complaint calls he was getting. That was yet another occasion when I was fortunate that my career did not come to an involuntary end.

We would occasionally welcome celebrities to the restaurant and the hotel when they were appearing in local productions. Among them were the acclaimed stage actress Helen Hayes and Hollywood actress Jayne Mansfield. Mansfield, plus her entourage and dogs, left her suite in utter shambles. I don't think they ever properly walked the poor dogs.

At that time, we hosted a daily, live, remote local radio show from the lounge from noon to two and the disc jockeys became good friends of ours. One was Jack Lazar, who for many years had been with Station WNEW in New York which was heavily involved with the pay-for-play scandal of the 60s. The other was a wonderful fellow with a great sense of humor, Gene Stewart. Due to an accident, Gene had lost his left arm. You could tell how well we got along, as on one occasion I went to shake hands with him and held out my left hand. Of course, he held out his right hand and we both collapsed laughing. (Was that sick or what?) We also had a fine restaurant captain, Steve Hogan, who walked with a pronounced limp, also due to an accident. The restaurant was known for having a lavish brunch buffet on Sundays, and we often had a line at the door waiting to get in. One Sunday Gene and Steve pushed their way to the front of the line, Gene copying Steve's limp and Steve, with his left arm under his jacket and his jacket sleeve tucked into his left jacket pocket, loudly asked Lee Cassalini, our maître d'hôtel, for a table for a pair of bookends!

I am rather embarrassed to say I don't remember quite how or when I proposed to Anita. We had known each other for about five months and, it was just understood between us. We agreed we should get married and the next formal requirement was to get an engagement ring. We set off to New York and headed for the famous Tiffany and Company jewelry store on Fifth Avenue where we looked at a huge array of options. Anita finally selected one, which she tried on to see if it fit. Yes, it did! So we bought it, or I should say more correctly, I bought it. Upon exiting the store, I asked Anita to remove it and give it to me so that I could present it to her at a more private and intimate moment. She not only refused, she emphatically refused, so the 'deal' was done and the ring stayed on her finger. Anita 1 – Bill 0. Just ten minutes after getting her a beautiful diamond ring, I am already one down. Is this really going to work?

That week President John F. Kennedy was assassinated while on an official visit to Dallas, so our excitement was mitigated by this

With Anita, poolside at The Stratford Motor Inn

senseless tragedy. Anita and I mutually decided that I should 'fire' her so that we would no longer work together, as such relationships could present a conflict of interest. Some of our employees in the restaurant were not aware of our relationship and when she was 'fired,' they really could not understand why. One elderly fellow, Bill Stansfield, the front office manager, adored Anita and, as a result, he immediately took a serious dislike to me – and showed it. After a few days, I saw him sitting alone in a corner of the restaurant having his lunch and I went over and asked, "May I join you, Bill?" He didn't say a word, but I sat down anyway. I said, "Did you know that Anita and I are engaged?" He loved Anita and hated me so much he just didn't know how to react to that, and it was quite funny to see. Happily, the animosity he had towards me dissipated and he eventually got over it.

Anita lived in Devon, a small community near Stratford and Bridgeport, with her parents, Frank and Margaret 'Peg' Herb. Her father was a soon-to-be retired Army Colonel and was of German descent. Her mother's maiden name was Conroy and she came from Dublin, Ireland and never fully lost her wonderful Irish brogue. They were always wonderful to me even though I was going to take their 'baby' away from them. Anita's older sister Barbara and her husband, John Stompoly, an attorney, lived in Point Pleasant, New Jersey. Her younger brother Frank was still living at home.

Then it struck me. What was it my mother had said about an American girl just before I boarded the ship in Southampton two years ago? Oh dear! Well, I had better arrange to take Anita to the U.K. to meet her and remove any preconceptions she may have. I received permission from the company to take a leave of absence to do this. I was advised that I would have to leave my job running the Mermaid Tavern but, that on our return, I would be reassigned to another, yet to be determined facility.

We spent several weeks there in the early months of 1964. My mother quickly came around to approve of my important selection. It was a wonderful time, during which we also flew to Dublin and looked up a couple of the families known to Anita's mother. One was the Roche family who owned several chemist shops in Dublin and a little dog they had named Kennedy after the American President. Visiting the second family was a rather interesting experience. When we contacted them, they invited us to their unpretentious row house for tea. During our conversation, we learned that the husband was a knowledgeable art enthusiast and that he had recently purchased an old and slightly damaged painting at a second-hand shop for a nominal ten pounds. He proudly took us upstairs where he brought it out from under their bed. With his experienced eye, he had identified it as a work by acclaimed artist Charles Willson Peale. It depicted George Washington standing with Princeton, New Jersey, burning in the background. He said this was almost an exact duplicate of the original, and had been done for John Hancock. He pointed out a barely perceptible difference from the original where the hilt of Washington's sword broke the horizon.

For comparison, he showed us a full-page color picture of the original, which had been published in National Geographic magazine, and pointed out the difference. He told us that the original was hanging in the Brooklyn Museum. We assured him we would go and look at it after we returned to America, and we did. He planned to do the necessary restoration work and then present it at auction. Imagine our surprise when back home in New York, we read in the airmail copy of the July 17, 1965 edition of the Daily Telegraph, that he had successfully sold it for 14,000 guineas! At that time, this would have been somewhere between $40,000 and $45,000; over $300,000 today. It was quite exciting. Thanks to his experienced eye, he had indeed made a handsome profit.

Upon returning to the States, I learned that I was being assigned to one of the finest Restaurant Associates' restaurants in New York City, *The Forum of the Twelve Caesars* on 48th Street. I would be the assistant to the director, Lee Hardy. This was a magnificent restaurant located in the famed Rockefeller Center, featuring large portraits of the twelve Caesars and offering an amazing menu formulated around the first ever cookery book from the Roman era written by Apicius. One of the more popular items was the pheasant baked in clay with the clay broken off tableside by our experienced captains. In 2010, the restaurant was recreated and featured prominently in a TV episode of "Mad Men".

Anita and I set our wedding date for the first Saturday in June 1964 and, although we did not realize it at the time, it was a perfect Anglo-American compromise. In the U.S, we print the date with the month first followed by the day and then the year. However, in England it is customary to write it day first, *then* the month and the year. This all came to our attention when we went to order our wedding rings and asked to have the date engraved on the inside of each one. Our wedding day was going to be the 6th of June so the engraving would be 6-6-64.

I had rented a small apartment on the east side, while Anita and I looked for an apartment where we would live after the wedding. We settled on a brand-new building, Lexington Towers at 160 East 88th Street and Lexington Avenue, in an area known as Germantown. There were some magnificent German pastry shops on 86th Street, most of which, sadly, are no longer there.

The developer was giving some rent concessions at the time to get the building fully occupied and we leased apartment 10K, a nice one-bedroom on the tenth floor, for $192.00 a month. There was underground parking available for an additional $30.00 a month and we signed up for that as well. That same apartment rented for over $3,000 per month in 2016.

With so many things going on, both a new job and preparations for the big day, June came along quickly. My mother and Aunt Gladys came over for the wedding, and my friend Norman Krohn, from my Palm Beach days, who was now also working in New York, agreed to be my best man. We were married in St. Ann's Catholic Church in Devon, Connecticut on a beautiful but very windy day. Our reception, naturally, was held at The Mermaid Tavern, in the banquet room on the lower level, known as Guildhall. Thank goodness, we have photographs of the event because it was all a blur to me at the time. It was so nice being served by our employee-friends, and I think they enjoyed it too. Having never attended a wedding in America, I was totally unaware of the traditional cutting of the cake and the process of the bride and groom feeding each other the pieces. I took mine and immediately stuffed it in my mouth, which did not go unnoticed. But it was too late then for Anita to change her mind. After the reception, we changed clothes, waved goodbye to all and headed off to Lake George for our honeymoon, still in my little Corvair. Somewhere in route, I was suffering through my usual spate of drowsiness after a meal, so Anita took over the driving. We arrived at The Georgian hotel on the banks of beautiful Lake George whereupon Anita rather unceremoniously poked me in the ribs and said, "Wake up, we're here." I think I was supposed to be more excited about the whole thing. Poor Anita. Before even 24 hours had passed she was probably already having second thoughts.

Key to Success #5

Be Prudent: *Always try to maintain good relationships. These could lead to future opportunities.*

5. Career and Married Life (1964-1966)

During the summers of 1964 and 1965, New York hosted the World's Fair in Flushing Meadows, adjacent to the New York Mets' baseball stadium. Restaurant Associates, for whom I worked at The Mermaid Tavern, had been successful in obtaining food service operating agreements at several of the pavilions. These included an exclusive 36-seat Four Seasons-type private executive dining room in the Ford Motor Company Pavilion, an innovative restaurant known as The Festival of Gas in the pavilion run by the American Gas Association, and a more casual dining venue at People to People in the Missouri Pavilion. The company also managed the "Top of the Fair" restaurant in the adjacent Port Authority Building. In the Festival of Gas restaurant, we used rolling trolleys specially designed by the Corning Company, which contained bottled gas, a hot plate and grill on which an entree could be cooked tableside. With current fire codes, I don't think one could do that today. That first summer, I was sent out to assist at the Festival of Gas Pavilion and I worked alongside Bert Laacks, who was managing the facility for the company. I got to meet some interesting people including Glenn Ford, the movie actor, and Herman Lay, founder and chairman of "Bet you can't eat just one" Lay's potato chips. After that, it was back to the *Forum*.

The following summer, I was appointed Director of the VIP dining

Ford Pavilion

room in the Ford Pavilion. This was a great opportunity. For one thing, I got to meet Walt Disney, whose company had designed the Ford Magic Skyway ride at the pavilion around the evolution of the wheel. Guests traveled in Ford model automobiles, straight from the assembly line. The cars were attached to a rail system that moved the passengers through time with narration by Disney himself. They began in the age of dinosaurs, progressed to the invention of the wheel, and after a series of dioramas traveled to a futuristic city before exiting the ride. It was quite a triumph for the Disney Imagineers. Our daughter, Wendy, had just been born on June 26th and Walt was kind enough to sign one of the fancy Ford Motor Company pavilion brochures for her. It is one of her most treasured possessions to this day. The ride, along with the General Motors and General Electric exhibits, was one of the most popular at the fair.

The pavilion was almost always on the VIP escorted tour. One of the most memorable visits was by Princess Grace of Monaco who visited with young Caroline and an accompanying caregiver. We had been notified of her impending visit that day, but having no more details, we prepared all kinds of fancy hors d'oeuvres with caviar, foie gras, smoked salmon and other dainty finger food plus platters of assorted delicate pastries. We were ready to provide practically anything she would have wanted.

They arrived with a cadre of security escorts from Ford, the World's Fair, New York City, and the State of New York. In addition, John Sattler, the Ford pavilion manager, and a representative of Robert Moses, chairman of the World's Fair Authority, accompanied them. There were certainly far too many people just hovering around. Princess Grace, Caroline and her nurse got seated comfortably, were presented all our elaborate food options, and then her highness asked if she could simply have a cup of tea. Caroline and the nurse had Cokes. It was summer in New York, hot and steamy. After relaxing for about 20 to 30 minutes, Princess Grace said they were ready to take the ride. The Ford Pavilion was on four levels. The ground floor level was the public entrance, the lower level housed the employee cafeteria and lockers, our VIP lounge and dining room were on the second floor and the Walt Disney ride was on the third floor. There were two elevators, one on each side of the building, both stopping at all four levels. The entourage entered one of the elevators, security personnel and all, and as the doors closed we wished them a pleasant ride.

Almost as soon as the doors closed and the elevator had started to go up to the third floor, the alarm bells went off and the elevator stopped about two or three feet from where it had started. Try as everyone might, no one could open the doors so we sent out an emergency call to Lou Columbo, the pavilion chief engineer. He was in the pavilion but far away from the elevators, and it seemed an interminable amount of time before he arrived on the scene and went to the basement to crank the elevator back down to our level. They were all in there for at least 10 minutes, which seemed more like hours for all concerned.

They emerged hot, sweating, flustered and apologetic, especially poor John Sattler who was a red-haired Irishman, now with a *red* face to match! Princess Grace, Caroline and the nurse retired to the ladies' room to do whatever repair work was necessary and then returned to the couch area where they had been sitting before. While they were relaxing, John Sattler was corralling the troops to determine the pecking order for those who would, of necessity, not be able to ride in the elevator, as he surely was not going to over-load it again. Finally, they had it all figured out and Princess Grace was ready to go. Once they were all in, the button

Artist concept of Ford Magic Skyway created by Disney

Princesses Caroline and Grace at the Ford Pavilion

was pressed and up they went to the ride. This time everything would be fine. No way!

Due to the time taken to load the elevator with everyone authorized to accompany her highness, someone had beaten them to it, so instead of going up, it went down. It opened on the basement level, the employee cafeteria full of vending machines and scattered with newspapers and all kinds of trash. One of the students employed by Ford as a pavilion attendant, looked up and in a loud voice exclaimed, "Look! Princess Grace!" which brought the folks in the elevator much more attention than they wanted. The doors closed again and this time the elevator did indeed move upwards. However, it had chosen the scenic route and the next stop was on the main public floor level where the entry was a mass of humanity. We had no idea of all this added excitement and we were going about our business putting all the royal trappings away. Suddenly, the elevator door opened and everyone was *still* there. At last, the next stop was the ride, which I am sure was less event-filled than the unscheduled 'tour' getting to it.

****

The pavilion was certainly the place to meet important people. Juan Trippe, chairman of Pan American World Airways, came in for lunch one day with his wife and son. I always thought that was an interesting name for a senior airline executive, as I thought it was pronounced "one trip" – perhaps not such a good slogan for an airline.

During my time at The Colony, I also had occasion to meet many people who were considered high society at the time and who flitted around the social scenes such as Palm Beach in the winter, Southampton in the summer and other high profile seasonal venues. One of these, Huntington Hartford, was a friend of Joe

Tankoos. I was quite happy to take care of him and his guests when they rested from the summer heat in the Ford VIP Lounge. I am not sure that he remembered me from The Colony, but we did talk about Tankoos and my association with him.

During our conversation, he told me he was looking for a manager to take over The Mermaid Tavern, a restaurant and bar discotheque he owned on Bay Street in Nassau. It was located by the dock where people took boats over to Paradise Island. I told him about my friend David Ward in London and he asked me to get in touch with him to see if he might be interested. He also asked if I had any letters from David to which I replied that I did. When I asked why, he replied: "I study handwriting, and I feel I can tell something about an individual by the way they write. Would you mind coming to my home sometime, so that I can look at one of his letters?" He gave me his address, Number One Beekman Place in Manhattan!

David and I shared a somewhat infantile sense of humor and our letters to each other reflected this. I tend to be a 'keeper', much to Anita's chagrin, and I had kept several of David's letters since coming to the States. However, I had great difficulty finding one that I could show to a third party that would not convey this immature style and perhaps hurt David's chances for the position for which he was being considered. I picked the best one I could and made an appointment with Hartford's secretary to follow up on his request. It was to be a five o'clock appointment one afternoon at Beekman Place, where he occupied a complete floor of this impressive building.

As the elevator door opened, I was met by a uniformed butler and obediently followed him to the living room. On the way, we passed Hartford's young wife Diane, a small group of musicians, who seemed to be practicing, and several Romanesque style statues. Hartford was on the telephone, and I was invited to sit down. He was still in his dressing gown and eating a bowl of cereal, much of which had spilled on the floor. He hung up and I showed him David's letter. To my relief, he actually did not read it but seemed to only study David's handwriting. The phone rang again and I sat there just listening to his side of the conversation. He finally hung up and said to me, "I'm thinking of selling part of Paradise Island, what do you think?"

Paradise Island is just across the water from Nassau and was formerly known as Hog Island. I was somewhat familiar with it, having visited it while in the Bahamas. At that time, other than the Ocean Club, a golf course and a restaurant called the Café Martinique, there was little there. However, it did have a large protected beach on the western end that was extremely popular. It was simply heaven on earth to take a dip in the crystal-clear waters, return to my chaise lounge under a huge beach umbrella and raise the flag to prompt one of the beach attendants to bring me one of their colorful rum drinks. Now it is home to up-scale resorts, including Atlantis, and high-end condominiums.

"Which part?" I naively asked, thinking maybe he was selling the section where the beach or the golf course was located.
"Forty percent." he said, clearly putting me in my place. "I'm thinking of selling part of it to the Mary Carter Paint Company." And he was asking *my* advice?

He evidently approved of David's handwriting and, to cut a long story short, he offered David the job. David accepted and moved from London to the tropical haven of the Bahamas; quite a change and certainly an interesting one. I took some vacation time after the World's Fair closed at the end of the 1964 summer and flew down to Nassau to spend a few days with David. The boats to the island left from The Mermaid Tavern, and I arrived in suit and tie with my suitcase as I joined the bathing suit and flip-flop clad crowd. I sure stood out among the mob on the crowded boat as I sat on the roof of it with my suitcase between my knees. Still, it was a break from the hustle and bustle of New York so I really didn't care.

One of Hartford's claims to fame was that he had inherited two massive fortunes. One was from his grandfather, who had developed the A&P grocery store chain, and the other from his father, who had invented and patented a shock absorber for cars. I had heard people say that Huntington Hartford II was in the process of losing it all, which seemed to be confirmed in an article appearing in the Washington Post. He had a tendency to invest in many diverse enterprises, many of which did not pan out. During David's tenure, he received a letter from Hartford's attorney congratulating him on showing a profit of a few thousand dollars and noting that, "...at present it is one of the few Huntington Hartford projects operating at a profit."

****

One night, as I was leaving the pavilion and heading for my car, it was raining heavily. I had not brought a raincoat with me, so I took a large black trash bag from the kitchen, punched a hole in the bottom for my head and joined the crowds scampering for the exits. I had pulled the trash bag down as far as it would go, leaving my hands and arms inside. This was fine, until I tripped over a curb and fell flat on my face. There I was with my nose sniffing the running water in the gutter, my hands and arms pinned to my side inside the trash bag. I had no way of either breaking my fall or getting back up in any sort of dignified manner. It must have been hysterical for those still in an upright position. I am just sorry there was no movie director around to hire me for a Peter Sellers movie. I would have been a perfect fit.

****

On another occasion, a couple of high ranking Ford executives, whom I knew well, needed a ride back to their apartments at nearby Lefrak City where many World's Fair executives were staying for the duration of the fair. I happened to be leaving at the same time and offered to give them a ride. It did not go unnoticed that my Chevrolet Corvair was a competing product and Jack Mulally kept muttering "Oh, Henry, (referring to founder Henry Ford) please, please forgive us, we don't know what we're doing".

****

Even with all the excitement going on around my World's Fair responsibilities, there was one even more beautiful and exciting event, which happened that summer of 1965. On June 26, Anita and I became parents when Wendy Sharon Margaret was born in Lenox Hill Hospital. As any newborn does, Wendy did her fair share of crying, and I made the comment to Anita's mother that we were thinking of getting Wendy a room of her own. This would not have seemed unreasonable, as our Manhattan apartment only had one bedroom, but when I told her it would be in the Bronx, she did not seem to be amused. I thought the Irish had a good sense of humor! Just another self-inflicted wound.

My position at the World's Fair that summer turned out to be almost as fortuitous as my meeting Tankoos in Paris in 1959. Each state was granted a special designated day at the fair and for Arizona Day both Governor Sam Goddard, and Phoenix Mayor Milt Graham, visited us in the VIP Lounge. While we were getting them some refreshments, Governor Goddard asked if I had ever been to Arizona. "No, I'm afraid I haven't but we're planning to drive out there after the fair closes in October. My sister-in-law and her husband recently relocated to Tucson and my wife's parents moved there after my father-in-law retired. He was a colonel in the Army and they wanted to be near the Davis Monthan Air Base where they could avail themselves of the PX and other military services."

Mayor Graham spoke up. "When you're there, if you've got time, why don't you come to Phoenix for a couple of days? I'd be happy to arrange for you to meet some of the principal hotel and restaurant people. Here, I'll give you my card. Just give me a call a day or two before you plan to arrive."

"Thank you so much," I said taking his card. "I'll certainly try to do that."

This development led to some more interesting aspects of my career that would never have happened to me otherwise. I have certainly been blessed with these opportunities.

Key to Success #6

Encourage: *Encourage input and suggestions from your associates; and, follow through. Implement as quickly as possible or explain why you cannot.*

6. Suriname? Where's That? (1966)

In October 1965, the Worlds' Fair finally closed after two busy summers. In many ways, it was sad, as the business community working there had, in large part, bonded. It was as though a whole town was being eradicated from the face of the earth. Ford had contracted with a large construction company to take over the entire pavilion lock, stock and barrel. On the last night, right after the fair closed for the final time, representatives of that company took over immediately; to the point that they did not even want to let John Sattler back into his office to get his raincoat. It was a sad night indeed. Earlier, Sattler had gathered our small group of Restaurant Associates employees together to thank us for our work. He praised us for how we had supported Ford in all their marketing efforts and, to our great surprise, presented us with beautiful gold Tiffany wrist watches. Mine reads, "L.W. Pullen – In appreciation –*the oval Ford logo*- New York World's Fair 1964–65." It is one of my most treasured personal possessions. I have since met some long-term Ford employees and they always say, "I never got one of those." Maybe theirs came in cash. As a small aside, I was given permission by Sattler to take one of the heavy marble-topped coffee tables from the VIP reception area before the fair closed. It seemed so small in that area but so big as I struggled to get it home. That table and a beautiful print of a painting of the Ford Motor Company

Pavilion are still in my possession and are cherished memories of my time there.

Then came vacation time; Anita and I packed up little Wendy, loaded some suitcases in the Corvair, and headed out to Arizona. It was an interesting trip with various stops along the way before arriving in Tucson, where we stayed with Anita's parents. This was perfect because Anita's sister Barbara lived right across the street with John and their two wonderful kids, Pam and Chris. Those were happy times. I also took Mayor Milt Graham up on his kind offer of a tour and introductions to local hoteliers in the Phoenix area. He set up a meeting with a delightful man, Fred Eberhardt, through the Phoenix Chamber of Commerce, and Fred was my personal guide for the two or three days I spent there. He scheduled several appointments for me, among which were two that developed into positions, which are now a part of my resumé. The first of these was with Jack Stewart, owner and original developer of the famous Camelback Inn in Paradise Valley, who offered me an assistant manager's position. The salary seemed fair but the problem was that it would only be a winter seasonal position. The other meeting was with Joe McGovern, general manager of the Executive House Hotel in nearby Scottsdale.

Fred also saw that I was introduced to Chuck Cronrath, the general manager of Del Webb's Mountain Shadows Resort, which was almost across the street from the Camelback Inn. He offered me a position in their banqueting department. This would have been a year-round position but at a lower salary than the job offered to me at Camelback Inn. The total compensation would have included gratuities but, at that point, I had no idea what these may have added to my total income. However, it did give me something to consider.

Our return trip to New York provided us with the scare of our lives. We had planned an overnight stop in Alamogordo, New Mexico. This is approximately 70 miles east of Las Cruces and, after leaving the outskirts of Las Cruces, there is virtually nothing in between. It was a nasty evening, with a black cloudy sky and lightning. I don't recall the rain but the lights of Alamogordo were indeed a welcome sight. We found our motel and pulled in to a parking space quite near the office to check in. Wendy had been quiet in her car seat in the back and when we went to check on her, we immediately thought she might be dead. She seemed to be unconscious; cold, as white as a sheet and waxen to the touch. I flew to the office to find out where the nearest hospital was and just as I was returning to the car, Anita came up and said, "It's OK, she's awake!" It took several minutes for us to compose ourselves as we checked in to our room. Wendy's color gradually returned to her cheeks and it wasn't too long before she was back to her normal self. We had a terrible scare. We speculated the cause was carbon monoxide poisoning coming from the engine, which, in a Corvair, is in the rear of the car behind the back seat. If that was it, and had we gone on further that evening, we could have had a devastating event in our lives.

Upon our return to New York, among our accumulated mail was a telegram from Jack Stewart changing the conditions of his offer to a year-round position. Not being sure of the gratuity issue with the offer from Mountain Shadows, I elected to accept the position at the Camelback Inn and soon after, we relocated to sunny Arizona. We moved into a small but nice ground floor garden apartment in Phoenix and prepared for a new and exciting experience in this desert paradise with its wonderful climate.

It did not take long to realize that Jack Stewart was, regrettably, a different type of boss. On my first day of work he assigned me to the Cholla Bar, which was adjacent to the swimming pool. I reviewed the bar's operations in the morning, and then he and his wife invited me to have lunch with them to report my initial observations. There were no meaningful controls in place at the bar, and I made my recommendations for correcting this situation. It would require a few days to accomplish as, at that point, I had no idea what volume was customary in that outlet. However, about two hours later, I received a telephone call from him asking if I had accomplished what I had proposed. I advised him I had not, as I needed time to determine certain information before I could. Out of the blue he said (quote) "God damn it man, if this isn't done immediately, I'll come down and do it myself!" and hung up. It seemed I was working for a nut. In speaking with some other management employees, I found this was not unusual behavior for him and that the large turnover of staff was largely a self-inflicted problem. Had we uprooted ourselves from a relatively secure environment in New York for this? I made an appointment to see Chuck Cronrath at Mountain Shadows to see if the job he had offered me in the banquet department was still open. Apologetically, he advised it was not.

"We assumed you had accepted another offer in the area. Where was it?"

"Across the street at Camelback Inn." I replied

"How long have you been there?"

"About two weeks."

"Then you are twice as smart as we took you for." he said grinning. "We guessed that was where you went, and we gave you a month."

Before I move on, I should mention that it was while I was there that Jim Durbin, a fine hotelier with the Marriott Corporation, was at Camelback Inn negotiating the acquisition of the iconic resort with the Stewarts. Marriott not only acquired it for their impressive portfolio, they took it to even greater prominence and still operate it today. It remains one of this country's great destination resorts.

But now what do I do?

My next step was to go back to meet with some of the other hotel and restaurant people I had met with Fred Eberhardt to see if there might be other employment opportunities in the Phoenix and Scottsdale area. It was my meeting with Joe McGovern at the Executive House which bore some unexpected fruit. He submitted my resumé to their corporate office in Chicago and, soon after, I received a telephone call saying that they would like to see me to discuss an opportunity in South America. Wow. I thought, maybe Buenos Aires, Quito, Montevideo, or some city with which I would be familiar, but I was not expecting Paramaribo, Suriname. "Where? How do you spell that?" I said.

I indicated I would be interested in meeting with them and immediately ran off to the nearest library to see if there was indeed such a place on the world map. I did find it, but everything seemed to be '90'; 90 inches of rainfall a year, an average annual temperature of 90 degrees, 90 percent humidity and situated just a smidgen north of the equator. It was surrounded by the tropical rain forest on the north-east coast of South America sandwiched between Guyana, formerly British Guiana, to the west and French Guiana to the east. Suriname had formerly been Dutch Guiana. So far, *not* so good! And there was only one real hotel in the whole country, the 81-room Suriname Torarica Hotel and Casino.

The interview at the corporate office in Chicago went well and I was offered the position of general manager. This would be my first opportunity to manage a complete property. The salary was $12,000 a year and we would be able to live in the hotel, so room and board would also be provided. Obviously, Anita and I discussed it in great detail, and finally we decided to go for it. Anita's mother thought we were totally crazy, reacting with "Are you all mad?" She was more concerned for poor little Wendy than for us. Regardless, we made our plans and headed south.

I could write a whole book on this part of our lives. Transportation was limited but Pan American had one flight a week out of New York's Kennedy Airport, and this was by far our best option. It was an exciting but nervous time, as we really didn't know what to expect. After a stop in Port of Spain, Trinidad, we landed at Zanderij International Airport in Suriname, about 28 miles from Paramaribo. Immediately we had a problem. Evidently their immigration regulations required foreign visitors to have return tickets. When they asked me how long we were staying, I could not tell them. It was now dark and hot and "tropical" and nine-month-old Wendy was getting a bit stressed, to say nothing of her mother. I told them I had come to take over as general manager of the Torarica but they weren't impressed. We were still waiting for someone to tell us what to do after everyone else on our flight had left the airport for their own destinations.

Finally, we were cleared to go and we just managed to get the last vehicle leaving for town. It was a station wagon and Anita sat up front next to the driver with Wendy in her lap. I sat in the rear jump seat facing backwards next to a large black gentleman. He had his brief case on the seat next to him, which he was not about to move, so one of my 'cheeks' was actually sitting on it. I was uncomfortable and it was quite stressful. It was pitch black outside,

Torarica Hotel and Casino

except for the reflection of the headlights, and I remember seeing dogs and chickens scattering back into the road after surviving our vehicle, passing like a speedboat cutting through the surf. Thankfully, the ride came to an end under the entrance lights of the Torarica, and we reached the civilization of the welcoming lobby. Yes, we had been expected and from then on things improved dramatically.

After a much needed, good night's sleep, we received a warm welcome from Marcel Wortman, the general manager whom I would be replacing. It was a delightful hotel with three floors of guest rooms connected to the commercial area by a glass corridor bridge over a beautiful pool, which was host to some healthy gold fish. In the commercial area was a lounge featuring nightly entertainment, an excellent full-service restaurant, a coffee shop, a casino and the administrative offices. The hotel was situated on the banks of the mile-wide Suriname River with an expansive view over it to the rain forest on the southern bank. The large, circular swimming pool was set in a colorful tropical garden on one side and a wide terrace area adjacent to the restaurant, used frequently for private parties and special events, on the other.

Before coming to Suriname, the company had allowed us to stay at their Executive House hotel in Scottsdale, after we had moved out of our apartment. Scottsdale is considered to be 'up market', yet here we were immediately adjacent to the tropical rain forest, in an out-of-the way destination and we found the quality of the white glove service in the restaurant vastly superior to what we had just experienced. The difference was simply amazing. Later, we found out that before the Torarica Hotel had opened, a professional Dutch hotelier had come over to train the staff and he obviously did an outstanding job. Since this was the only hotel in the country, one could not just hire trained bartenders, waiters, housekeeping staff and so forth. They had to be trained on site. The funny thing about that was the staff did not know just how good they were because this was the *only* way they knew.

Since we could not carry all our luggage with us on our flight down, we had made arrangements, thanks to a referral from the hotel, with a fellow by the name of Hank Goodman. He had his own plane and flew consignment freight to Guyana, Suriname and French Guiana every two weeks out of Miami. We had enough clothes to get by until his next trip, the following Tuesday. But Tuesday and Wednesday came and went with no pilots checking in to the hotel. Typically, their arrival was an indication that any freight being brought in for the hotel was here but just waiting for customs clearance. At this point, Marcel had become concerned and made some inquiries and we received word that the plane was reported missing and therefore so was all of our 'stuff.' Because flights from Miami to northern South America either went around or over Cuba, I said, *"If ever I see Fidel Castro on TV wearing my tuxedo, we'll know what happened"*. Of course, this was no laughing matter, as the pilot and co-pilot were sadly also missing. Fortunately for Hank Goodman, he had not taken that flight. That made the loss of all our belongings seem unimportant. U.S. Coast Guard vessels were sent out in search of the plane but, after a few days, had found no trace. They were, eventually, called to assist a cruise ship that was on fire elsewhere in the Caribbean. Speculation was rampant about the plane getting lost in the infamous Bermuda Triangle. As far as I know, no wreckage was ever found.

Marcel had arranged a grand welcoming reception for us to be introduced to many local business and government officials. This presented a problem, as we only had the clothes we had brought with us and really nothing which would have been appropriate for this event. However, it was a welcoming subject of conversation and we got through it all right. The guests were most understanding.

The makeup of the staff was a perfect cross section of cultures as represented in the emblem of the national Suriname flag, which was an oval symbolizing unity, with five stars of different colors representing the five ethnic groups. The stars were red for Amerindians, yellow for Asians, black for Bushnegroes, white for Europeans and brown for those of mixed Spanish and French descent. The Amerindian tribes were the indigenous inhabitants. In the 17th century, the country was colonized by Europeans and it was then that an estimated 300,000 negroes were brought over from West Africa as slaves. Over time, many of these slaves ran away into the interior and settled their own Bushnegro villages keeping many of their cultural traditions, even today. When slavery was abolished in 1863, laborers were imported from China, India and Indonesia, each bringing their cultural heritage with them. This incredible diversity created a wonderful, friendly and colorful population and they all lived and worked in harmony as Surinamers.

When Era Bell Thompson, a writer with Ebony Magazine, came down to do a story, "SURINAM: Multiracial Paradise at the Crossroads", she featured many of the beautiful girls in Paramaribo. This included Marijka Schneiders, one of our receptionists, and Gusta Gemerts, one of our telephone operators and part-time gift shop assistant. They appeared in more than one issue and Marijka was featured in full color on the cover of the February 1967 issue. She had a Dutch-German-English-French father and a Suriname-born mother. It just so happened I was in New York when that magazine came out, and it was great to see Marijka, one of *my* employees, so prominently displayed on all the sidewalk newsstands. I took several photographs to show her when I returned to the hotel. I still have copies of these magazines.

The official language was Dutch although the local dialect was Taki Taki, which had primarily evolved from Dutch, English, French, Spanish, Yiddish, Portuguese and West African dialects. Most of the Bushnegroes and Amerindians in the interior spoke Taki Taki but, in the more urban and business environment in Paramaribo, English was widely spoken. The currency was the Suriname guilder, which, at the time of our arrival, was approximately 1.80 guilders to the dollar.

The multiracial environment that had been our home for a while was emphatically brought home to me several years later when one of our accounting employees, Frank Robles, visited us with his delightful wife Gloria and their young daughter. We were living in Port St. Lucie at the time and invited them to use our beachfront condominium in Jensen Beach. We picked them up at the airport and took them to our unit on Hutchinson Island and when Anita and I got in the car to drive home, I turned to her and said, "That's amazing! Truly amazing."

"What do you mean?" she asked.

"I don't remember Frank being black. I just remember him as Frank."

That was indeed an enlightening moment for me.

Key to Success #7

Preserve: *It is better and more economical to work at keeping your existing business than marketing for new.*

7. Challenges in the Tropics (1966-1968)

I settled in to my new, exciting responsibilities as quickly as possible to take advantage of Marcel's local knowledge and the hotel's operating systems before he left. His new assignment was as general manager of the company's beachfront Aruba Caribbean Hotel. One rather unusual challenge in Suriname was that, unlike hotels in the U.S., which get their supplies from local vendors, in Paramaribo there were limited sources for many of the needed items. Consequently, we had to import relatively ordinary products from a supplier in Miami, which were then transported to Suriname by our friend Hank Goodman's airfreight company, Kimex, Inc. We purchased our meat products just three or four times a year via freezer cargo out of New York; thankfully, the hotel had a large walk-in freezer. We would have to check to see how much of an item we still had on hand before we could quote for a banquet.

All arriving supplies had to be cleared through Customs, which required a special agent hired by the hotel, and the payment of any assessed duty. This often presented some interesting challenges, as was the case when we imported baking potatoes. Our paperwork listed "4 cases of 60 count baking potatoes" but Customs required the weight in kilos. Although this was an honest and simple discrepancy, Customs would not release the potatoes and they sat in the rat-infested warehouse on the docks for weeks. When finally, we received a telephone call to come and get them, about 30% of the weight had been lost to the rats. The entire shipment was thrown out.

A similar situation arose after we had been successful in booking a meeting of the Caribbean Lions Clubs. With limited choices for guest accommodations in Paramaribo, we needed some additional folding rollaway beds to supplement what we already had at The Torarica. We ordered 30 of these from our supplier in Miami and Hank Goodman transported them to Suriname well ahead of time. I was a little dismayed then when our agent came to tell me he was unable to clear them through Customs. The problem was that we had declared them as "30 folding beds complete" with the purchase price on the required clearance forms. He said because the frames would be assessed a 25% duty and the mattresses, being an upholstered product, a 40% duty, the beds had been incorrectly declared. Customs had no way of separating the value of the frames and mattresses from the unit price. Despite numerous efforts to get the beds released, we were never successful and the small convention came and went without them. However, since we had paid for them and still needed to get them to the hotel for any future needs, I made an appointment to personally meet with Tjon a Ten, the head of Customs, to appeal for his assistance.

This meeting was like something out of a movie. He was in uniform, like an admiral, reclining in his chair, with his legs crossed and his feet on the desk. He wore an official military type cap pulled down over his eyes and had a big cigar in his mouth. A huge fan in the ceiling was turning so slowly it provided no cooling at all. The first thing he said as I walked in was, "We're going to fine The Torarica."

"For what?" I asked.

"For incorrectly declaring the beds" was his snarled retort.

Our conversation went downhill from there. When we finally got a call to come and get them out of the warehouse, the beds were scattered all over the place, some with rat eaten mattresses. Even if we took them to the hotel, they would not have been usable. We decided to leave them there and I assume they eventually threw them out.

Because we lived in the hotel, Anita would join me for dinner in the evening and for many social events; we needed to hire a babysitter. Wendy had two, one was Charlotta and the other was Lucia, who also had a young daughter, Joyce, about Wendy's age. They were both wonderful and they took to little "Vendy" as if she was one of their own. Because Wendy would often play with Joyce, she began to speak Dutch just naturally although, when we later made a trip back to the States and tried to get her to show off her linguistic skills, she wouldn't utter a word in Dutch.

Paramaribo, Suriname is not the first place a travel agency would think of as a destination for their clients but, in its own special way, it did, and still does, have much to offer. From the colorful traditions and costuming of the different cultures, the natural friendliness of the people and the adventurous trips into the interior, Suriname is a fascinating and relatively unknown travel venue. The interior is host to several interesting sites. These include Joden Savanne, the first Jewish synagogue built in the western hemisphere, many native villages, a multitude of beautiful areas in the tropical rain forest and the rich bauxite deposits.

We naturally did everything we could to promote our destination and we were successful in being included in one of Travcoa's 54-day escorted tours of South America. We were the last stop before the group returned to the United States. One of these groups was led by a young man who was doing it alone for the first time. As they traveled down the western side of the continent and back up the east side, we kept getting telegrams from him revising the guest list downwards. There was an interesting assortment of reasons given, such as, "Mr. and Mrs. So and So got mad at me and returned to Chicago on their own." By the time they arrived at the Torarica there were only nine people plus himself left in the group. He was totally frazzled and exhausted, and I am sure he went into another profession upon his return to the states.

The Florida Audubon Society, led by Orville Crowther, had similar problems. When I greeted him brightly at the front desk with, "Welcome to Suriname, Mr. Crowther, are there still 17 in your group?" he looked kind of glum and said, "No, I'm afraid not. We're down to 14. One of our party died in Argentina and a couple accompanied the body home." Crowther was rather short, stocky and balding. Sweating, with his camera around his neck on one side and his binoculars on the other, he would have been perfect in the title role of a movie about a bird watcher.

In Suriname in 1966, access to world news in English was rather limited. Although there was a mimeographed two-sided sheet, published and distributed periodically, it probably would have mentioned somewhere inconspicuously that the Third World War had been declared four months before. Otherwise news mostly came from our guests who arrived from Europe and America. At that time, we had no television service. and the newspapers and radio stations were mostly in Dutch. However, there was one exception.

The Dutch airline, KLM, was initiating a once-a-week service from Amsterdam to Caracas. There were stops in Frankfurt and Lisbon, before arriving in Paramaribo. The plane turned around in Caracas for the return flight to Amsterdam with the same stops in Europe. There was no catering facility in Suriname able to provide meals for these flights, and I was approached by some of the airline's executives to see if our hotel could provide this service. They required a light snack consisting of a dainty sandwich, a sweet pastry and a choice of beverage for the relatively short flight to Caracas and a full dinner meal for the return flight to Europe the next day. It would be a feather in our cap and an excellent source of additional business but there were challenges to overcome.

Transportation from Paramaribo to Zanderij Airport would take close to an hour and, given the heat and the humidity, food would certainly not be in its prime condition by the time it arrived at the aircraft. There was only one refrigerated vehicle in the country, a small van, belonging to a pork-processing facility in Paramaribo called Gwamba. Fortunately, the van was available for rent, so we worked out all the related logistical issues and confirmed with KLM that we would be able to do it. I promoted one of our restaurant captains, Jules Hasselhof, to be responsible for this operation, and we set about providing this service two days a week. The flight departed Amsterdam in the morning and arrived in Paramaribo in the early evening, at which time Jules would put the food on board. As a bonus, what would he find on board, but that morning's European newspapers! These usually included the London Daily Telegraph, the Times and the Daily Mail, and Jules would bring them back to the hotel. Many of our guests were English, company sales representatives traveling the Caribbean circuit regularly. I would take great pleasure in walking into our restaurant that same evening with one of the London newspapers under my arm and start talking to them. Noticing the newspaper I was holding, they would typically ask, "How old is that Daily Telegraph?"

*Loading meals on KLM flight at Zanderij,
Paramaribo's International Airport*

"What do you mean?" I would reply, feigning surprise at the question. "It's today's of course. I'm not going to read yesterday's paper today am I?"

"Oh, Come on! How old is it?" would be the usual follow up, believing full well there was no way the same day's London paper would be available in Paramaribo.

When I would show them it was, indeed, that same day's edition, they just couldn't believe it! Of course, I could only pull this trick one day a week!

****

While many areas of the hotel had hard floors, with tile in our public areas and hardwood floors in our guest rooms, our restaurant and casino were carpeted. Because of the limited availability of carpet cleaning services in Paramaribo, I decided I would purchase a commercial carpet cleaning machine so we could clean these areas ourselves. I selected a good Hild model, and after we got it cleared through Customs, I decided to demonstrate how it should be used to some of our housemen, many of whom were Indonesian and rather small in stature. We moved some of the tables and chairs from one section of the restaurant, and I showed them how to fill the tank with shampoo. It had various attachments so it could also be used to mop and polish tiled and wood floors. As this was carpet, I attached a stiff round brush to the machine. Being sure I had their full attention, I turned it on.

I was not prepared for what happened next. Up until this critical point in my demonstration, I had been in total control. However, as soon as this awful machine came to life, it took over and had me holding on for dear life, as it ran me all over the restaurant. To complicate matters, I was being jerked around so much I could not find the 'off' switch and didn't have the good sense to let go. After fumbling with the machine, I found the switch and turned the damn thing off, only to find my audience doing everything they could to suppress their utter glee at seeing their boss in such an awkward predicament. After the group settled down, one of the housemen asked me if he could try it. At this point I was glad someone else was prepared to be as embarrassed as I was and I happily turned the whole thing over to him. My humiliation only got worse, as he calmly and easily moved the unit back and forth in the same manner as outlined in the operating manual. I quickly retreated to the relative calm of my office, hoping that by the next morning there would still be a few of the employees who had not heard of my fiasco.

One rather interesting aspect of this resort, not typical of a hotel in the States, was the development of our 'zoo'. Periodically, one of our tourist visitors going on trips up the rivers and into the interior, would get carried away and return to the hotel, not just with intricate wood carvings and such, but with 'pets.' These included parrots, monkeys, sloths, iguanas and other creatures they felt at that they could not do without. When they realized their live souvenir would not be welcome on their return flight, and would be equally unwelcome in our hotel's "Lost and Found", we had no other choice but to house them in our lush, riverside garden. Housed in cages built by our head gardener and his crew, they then became an added attraction for the hotel.

One of these animals was a monkey named Jope (pronounced 'Yopee'), and for some inexplicable reason, he hated women. He was a devil and had somehow escaped a few times, only to be caught again by our grounds crew. He got out one time when Anita was sitting in the garden outside our room reading a book. She saw him headed her way and quickly fled back into the safety of our room. Through the glass door she saw him meticulously going through her purse with a seemingly critical eye and tossing most everything out. Anita smoked in those days, and he was probably looking for a cigarette. Thankfully, our staff returned him once again to his 'home'.

On another occasion, he was even more of a problem. I had returned to the States for a managers' meeting at our headquarters hotel, the Executive House in Chicago, when he escaped again and decided to venture off our property. Anita asked some of our staff members to go out to try to find him, but with no success. Then the phone rang. It was the switchboard operator.

"Mrs. Pullen, I'm sorry to trouble you but I have Mrs. de Vries, the Governor's wife, on the phone wanting to speak to your husband. I explained that he was away in the States for a meeting and she asked if she could speak with you".

"Certainly, put her through", replied Anita.

"Mrs. Pullen, I am so sorry to bother you but, as your husband is away, I thought maybe you could help me." Mrs. de Vries started. "We have a stray monkey over here at the Governor's House and I wondered if any of your employees could come over and catch him. We only have a limited number of people here and they need some help."

"I will be glad to," Anita answered. "Our monkey, Jope, escaped this morning and so far, our employees have not been able to find him. That is probably who it is. I hope he's not doing any damage."

"No, not really" Mrs. de Vries answered, "He is just tearing up some of the potted plants around the verandah."

"I'll send some of our maintenance staff over there right away." Anita promised.

145

The Governor's House was a magnificent colonial structure right in the middle of town, surrounded by beautiful grounds. The tiled and meticulously maintained verandah went completely around the house and was decorated with huge white pots containing various tropical palms, so you can imagine the disaster awaiting our hotel crew when they arrived. Sadly, Jope was one step ahead of them and, search as they might, they not only could not catch him, they could not even find him. Dejectedly, they returned to the hotel empty-handed. Reluctantly, Anita called Mrs. de Vries back to report on their failed mission and discussed with her further options toward solving this problem.

"Mrs. Pullen, you know, Minister Pengel may be able to help." Mrs. de Vries suggested. "He has a small zoo on his property and he might have a suggestion for us."

Suriname Prime Minister Johan Pengel was a large and imposing figure, and Anita was justifiably apprehensive to approach him with the problem.

Somewhat aghast, Anita pleaded, "Mrs. DeVries, I'll do anything I can to help get this monkey but please, please don't ask me to call the prime minister."

Jope was never caught, at least not by our staff, and we assumed, continued to live happily ever after somewhere in Paramaribo.

✳✳✳✳✳✳✳✳✳✳✳✳✳✳✳✳✳✳✳✳✳✳✳✳✳✳✳✳✳✳

Early in 1967, I received a call from The White House to inquire about the availability of our hotel facilities. President Lyndon Johnson would be returning from a South American summit meeting in Punta del Este, Uruguay, and Air Force One needed a quick stop for refueling before proceeding back to the States. This stop had originally been planned for Georgetown, Guyana, but the advance party determined that the landing strip could not safely handle the weight of Air Force One, so they needed to find an alternative. After verifying the airport at Zanderij would be acceptable, their next step was to investigate ancillary needs. Even though the stop was only anticipated to last for about two hours, security and communications people needed to be there well ahead of the event.

After finalizing their requirements, and finding we could accommodate them, we received a "Go" signal. In fact, I knew about this potential event before Mr. Kuppinger, the American vice consul in Suriname.

I was amazed to learn of all the advance arrangements that are required before a simple two-hour refueling stop. Numerous White House staff, security personnel, Secret Service and communications professionals stayed at the hotel, and were there almost a week in advance. Two connecting rooms on our top floor were stripped of their furniture and set up with equipment for direct communications to the White House switchboard. There seemed to be no end of people running around the hotel holding walkie-talkie radios. They stood out like a sore thumb, which seemed in direct contradiction to their insistence on confidentiality and that, 'We don't want anyone to know that we're here.'

I got to know them well, as it became almost my full-time job to coordinate their activities and provide local contacts for some of their off-property needs. One of our rooms was dedicated for President Johnson's use in case of an emergency. Also, our hotel station wagon was to be parked at the small grass landing strip in the Zorg en Hoop neighborhood in town to be available to transport him to the hotel, if needed. The advance team also had a helicopter standing by at the airport to bring him to Paramaribo, if necessary.

While chatting with some of the communications people in a quiet moment, after everything had been set up, it came out that I still had family in England. They asked if I would like to speak with my mother, as they could hook me up through the White House to the switchboard at No. 10 Downing Street in London, the British prime minister's residence. From there they could dial my mother's phone number. I was naturally excited about this, as telephone communications in 1967 were nothing like they are today. There were however some rules. Number one, I could not mention *how* I was able to make the call, as the lines going through the White House and 10 Downing Street are kept open for security reasons and should not be used for frivolous purposes. The other condition was, because this would be done using two-way radio, only one person could speak at a time. This meant the speaker had to say "over" before the person on the other end could talk. This seemed a little complicated but we went ahead and, allowing for the time difference, called my mother. Well, I think this scared her out of her wits, as she just couldn't comprehend receiving a call from me in Suriname just to say "hello", let alone deal with the "over" business. Not being able to tell her how I was able to call also made it difficult. It didn't go smoothly, but the people at my end were helpful and I did manage to make a similar call to my brother Jim, which went much better.

The day came for President Johnson's arrival and it was pouring with rain. Nothing unusual about that, as it seemed to rain most days at that time of the year. All the local dignitaries in town were invited to the airport to greet the president, and a small stage with a podium was set up, from where he would make some remarks. It was a big deal for Suriname, even though it would only be for a couple of hours, and it went on in spite of the weather. He gave a short speech under a huge umbrella held by one of his security staff and then stepped down to personally meet some of those in attendance.

Finally, the event over, Air Force One flew back to Washington, fortunately without any of the carefully arranged contingency plans being needed. Most of the technical staff remained to tear down their equipment, but the White House and Secret Service people all left, and life went back to normal. I was given some personalized gifts carrying the president's signature in appreciation for what we had done. A few weeks later I received a thank you letter on White House letterhead from Sherman Markman, assistant to President Johnson. Also, Colonel Jack Albright, who was involved with this event, wrote a complimentary letter to Carl Devoe, president of the Executive House Company, congratulating us on our performance and individually naming several members of our staff. It had been an exciting interlude for all of us and great fun just being exposed to everything that went on. (Both letters are included in Appendix II.)

****

Towards the middle of 1967, we found that Anita was pregnant and Diana Mary arrived on January 26, 1968 at the St. Vincentius Hospital where the nurses simply gave Anita one aspirin to assist her in childbirth. Fortunately for her, she had a relatively easy time. I waited patiently at the hotel for news and as soon as we received word that we had a new member of the family, I went immediately to the hospital to find out if we had a son or daughter. At the main desk, however, they were more interested in getting me to pay the bill than telling me but finally they said it was a 'meisje,' meaning Wendy had a little sister. Being born in Suriname was quite significant for Diana. She could officially have four different nationalities, American, English, Dutch and a

Surinamer, as all four countries recognized her particular circumstances.

At that time, it was more practical for us to stay in the hotel, as it would be easier for Anita to take care of Diana, but the company had approved our renting a house nearby when we were ready. We found a nice one on Van Roosmalenstraat, owned by the brother of Harry Radikashun, the minister of agriculture, who we knew quite well, and after a while, we moved in. I used the little blue Opel station wagon owned by the hotel for my transportation. Because of Diana's unusual circumstances regarding her nationalities, I had her included on both Anita's and my passports. The British vice consul based in Georgetown, Guyana was a regular guest at the Torarica, and he took care of the English part of this for me after which I went in to show Anita my British passport and kiddingly said, "See, now we are tied - 2 to 2. Two Americans and two Brits!" She didn't like that one bit and said, "You're not funny!" (Again, where's that good old Irish sense of humor?)

****

We had a great group of employees at the hotel, and one of them was a young man by the name of George Gambier. He only had a limited knowledge of English, but he had a beautiful velvety singing voice and had composed, in his head, several calypsos in Taki Taki, the local language. Most of Suriname's entertainers, at that time, tended to imitate the popular stars of the day such as the Beatles and Elvis Presley but he had a latent and raw talent, singing about local stories in his melodious calypsos. He called himself Lord Cammy. We had a permanent six-piece house band, and I suggested he transfer to the Saramacca Bar where he would have an opportunity to better develop his understanding of English and occasionally sing with the band. This would further develop his skills plus it would be an added attraction for the hotel to have some local entertainment for our guests. He was thrilled with this opportunity. In the beginning, he was extremely shy and stood in the corner out of the spotlight modestly singing his songs. Having the typical Caribbean beat, the band quickly adapted their accompaniment in support. As his popularity grew, he became more confident and his show presence improved tremendously.

About the same time, Suriname was building its first television station using Philips sound equipment imported from Holland. Their chief sound technician, Ewald Stomp, was a wonderful fellow and, as we were talking one day, I asked him about the possibility of using their facilities to record some of Lord Cammy's Taki Taki calypsos. Once the TV station was up and running, their programming was set for limited hours, I think it was something like 6 a.m. to 10 p.m., so after that time the station was shut down. Ewald had access to the building and one night, after we closed the lounge, the six musicians in the band, Lord Cammy and I went over to the station. It took a while to get everyone in the mood, as the sterile atmosphere of the studio was quite different from our lounge, but after several attempts to get four of his calypsos recorded, we were all satisfied with the final tape and left some time in the early hours of the morning.

One of the more widely popular Caribbean groups at that time was the Merrymen. Their albums were produced by the West Indies Records Studios in Barbados. I sent them the tape and asked if they would cut a 45-rpm record, which they agreed to do. I then contacted a talented local artist, Rudy de la Fuente, for his help in producing a professional sleeve for the record, and I drafted brief, rough translations of the four calypsos. Eventually, we received the finished product and made it available for sale at the hotel. Because the recording had been made without the permission of the TV station manager, who, by the way was the prime minister's brother, we labeled it *"Recorded from the Saramacca Room of the Torarica Hotel-Casino in Paramaribo, Suriname, South America"*. Thankfully, no one ever questioned it and the record became a hit with both our hotel guests and the locals.

In some ways, I take some satisfaction in helping him launch his career, as he subsequently left Surname for Europe and ended up owning and operating his own nightclub "Rock-Palast" in Meppen, Germany. We were able to get in touch with each other again and I was happy to find him doing well. (If the reader has any interest in hearing these calypsos, go to YouTube and search for "Lord Cammy at the Torarica" There you will find a video along with a photo of the cover we produced.)

****

The Torarica was by far the primary site for special events and parties and we hosted several outside on the wide poolside terrace. Once we even built a special wooden platform over the pool for the local military band. We frequently hired the Shell Invaders steel band, a colorful group, which provided rhythmic island music on their steel drums. Sometimes, if we had tour groups in the hotel, we would bring in some of the Bushnegroes from the nearby village of Santigron to perform their fire dance, which was most entertaining. They would start a fire on the terrace into which they would place an axe head until it became red-hot. The men would dance to the beat of their drums, gradually getting into a trance so that they could dance into the fire, without feeling the pain. Their wives would come with them to keep them from serious harm. One of the performers would take the axe head out of the fire with his bare hand and walk around the audience, seemingly unhurt, although you could smell the burning flesh. Drinks were served to the audience, and often the performers would take the glass out of someone's hand and 'eat' it, spitting out the broken pieces. The audiences were spellbound.

****

I had several unusual challenges during my time there, which provided many great opportunities to do some different and exciting things. These included the slaughtering and roasting of a suckling pig on a rotating spit on the pool terrace. Also, we flew in live Maine lobsters on the one weekly Pan American flight from New York for an event hosted by Royal Dutch Shell to celebrate their off-shore drilling contract. I believe live Maine lobsters had never been seen in Suriname before.

The most ambitious event we were asked to handle was a cocktail reception and service for an ultra-VIP event on the *E.W. Thornton*, the largest ocean-going catamaran oilrig in the world at that time. This imposing 278 by 105-foot vessel, which was moored at the main dock in town, would give us many nerve racking challenges. The list of invitees started with the governor and his wife, the prime minister, and proceeded right down the entire protocol list. Anybody who was *somebody* in Paramaribo was on the invitation list.

Upon inspecting the facilities on board, it was apparent that we were going to have to cater two parties rather than one, due to the dual hull construction of the ship. With an estimated guest list of 300, it would have been impossible for everyone to get from one side to the other to enjoy our hors d'oeuvres and to get easy access to the bars. This meant that everything had to be done in duplicate, including the ice-carving centerpiece. Our chef, Roland Laurenceau, had to sculpt these himself, in addition to all the food preparation going on in the hotel's kitchen.

The morning of the event we transported the various tables, linens, chafing dishes and other pieces of equipment required for the set up to the dock. We had planned to take the smaller items such as the plates, silverware, serving utensils, napkins and so forth in the afternoon. Our little station wagon was loaded up and off to the dock we went. However, upon our arrival at the dock, the Thornton was noticeably absent.

What on earth was going on? We looked around only to find the catamaran now at anchor out in the middle of the mile-wide river. We went to the marine administrator's office where we were told that they were forced to move it because a freighter was expected to arrive later that day and the space at the dock was needed. There was absolutely no chance to bring the ship back for the event that evening. This presented not only the challenge of getting the party set up and the food delivered in a first-class presentable manner, but also of getting the guests out to the ship later. Fortunately, in these colonial-type venues, evening events tended to be scheduled later than they would normally be here in the States, so we had a little more time to work on solving these unexpected logistical problems. Everyone started scrambling to find suitable boats to deliver the service items, food, drinks, ice, and personnel; plus boats to transport the guests in as dignified a manner as possible. It was a frantic time, but we managed and, believe it or not the event was a success. I think this was probably the most challenging situation I encountered in my entire career. (A letter from Mr. D.G. Bokenkamp, the operations manager for the Reading and Bates Exploration Company to Mr. Morris DeWoskin, Chairman of the Executive House Hotel Company is included in Appendix II.)

****

Native fire dancers

E.W. Thornton

About that same time, there was a minor military skirmish between forces from neighboring Guyana, and the Suriname military concerning a border territory, which had been in dispute. The Corantijn River divided the two countries and split at a fork. The two tributaries then flowed out to the coast. It was the sovereignty of the land between the two forks that was in dispute. Prime Minister Pengel, decided to use the new television facilities to address the nation on the issue and, to our pleasant surprise, broadcast Lord Cammy's calypso, "The Border Question," which he had composed about this problem. It was the best promotion we could have asked for, and we sold out of the records soon afterwards. I reimbursed the hotel for any out-of-pocket expenses incurred, gave Lord Cammy a nice check, and split the balance six ways for the band's participation in the project.

****

The primary contributor to the country's economy was its natural deposits of bauxite, the ore used in the manufacture of aluminum. The company developing this resource, Suralco, was a national subsidiary of Alcoa. Before we arrived in Suriname, the company had developed a smelting plant at Paranam and had built a dam for hydroelectric power at Afobaka, a critical part of the Suriname River in the interior. When this was done, it created a natural reservoir of over 600 square miles behind the dam. This, in turn, raised the levels of the river back upstream for miles putting many of the animals living in the rain forest in danger.

A young fellow by the name of John Walsh, representing the International Society for the Protection of Animals (ISPA) based in Boston, was brought down to Suriname to see what could be done to save them. He put together a great crew of Bushnegro helpers and they rescued almost 10,000 animals of all different species under the project title "Operation Gwamba" (gwamba means wild animal). Living as he did, mostly in the interior, he quickly acquired the skill of communicating with his native crew in Taki Taki. CBS television network did a one-hour special, hosted by Walter Cronkite, on this adventurous and exciting project. John later wrote a book entitled *Time is Short and the Water Rises*. The special was recorded before we arrived in Suriname, so we met John when he returned with his co-writer, Robert Gannon, to write the book.

One of the first things they did when they returned was to get in touch with as many members of the former crew as were available. Several of them came to see him at the Torarica where John and Robert were staying. As I mentioned earlier, the hotel had a decorative outside pond with numerous large golden carp. These poor fish were the cause for our head housekeeper, M. Frau Osterling, calling me to say that there was a strong odor coming from some of the guest rooms. She thought some of our guests were cooking in them. Upon investigating, it proved that this was indeed correct which, of course, violated the local fire codes, as well as creating a rather unpleasant environment for our other guests. It seems that some members of John's former crew had been down at the pool earlier and, using natural skills learned in their home villages, had speared the fish. Just another attraction for our visiting tourists! (As John Walsh says in the acknowledgements at the beginning of his book, *"Bill Pullen, new manager of the Torarica, who always kept his temper despite adversity."*). John also signed a copy of his book for me with the following message:

To Bill Pullen;

As Operation Gwamba becomes a memory, I will never forget

weekends at the Torarica with my Bushnegroe "Tourists". I am sure
they enjoyed the hours they spent riding on your elevator, washing
their clothes in the swimming pool at night, and the delicious fish
which you so kindly provided in the fish pool. Thanks also for making
my visits to Suriname so enjoyable.

With Best Wishes, John Walsh

One evening John and a guest came into the restaurant for dinner.
He introduced this attractive Indian lady to me, as one of the local
Paramaribo police officers. He explained to me how they met. For
the duration of their visit, John and Robert had acquired the use
of a Jeep; John was alone and driving through town way above the
safe speed limit as, it seems, he frequently did. At some point, he
noticed that he was being followed by a police officer on a
motorcycle and after some distance, not being able to shake the
officer off his tail, he stopped quickly and ran into a small local
store with which he was familiar. The police officer arrived at the
scene, got off the motorcycle and was in the process of writing
down the particulars of the vehicle for the required report when
John came running out of the store, threw his arms around the
stunned officer in a hugging embrace and in fluent Taki Taki said,
"My truck. You've found my truck!" John, being a tall, young,
white American, not much older than a college kid, so shook this
poor lady police officer that she dropped the idea of writing the
ticket and after an enlightening conversation, he invited her to the
Torarica for dinner. I don't think that would have worked in
Boston.

****

We spent a great deal of time talking to our visitors about, and
promoting, the adventurous river trips into the interior by
motorized dugout canoe. As it came closer for us to be
transferred back to the states for another assignment, we were

determined not to miss this opportunity ourselves. We invited our dear and good friend, Agnes Guardiola, a prominent local executive with the Suriname Bank, and Milton Fluekigger, who had just arrived to replace me at the hotel, to join us. Agnes had some apprehension about the trip, as she couldn't swim. Putting that fear aside and stocking up on some alcohol for the trip, she decided to come. We were glad she did, as she added so much to our enjoyment. It was an unbelievable experience as we went up about 600 feet in altitude through the many rapids and visited many Bushnegro villages along the way. We took a personable young Paramaribo-based tour guide, Artie, and drove down to the town of Albina on the banks of the Marowijne River, which separates Suriname from French Guiana to the south. While we were there, we took a canoe ferry across to St. Laurent on the French Guiana side and visited what had been a former penal colony like the more famous one on Devil's Island. The conditions for the inmates must have been horrendous, given the terrible heat and humidity, and their primitive accommodations.

We returned to Albina and spent our first night under mosquito netting, a must in this part of the world, at a small hotel. We were surprised to see our breakfast, consisting of cold cuts, cheese and bread, already set up for the next morning. Observing the daily life of the locals was very interesting. Many women were walking with huge baskets balanced on their heads containing fruit, clothes and other items, often without any support from their hands. Down at the river's edge many of them were doing their weekly wash, and I recorded some of this activity on my movie camera.

Artie had arranged for us to take a covered canoe with two expert local crewmen for our trip up stream to our Stoelman's Island destination, a few days away. Watching our crew was really fascinating. When going through the many rapids on the river, one stood in the bow with a guiding pole and his partner sat in the stern holding on tightly to the outboard motor. The motor would then be raised and lowered to avoid hitting the large rocks.

Our second night was spent at a government guesthouse at Tamara, a small island sitting in the middle of the Marowijne River and we were told that the granman (chief) of the local Paramacca tribe would come and greet us. He spoke mostly in Taki Taki, but also some French. Because of his elevated status, it was made known to us that we could not speak to him directly but only through his son. We would ask a question and Artie, translating for us, would speak. The granman would obviously understand what Artie had said but would not respond until his son would say something we did not understand. This evidently cleared the way for the granman's reply, which the son would then pass on to Artie. It was a beautiful, quiet and calm sunny evening with the stillness only being broken by our own voices and the occasional sound of outboard motors on passing canoes. The rivers in Suriname serve as highways and all food and supplies were transported to and from the villages by this method.

It was here that Artie demonstrated for us the voracity of the piranha. He cut up a raw potato, which he put in the water at the end of a pole, and very quickly hooked a small piranha so that he could show us its amazing set of teeth. He then cut the fish into pieces and threw it back into the water, whereupon there was an immediate violent reaction for just an instant, as other piranha came in for a feeding frenzy and, as quickly as it had started, all became quiet and completely still again. It had all happened so quickly, it was quite frightening. They devour any unfortunate animals the same way, even cattle, if they venture into the water.

Bushnegro fishermen

On our way to Stoelmans Island, we visited Langatabbetje and a few other villages and marveled at the intricate wood carvings done by the inhabitants. These were found on many of their huts, tools, pieces of furniture and their canoe paddles. Anita and I purchased two of these paddles. When I asked one of the natives who spoke a little English, to translate what the carving meant, all he would do is look at it wide-eyed, put his hand over his mouth and giggle. Artie said it was something romantic but obviously, nothing they were prepared to tell us. We never did get a proper translation and perhaps that is just as well.

The facilities at Stoelman's Island were more than adequate, and we spent a few days there relaxing and exploring the area. One morning I was down by the river in an area immediately adjacent to a rather steep rapid when two large canoes, heavily loaded with supplies, negotiated their way up stream with some difficulty. I was sitting in the crook of a palm tree that bent out over the rapid with my movie camera and recorded the effort as the men struggled to get to the top of the rapid and calmer waters. They were so close to me I was lucky they didn't knock me into the river.

Our expedition finally came to an end and one of Suriname's newly acquired de Havilland Twin Otter aircraft arrived on the grass landing strip to pick us up and take us back to Paramaribo. We had been away for five days and had a marvelous adventure and some thrilling times. I don't think there was any alcohol left to take back with us; and I was dying for a shave.

****

One day, not long before we would be leaving Suriname, I noticed a Hindustani gentleman standing in the lobby with a cardboard box at his feet. He did not seem to be bothering anyone and actually, was barely noticeable. As I went about my duties I kept passing him and, finally, I asked the staff at the front desk if they knew what he wanted. They said they didn't but that he had been standing there quietly all morning not speaking to a soul. I walked over to him to see if he needed any help.

"Do you want to buy bottle, mister. I have good bottle!" he said.

I said no that I did not want to buy any bottles, but he persisted, "But I have good bottle, mister. Good price!"

Again, I insisted that I had no interest in buying any bottles.

"Let me show you, mister" he continued, as I was beginning to regret that I had started this conversation. Our bantering continued in this vein and at some point, I just wanted to get him out of the lobby, so I said, "Let's go back to my office."

That seemed to be an even bigger mistake. Once in my office he started to unload his bottles on to my desk that was already covered in my papers.

"Good bottle, mister! All bottle four hundred guilden, mister," he said in his heavy Hindustani accent, never having expected to have gotten this far. (His accent sounded pleasant and it reminded me of Peter Sellers when he went through his Mr. Banagee and Mr. Lalcakka routine on the BBC's Goon Show back in the 50s).

"I don't want any bottles," I insisted, "Please put them away."

"Oh, mister," he cried, as he started to put them back in the box. But he wasn't giving up!

"Mister, three hundred fifty guilden, mister. All bottle, mister. Good bottle." and he started putting them on my desk again.

Well, not to belabor the point but this went on and on. Various staff members kept coming by my office to see me about insignificant issues like "the hotel is on fire" or something, and he kept putting the bottles back in his box and then back on my desk again, crying with his "Oh! Mister." and each time bringing the price down a notch and insisting they were indeed "Good bottle." It seemed to go on all day. Finally, yes, you won't believe it, but I ended up buying his damn box of "all good bottle" just to get him out of the office. Phew!

Do you think he would come back again? Oh, yes. And more than once.

The bottles were all hand blown European black glass from the late 17th and early 18th centuries. They had ended up in Suriname mostly by way of the sailors whose ships came over with bricks as ballast to pick up lumber and various crops grown in Suriname at that time. Several of the buildings in Paramaribo were built with these bricks. The bottles are some of the first individually hand-blown glass bottles ever made in commercial quantities. As such, each one was different and unique, designed to hold various wines, beers and liquors. Once the product inside of these bottles had been consumed, they would be tossed overboard where they reclined on the riverbed for a couple of hundred years. It seemed there was a small local "cottage" industry where enterprising Hindustanis would go out and dig in the mud to find them. Paramaribo sits on a curve on the north bank of the Suriname River and, as the river flows around the bend, it gradually deposits sediment on the outside of the curve so that portions of the river that were at one time mid-stream were now in shallower waters and reasonably accessible for these entrepreneurs. Having now acquired many of these "good bottle," whether I wanted them or not, I learned that they were relatively valuable to avid bottle collectors back in the States. So, what did I do? Yep, you guessed it, I bought more.

Hank Goodman found a source in South Florida quite interested in acquiring some of them. When preparing for our return to the States, I sorted them with my amateurish eye and packed them carefully into four large moving van type boxes. I had about 80 and divided them into two categories. I placed the better half into the two boxes I intended to keep. The rest I placed in the two boxes marked with an "X" indicating they could be sold. Hank and I had agreed we would split the proceeds 50/50. It was no big deal but Hank did not remember which were the boxes to sell and which to keep and wound up selling the wrong bottles. Anyway, we split the proceeds, which just about covered the acquisition cost for all of them.

Recently, I did a little research and found that some of them could sell for over $100 a piece, depending on condition. I ended up splitting the various types among Wendy, Diana and myself as remembrances of our Suriname experience and then sold the balance to a dealer at a local flea market here in Webster, Florida. All in all, it had been a most interesting experience and a good story in the telling. In Appendix II you will find a photo of me with 'good bottle' which appeared in The Villages Daily Sun, November 30, 2008.

****

Leaving Suriname was difficult. We had only been there just a little over two years but the friends we had made, both local residents and our hotel employees, were friends for life and the bond we felt was extremely strong. I was being transferred back to Arizona to take over as general manager of the 212-room Executive House Hotel in Scottsdale, another step up the career ladder for me. Notwithstanding all the wonderful times we experienced in Paramaribo, it certainly was a different and somewhat isolated world and, after a while, it became necessary to return to the rest of civilization. It had been a priceless experience, which we were privileged to enjoy again when we returned with our whole family in 2004 in celebration of our 40th wedding anniversary. The manager then was Frank Robles, a local fellow who had been in our Accounting Department when we were there in the 1960's. He took such wonderful care of us and it was so exciting for Wendy and Diana, who essentially lived their earliest years there, to see it in a different light. He even put on a special lunch for us and invited as many of our former employees as he could find. Obviously, some had since passed away and those still there had retired but it was a moving moment for me.

I have a huge place in my heart for Suriname and the wonderful people there.

It Started at The Savoy

Key to Success #8

Support: *An effective manager must both lead and follow. Obviously, good leadership is critical but by follow, I mean it is equally important to be sure your associates have the tools and support they need to do the job you expect.*

8. From the Tropics to the Desert (1968-1970)

June of 1968 found us back in Arizona in the beautiful resort community of Scottsdale where I succeeded a fine gentleman, Joe McGovern, as general manager of the Executive House, another hotel in the company's portfolio.

One of the most unforgettable individuals I have ever met was Jim Turchi; known for much of his professional life as Jimmy Tattler. Jimmy was a little fellow, just four feet eleven inches tall, and was often mistaken for the diminutive bellboy character in the *"Call for Philip Morris"* TV commercials, something he never denied. He had made a name for himself while working as a wine steward at the Pump Room of the Ambassador Hotel in Chicago at a time when it was one of the most renowned restaurants in America and often frequented by celebrities. At that time, a journalist by the name of Nate Gross wrote a gossip column under the banner "The Town Tattler" for The Chicago Herald American. He frequently gleaned his material by calling Jimmy to see who had been seen in the Pump Room the night before. Hence, Jimmy's adopted name; it was rumored that he had it legally changed. When Jimmy's health started failing, the chairman of the Executive House Board of Directors, Morris DeWoskin, suggested that he move to Arizona to a better climate and promised him a job for life at the company's hotel in

Scottsdale. That's where we met. One of his personal trademarks was his enormous collection of cuff links, many of which had been given to him by famous restaurant customers over the years. He was kind enough to give a few from his treasured collection to me, one of which is a pair of miniature pistols, which fire real blanks.

Before I left Scottsdale, one of the Phoenix TV stations invited Jimmy down to be interviewed and to do what they believed was his famous *"Call for Philip Morris,"* supposedly for the last time. When he got back to the hotel, I said,

"How did it go, Jimmy?"

"Say what, Pops!" he answered with a chuckle, "They think I did the 'Call for Philip Morris' for the last time. Little do they know, I actually did it for the <u>first</u> time!" His secret was safe with me.

Jimmy was so charismatic that his presence at the Executive House often attracted celebrities. Bob Hope, who had known Jimmy from his days at the Pump Room, would come to Arizona to play in the Phoenix Open Golf Tournament pro-am and always made a point of stopping in to see him. One evening, of special note, Hope came in with some friends and settled himself in the lounge where Billy Shepard and Judi Jourdan, were performing. They were a very talented husband and wife duo and were friends of ours, as Anita and I had known them from their appearances at the Torarica Hotel in Suriname.

Jimmy introduced me to Hope, who then graciously introduced me to the other members of his party. "Mr. Hope, it's so nice to have you here." I said, "Would you mind if our performers recognize you from the stage? I realize you may prefer others not be aware that you are here so that you can enjoy the evening quietly with your friends, but I wanted to ask."

"Oh, that's fine!" he answered with a smile, "I think almost everyone in here now knows I'm in the room, except for that young couple in the corner, and I'm going to write them a letter, so go ahead."

When I shared the good news with Billy and Judi, they thought I was kidding. After much "crossing my heart" and swearing it wasn't a joke, I finally convinced them. They gladly acknowledged Hope and were thrilled to perform in front of him, being mindful of possible future opportunities.

Prior to his moving to Scottsdale, Jimmy worked for a while at the plush El Mirador Hotel in Palm Springs, owned by his friend, oilman Ray Ryan. He started work there the same night the singing maestro Eddy Howard and his 15-piece orchestra opened for the season. It just so happened that Bing Crosby and his wife Kathy were there too and upon seeing Jimmy, Crosby yelled out, "What's the matter, Jimmy? Did they close the Pump Room?"

There was one little known fact about Jimmy; although he was probably one of the better-known wine stewards of his day, he had very little knowledge of wine. It was his personality that attracted people to him. He was always dressed in his colorful vest with his silver chain and key to the wine cellar around his neck. Often, when asked what the big key opened, his typical reply would be, "Only conversations, my dear. Only conversations."

We became close friends while we worked together at The Executive House and again later at the Hotel Valley Ho. It was a sad day when Jimmy passed away in January 1980 at the age of 64. He was truly one-of-a-kind. His smile and bubbly personality touched every-day patrons and celebrities alike.

With Jimmy Tattler and Bob Hope

Of course, Jimmy wasn't the only reason to come to the Valley area. Scottsdale was fast becoming a very popular winter resort and many celebrities were drawn to the wonderful climate, luxurious resorts, great golfing venues amid beautiful scenery and many fine restaurants. While I was there, I developed good relationships with the two social column writers for the principal newspapers, the Arizona Republic and the Phoenix Gazette. Larry Rummel was associated with the entertainment scene around the Valley and Vic Wilmot covered the social scene and celebrity sightings. As such they were always willing to publicize any interesting events at the hotel. On one occasion, I saw we had a reservation for the movie actor 'tough guy' Robert Mitchum and I mentioned this to Vic, and said that if he liked, I would see if I could get him an interview. He said he would and then included information about Mitchum's impending visit in his columns. When any VIP would be checking in I would ask the front desk to alert me when they arrived, so that I could go out and introduce myself. I would welcome them to the hotel and ask if there was any way I could be of assistance during their visit. On this occasion, I greeted Mitchum with a big smile, and said,

"Welcome to Scottsdale Mr. Mitchum. Thank you for staying with us. We are delighted to have you here."

He didn't seem too thrilled.

"Thank you! But some asshole told the paper I was coming. My sister lives here and she is a devoted member of the Baha'i faith. She can be a real pain in the neck in trying to get me involved. I was hoping I could come here without her knowing!"

I said, "I'm so sorry!" and left it at that, never admitting that, in fact, I was that asshole. Oh, well!

Although we had not done anything special to promote ourselves to celebrities, we were often the beneficiary of their visits. Some of them included comedians Godfrey Cambridge and Jonathon Winters, entertainers Wayne Newton, Rick Nelson and Rusty Warren, movie actors Dana Andrews, Jay Silverheels (aka Tonto in the Lone Ranger movies), Amanda Blake (Miss Kitty in the "Gunsmoke" series), Rex Allen, Diane McBain and Dick Van Dyke. Also, there were personalities such as J. C. Penney, founder of J. C. Penney's department stores, politician and presidential candidate Barry Goldwater and Chief Nino Cochise, the grandson of the famous Indian Chief, Cochise. Another very popular local personality was Chief Shatka Bearstep who, in his elaborate tribal costume, performed a wonderful Malotte's version of the Lord's Prayer in Indian sign language. Letting it be known that we were hosting such celebrities could only be good for business.

****

Broderick Crawford was well known for his Hollywood movie roles but especially for his popular TV series "Highway Patrol". This ran from 1955 to 1959 and featured stories of a law enforcement officer, Chief Dan Matthews, with his patrol car on Route 66. When a Hollywood production company, General Film Corporation, brought its cast and crew to the hotel for several weeks to make a movie titled *"Ransom Money"* starring Crawford and Rachel Romen, I got to spend a great deal of time with him. He was indeed a talented actor but I also got to see a side of him that movie and TV audiences didn't. He drank a lot; and I mean a lot.

While in Arizona, Crawford was invited to Tombstone, the old western town known for its famous gun battles, for some publicity shots. The town officials planned to make him an honorary marshal. A small private plane had been leased to take him to Tucson and from there a car would be rented to drive to Tombstone. He invited me to go with him. We boarded the small plane at Sky Harbor Airport in Phoenix and set off for the short flight to Tucson. There was little conversation on the plane both because it was noisy and he had his eyes closed for most of the time. When we got off I said to him,

"You had a nice little nap there, Brod!"

"Nap? Hell no!" he said, "I was praying!" It *was* a very small plane.

It turned out to be lucky that I did go with him, as I think he would otherwise be holding up one of the head-stones in Tombstone's infamous Boot Hill cemetery. I drove and it did not take long for me to get the first inkling of his drinking habit. We had just left the Tucson metropolis and were in the surrounding desert, heading south towards Tombstone, when he noticed a closed up, rather dilapidated building from which was hanging, at an angle, an old rusted Budweiser sign. It was still quite early Sunday morning and, even if the place was still in business, it was obviously closed. There were no cars parked anywhere near. However, Crawford insisted that I go and see if there was any form of life where he might be able to get something to combat his 'thirst'. No luck!

On we pressed to Tombstone, where his celebrity status was on full display. After being welcomed, he was installed as an honorary marshal and posed for numerous pictures during the event. Around midday, he approached the town's mayor and, using his newly granted authority, prevailed on him to go and find a bottle

Waiting to board plane to Tucson

of something stronger than anything most of us would drink that early on a Sunday. Most stores were still closed but the mayor used his local influence and produced something that would soothe my famous companion for a while. I don't think it would have mattered what it was but, in this instance, it was vodka. He continued to drink all day.

The afternoon's activities went on and on, with much posing, handshaking, gunfight reenactments, speeches...and the partaking of 'refreshment'. So much festivity, in fact, that when we were supposed to catch our small plane in Tucson, we were still in Tombstone. After spending a great deal of time on the phone, I finally found us seats on the last commercial flight of the day leaving for Phoenix. It was evident that I would have to assist Crawford into the car if we were to make our flight. He was a heavy guy and when I tried to assist him, his arm would swing wildly towards me. I realized he didn't want the help, even if he desperately needed it. I think it was one of my most humiliating experiences walking with him down the concourse of the Tucson Air Terminal towards the departure gate for our flight. He could barely stand, and to make matters worse, the town brass back in Tombstone had given him an unopened "to go" bottle which he clutched for dear life. Unfortunately, he was recognized as we walked through the airport and, I am sure, he lost much of the esteem these good people had for him. We finally arrived at the gate where he prevailed upon the counter gate agent to open the bottle protruding from its paper bag. I was mortified. The agent politely complied and with minimal help, Crawford poured himself on to the plane and off to Phoenix we went. What a day!

****

Another one of the movie studio's promotional opportunities

with Crawford was an invitation for an on-air interview on the local TV affiliate morning show in Phoenix. The evening before, Anita and I had invited the actors and crew back to our apartment for a nightcap. One by one they thanked us and politely departed for their own rooms until the only ones left were Anita and I, Wendy and Diana asleep in their room and – Broderick Crawford. He didn't want to, or I should say more accurately, couldn't leave. He had been drinking all evening and it probably had not been a good idea to host this small get-together in the first place. Finally, he was practically unconscious and, somehow, I had to get him back to his own room so that we could go to bed. He couldn't stand and there was no way I could handle him by myself. I called our night auditor to come and help me. We found a rug, rolled him on to it, pulled him and the rug down the ground floor corridor, out into the night air, into the connecting building and on to his room. I opened the door with my master key, pulled him inside and, putting a pillow under his head, wished him a "good night" and left. It had to have been about 3 am.

Goodness only knows what shape he would be in in the morning when the limo came to pick him up. I thought I had better be up early myself to try to assist in any way that might be necessary. When I walked into the coffee shop around 6:30 the next morning there was only one guest, so far, having his early morning cup of coffee and – you've guessed it - it was Crawford. He was all ready to go and, when the limo arrived, off he went to his interview. No mention was ever made about where the rug had come from or any reference to the activities of the night before. Amazing.

****

As any hotel manager who has been in the business for a few years can tell you, there come situations from time to time, which are a little different from the norm. As you read these pages, I am sure you will realize that I am no exception. A reservation for a Henry Hite, who was in town doing a promotion for Corn King Foods, proved to be one of those occasions. Imagine my surprise when Hite arrived and I found myself welcoming a gentleman who was a mere 8 feet 2 inches tall. He held the title of the world's tallest human. Once I regained my composure it occurred to me that, to assure a good night's sleep, he would require special sleeping arrangements. Thankfully, he was not traveling with his wife, and while not a perfect solution, he accepted one of our king size beds in which he could sleep corner to corner. He was a real charmer and projected the natural talent of a former vaudeville performer, having been a member of the comedy team of Hite, Lowe and Stanley. He weighed 300 pounds, wore size 22 shoes and, as seen in the photo on page 180, had a splendid sense of humor, though I am sure he faced many challenges. Sadly, he passed away in May 1978 at the relatively young age of 63.

****

Piko Krabama. What *is* Piko Krabama? I had been asked to put up "Welcome Piko Krabama" on our hotel's street side marquee and, at first, I wondered if someone was pulling my leg. It certainly didn't make me any more comfortable when I was advised that it was the name of a horse! We were going to have a horse arrive at the hotel? I don't think so. However, the mystery was finally solved when I met the famed movie actor, Walter Matthau, at the front desk and welcomed him to the hotel.

"You have a horse named Piko Krabama?" I asked.

"No, not a horse. It's a consortium, the Pico Krabama Stable. We

Exchanging jackets with Henry Hite

With Walter Matthau

have two of our horses, *Speak to Me* and *Reram,* running in the 5th and 7th races at Turf Paradise this weekend. I am supposed to be in the winner's circle after the 8th race, which, I'm told, they have dedicated to me."

The consortium owned about 15 horses and the name was derived from the names of his principal partners. I regret I do not recall the name of the person who contributed the "Pi" but the "ko" was for Howard Koch of Paramount Pictures Corporation. He was the award-winning screenwriter of "Casablanca" and "The Odd Couple", among many others. The "Kra" was for Stanley Kramer, the Hollywood producer and director. The "ba" was for Shirley Baskin of Baskin and Robbins ice cream fame and, finally, the "ma" was for Walter Matthau. I do not recall if their horses won or not, but, thankfully, they were not among the group staying with us that weekend. I needn't have been concerned.

****

In the late 1960's the hotel business in Scottsdale was seasonal. This created some turnover among the employees, as staffing had to be cut back in the hot summer months. While I was recruiting for a new head housekeeper, one of the applications, which piqued my interest, was from a Ms. Peggy Carey. She was in California where she was working as regional director of housekeeping for the Sheraton Corporation. She wanted to relocate to Scottsdale to be closer to her mother who was in ill health. She was certainly over qualified for our 212-room property but her motivation was not career-based. I invited her over for an interview, and I liked her immensely. After doing my due diligence in checking her references, I made her an offer, which she accepted and we established a mutually acceptable starting date. I was thrilled, so you can imagine my utter surprise when one evening, as I was relaxing in our apartment watching the CBS News with Walter Cronkite, I heard him say *"Today, the White House announced the appointment of a new Executive Housekeeper. Miss Peggy Carey of Long Beach, California etc. etc..."* What on earth is going on?

I got in touch with her and she explained that indeed she had been spoken to about that position, but she had never expected to be offered it and had, in fact, been making her plans to move to Arizona. She had her concerns about her mother, but she had been convinced that she should not decline this prestigious White House appointment. I was happy for her and we kept in touch during the early days of her new responsibilities. She later told me that the job was not so much about housekeeping as it was about public relations. Still, it was the chance of a lifetime for her.

****

One day, about mid-morning, between the breakfast and lunch business, I went in to the coffee shop to get a quick bite to eat. Seating myself at the long 'U' shaped counter, I was deep into reviewing the sports pages of a newspaper when the only guest in the coffee shop said, "Don't look so worried. The market will pick up again soon." or words to that effect. I smiled and said, "I'm not looking at the financial pages. This is a recent English newspaper and I am looking at the sports pages. I'm originally from England."

My first observation was that he obviously spent a great deal of time in the outdoors. His deeply tanned face was somewhat wizened and cracked and I felt he probably looked older than he really was. His eyes sparkled and a faint smile flirted with the corners of his mouth. I told him I was the manager of the hotel and we got into a conversation. He was Claude Neal, a rancher from Kingman in northern Arizona where he raised cattle on several thousand acres. He explained to me how the land east of Kingman was divided into square miles, checker-board style, where the federal government owned alternating square mile blocks and the others could be privately owned. I surmised this was done to prevent any uncontrolled development. He could lease the government property and use it along with his own for raising cattle. He had recently had some health issues and had just been released from the Arizona Heart Institute in Phoenix where Dr. Ted Dietrich, an internationally renowned cardiovascular surgeon, was making a name for himself. His tests had shown that heart surgery was not going to be needed and he was planning to head back north in the next few days.

During our conversation, he related a hilarious prank he had hatched while at the Heart Institute a few days before his release, which clearly displayed his unique sense of humor. Remember, he was supposed to be pretty sick. Right after a nurse had brought him his breakfast tray, another nurse came into his room and asked him to give her a urine sample when he was ready. On his breakfast tray was a glass of apple juice and looking at the bottle to be used for his urine sample, and then at the apple juice, he poured the apple juice into the sample bottle and continued to eat his breakfast. His breakfast tray was subsequently cleared and a little while later, the nurse returned to collect his urine sample. On entering his room, the nurse said,

"Are you ready for me, Mr. Neal?"

"Yes nurse," he answered, "but don't you think that's just not dark enough? Maybe I should run it through again." whereupon he drank it.

The nurse almost passed out but his twinkling eyes and his smile gave him away, so she quickly recovered and joined in with laughter. I'm sure this is a story she has told many times. Some months later, Anita and I had the great pleasure of visiting him and his wife, Rita, in their home in Kingman and spent two wonderful days with them on their boat on Lake Mohave, between the Hoover Dam to the north and the Davis Dam to the south.

Before I took over the management of the hotel, live entertainment had been established as an important part of our food and beverage operation. The layout of the lounge and dining area was such that the guests in both areas could benefit from the attraction. A special and talented local entertainer by the name of Nadine Jansen had been entertaining audiences in the Phoenix area for quite a while, including extended engagements at the Band Box in Phoenix and the Black Cat in Scottsdale. The Black Cat Lounge was owned by Ed Ravenscroft, who was a retired senior executive with Abbott Laboratories in the Chicago area in Illinois. His younger son, Ed, was an excellent drummer and part of the trio. However, after some time, Ravenscroft decided to close the Black Cat and he approached me to see if I would consider hiring the Nadine Jansen Trio for our lounge on an extended basis. Typically, we hired only short-term entertainment, so this would be different, but Nadine's local following was considerable, and after careful consideration, I agreed.

Nadine was a fantastic pianist; she also, had the unusual talent of being able to play piano with her left hand and either a trumpet or flugelhorn with her right hand simultaneously. This was not a gimmicky thing; it was outstanding talent. She was not only an exceptional musician but also a wonderful person. With her large, loyal fan base she was always ready to expand her horizons through special events. Her occasional concerts on off- peak season holiday weekends, like the Fourth of July and Labor Day, became wildly popular and gave our business a boost on days which were typically quiet. Most often, local residents would head for the cooler mountain climes but if she had planned a concert, many stayed and we would fill the room, often as many as three times. She would invite other talented musicians to join her on these occasions, such as the California-based Pete Jolly Trio, well known as the base trio behind the renowned Herb Alpert and the Tijuana Brass. That weekend we had scheduled three concerts and after the first performance a gentleman in the audience approached Nadine to ask if his houseguest, a trombone player, could sit in with them. Nadine politely explained that, although they did do a lot of improvising, the concert had been well rehearsed and it would not be appropriate under the circumstances. Pete Jolly was standing by during this conversation and asked, "Is this anyone we know?"

The man, who was a local doctor and an avid jazz fan, replied, "It's Kai Winding."

Pete perked up. "Is this the real Kai Winding or just someone named Kai Winding?"

"No, this is for real. It *is* Kai Winding. He's presently with the Merv Griffin Show and he is staying with me while the show is moving its base from New York to California".

"Then tell him to get here and bring his instrument".

Kai Winding was probably the finest trombone player in the

country and he had recently been featured prominently by *Playboy* magazine in their story identifying America's top musicians. Both he and Pete Jolly were under contract with A&M Records. That next concert was purely magical and I have Ed Ravenscroft to thank for recording the event, which I have repeatedly replayed, relived and enjoyed over the years. Another of these concerts featured a dual piano routine with Nadine and another outstanding pianist, Betty Bello, who had studied under Erroll Garner. Their rendition of Jerome Kern's and Dorothy Fields' *"The Way You Look Tonight"* was absolutely spectacular and is still today my favorite piece of music as they played it. It gives me chills. Thankfully, Ed Ravenscroft recorded this one too.

Having Nadine and her trio at the hotel gave us so many wonderful opportunities for promoting our restaurant, which had been re-branded as *Cactus Charlie's - Casa for Beef* shortly before I took over. Dear old Cactus Charlie was a fictional gun fighter of the old west. He was supposedly buried just outside the entrance to the restaurant where his headstone read,

> *"Here lies Cactus Charlie –*
> *We buried him raw –*
> *He was quick on the trigger –*
> *But slow on the draw!*

****

We also hosted the popular syndicated Washington Post columnist, Art Buchwald, known for his political satire. He had spent several years in Paris writing for the European edition of the New York Herald Tribune and in 1959, during my time there, I was invited, with a number of other friends, to a party at his apartment. He was out of town and we had been invited there by his assistant, Connie, a delightful Irish girl. Nothing really got out of hand but I recall someone putting their foot through one of his typewriters, which happened to be on the floor in a hallway. I later bumped into Connie again when I was working in New York where she was working for the Irish Tourist Board. I am not sure if the party had been arranged with his permission or not but meeting him at the Executive House gave me a chance to confess that I had been one of those in attendance.

"I too spent some time in Paris." I said. "In 1959, when I was working at the Plaza Athénée, your assistant Connie invited a few us over to your apartment for a party. I hope it was with your permission."

"Probably not." He replied, "but I hope you had a good time."

"Oh, yes. And I remember that someone, not me, put their foot through your typewriter that was on the floor in one of the hallways."

"I can't say I remember knowing about that but I guess it's fortunate I had more than one."

****

Being accorded a live-in position in the hotel business has many advantages, especially financial ones, as our accommodations and meals were part of the arrangement. However, it also had its down side, as one is always on duty – or so it seems. Our apartment consisted of four connecting rooms on the ground floor looking out over the lawn and the pool area. It had a small kitchen and dining area in the first room, then a living room and then our two bedrooms. Just before our first Christmas, Anita and I thought it would be fun if we had a pet and, answering a newspaper advertisement for golden retriever puppies, we went to look. Oh my! Were they ever cute. We just could not walk away from these furry little ones empty handed and we picked out "Andy" and took him back with us to the hotel. We were thrilled for the moment. Nobody told us that these little ones tend to grow up to be huge, and dear Andy was no exception. He grew bigger by the day. We soon realized that having a boisterous dog in a hotel was not the smartest idea we had ever had. Fortunately, Anita's brother Frank and his wife Kathy agreed to take him. They were living in the gorgeous mountains in Prescott, just a few hours' drive north from Scottsdale, and they had a much more suitable environment for him. We missed him, even after so short a time, but it was the sensible thing to do.

However, the pet idea did not go away just because Andy did. Not long after, Irene, one of our waitresses, told me that her cat had just delivered kittens and wondered if we would be interested. We thought this would be easier and, right or wrong, it would be less of a potential 'guest conflict' issue. We picked out a brother and sister and, with Wendy and Diana's input, named them Candy and Favorite. Favorite was so named, as he *was* their favorite. We were right about them being easier to handle but, guess what? The guest conflict part was not completely resolved. We rarely let them outside but we did, on occasion, and, when they wanted to come back in, they would jump up on the patio's sliding screen door, and rattle it until we let them in. One problem! They did not seem to remember which were our rooms and which rooms were occupied by paying guests. This was brought home to me vividly one day when I was in the hotel's lobby and a guest approached the front desk and complained loudly about the damn cats rattling their screen door while they were trying to sleep. I was standing close by but, thankfully, the clerk on duty did not identify me as the person responsible for the cats. He assured the gentleman that management would be informed of the problem and that it would be properly handled and wouldn't happen again. He was right there. Poor Candy and Favorite had to suffer house arrest from then on.

Key to Success #9

Be Patient: *When taking over a new assignment, do not institute changes too quickly. Certainly, retain first impressions, but wait until you have time to thoroughly evaluate them before making changes. Something that worked elsewhere might not be applicable here.*

9. Playboy? Yes, Really. Playboy! (1970-1972)

It was the late summer of 1970 and I was well into my third year at the Executive House when I received a call from Ken Abrams. I knew Ken well from my days in New York with Restaurant Associates where he had been the vice president of human resources. He also knew Anita because of her role as Banquet Manager at the Mermaid Tavern. Like any good executive responsible for senior staffing in corporate America, he had kept in touch with us after we were married and we had moved out to Arizona. For obvious reasons, these contacts are often mutually beneficial. He too had moved on to bigger and better things and was now the vice president of human resources for Playboy Enterprises in Chicago. He called to tell me that the general manager of their company's new showpiece resort in Lake Geneva, Wisconsin was being promoted to a corporate position and they were looking for a replacement. Institutions Magazine had just done an extensive cover story on the property. The feature showed it to be a huge, beautiful conference resort with its own airport, many fine recreational amenities and 650 employees, of which 130 were "bunnies".

The resort was located on thirteen hundred acres in the beautiful rolling hills of southern Wisconsin. The hotel had over 300 rooms, several restaurant outlets including a 450-seat Las Vegas type showroom, a second-floor gourmet restaurant overlooking both the indoor and outdoor pool areas and many others, including a small interior sidewalk café. In addition, there were several meeting and banquet rooms. Outside there were two magnificent golf courses, one of them designed by Jack Nicklaus, and a ski area with a ski chalet, which housed a restaurant, lounge and discotheque. These were creatively named The Loaf of Bread restaurant, The Jug of Wine lounge and Thou, the disco. The ski hill had a 120-foot vertical drop with a chair lift, two rope tows and a fully operational ski school. The airport was home to the U.S. mail carrier Lake Geneva Airways as well as being used for private planes. There were also two outdoor tennis courts, a skeet and trap range and stables for the guests' horse riding pleasures. All this and construction was under way for more hotel rooms and a huge convention center addition, and all I was currently running was a small full-service 212-room hotel with about 65 employees.

Was I really going to be a viable candidate? I did not think so, but with Anita's encouragement, I went off to Chicago for my interview. There I met with Ken Abrams, Henri Lorenzi, the G.M who was being promoted, and Arnold Morton, Hugh Hefner's right hand man, to whom Lorenzi reported. For me it was rather intimidating. I could not believe they would select me for such a significant position. Of course, Henri Lorenzi would keep a close eye on me if I got the job, since his new responsibilities included oversight of the company's present and future hotel operations. He would, undoubtedly, be very helpful but critical of whomever took his place. After our meetings in Chicago, he drove me up to Lake Geneva for a site visit so that I could see what the job would entail. This was Playboy's newest and most dramatic addition to

Aerial view of Playboy Resort, Lake Geneva, Wisconsin

their portfolio, having opened just two years prior under his guidance. This was by far the most beautiful resort I had ever seen. I still feel this way today – and I've seen many of the best. It was an exciting, but humbling experience to be seriously considered.

I think those with whom I had spoken earlier in the day in Chicago must have put their heads together while I was still there as, after we had seen all that there was to see and while still sitting in his car, Lorenzi offered me the job.

WOW! Yes indeed, WOW is right.

My decision was instantaneous. The Lake Geneva Playboy Club-Hotel, here we come! Looking back now I firmly believe it was Ken Abrams whom I must thank. I don't think I would have been seriously considered without his recommendation. It was another example in my life of the benefit of maintaining good relationships.

With this new challenge ahead of us, Anita, Wendy, Diana and I packed up our things, including Candy and Favorite, and left Scottsdale for Lake Geneva. The winter months were almost upon us. Playboy had purchased the house of their former assistant manager, Jerry Steinweg, and they kindly turned it over to us. It was a delightful split-level home on a hill in the Sturwood section of Lake Geneva.

My first day at the resort, Lorenzi scheduled a full department head meeting. This was a fairly short and sweet meeting at which the different department heads were introduced, and I made a few generic remarks. Looking out from our head table, I saw a familiar face sitting in the front row. It was Michel Cipolla, who had just been introduced as the executive chef. My goodness, what were the odds of us working together again? When I had been working in Paris at the Plaza Athénée in 1959 as a *demi chef de rang* learning the restaurant service business, Michel was working in the hotel's kitchen as a *commis cuisinier* learning the critical food preparation side of things. I couldn't believe it. How great to have someone here I already knew, and a department head at that.

A much younger Michel Cipolla (far right front) and myself at the Plaza Athénée

I was blessed to have Henri Lorenzi as my overseer. He was by far the finest hotelier I had ever met, let alone worked for. He had the perfect combination of European trade know-how and American marketing and operations techniques. I remember that I had not been there long when we were walking the operation together on a busy Saturday night. As we passed through the kitchen situated between the Penthouse showroom and the VIP gourmet restaurant, he saw one of the cooks working on an order. Lorenzi's eagle eye saw that he was not making the dish correctly. He immediately went around the end of the line, grabbed the pan out of the cook's hand, threw whatever was in it away and proceeded to show the cook how it should have been done. There are few, if any, general managers today, me included, who could do that. He definitely got my attention.

This was indeed a big operation and at first I felt I was in well over my head. I remember in those first weeks walking around the resort on a Saturday night thinking, *I know we are busy! I just don't know what I should be doing.* On the main level, we had the 165-seat Playmate Lounge, which served as both our primary all day restaurant and an evening entertainment venue, and the Living Room, which had a beautiful permanent brass and copper buffet overlooking the indoor swimming pool. One of the appeals of the Playmate Lounge, as was typical in all the clubs, was the back-lit photographs of the monthly centerfolds displayed behind the bar. The Sidewalk Café was opposite on the other side of the central concourse. On the second floor, we had the 450-seat Penthouse showroom usually doing two shows a night and the VIP Room serving a gourmet menu on mirror-top tables. There were banquets being served on the lower level and a private party down at the ski chalet, almost a mile away. Such a lot of activity and it all seemed to be working fine. Should I just go home, hide in my office or just keep walking around? It was awesome. What do they even need *me* for?

My priority was to get to know my department heads, especially those with responsibility for operations that were totally new to me. This was October and winter would be coming on fast so I went to see the head of ski operations, Jerry Shanley. I admitted I had no knowledge at all about this activity, and that I needed to be educated as quickly as possible.

I told him, "Jerry, we need each other. I need you to help me understand the ski operations, and you need me to be able to properly evaluate and approve your budgets so that you can do your job. Let's get to it."

In the early months of the winter season, many of the employees who worked on the golf courses all summer were transferred to the ski department to get ready for the winter ski season. This allowed us to provide them with full time employment. As the temperature dropped into the mid to high 20's we would start to make our own snow. The crews would work 12 hours on and 12 hours off to build up a base. If the weather turned warm and it melted, they would start all over again. The ski school, rentals and ski chalet gift shop were all leased out. All I needed to do was to get to know these tenants and familiarize myself with the operating agreements that were already in place. That part of it was relatively easy. Quickly I was off and running and it wouldn't take long for me to have more work to do than I had time for. So much for just walking around!

Since the resort was the newest addition to Playboy's portfolio, the company put on many special events to get it maximum exposure as quickly as possible. The location, while physically beautiful was, after all, sitting amid the cornfields of Wisconsin. The large majority of our guests would need to come from surrounding communities, especially the Chicago and Milwaukee metropolitan areas, both an hour's drive away. Marketing for overnight guests would need both national and international exposure. The resort was open to the public, so not in any way exclusive to Playboy key holders, but bringing it up to the level of business needed for it to be profitable would be a challenge. One of the quickest ways to get the exposure we needed was with big name entertainment. In the summer of 1971, the Penthouse showroom booked some heavy hitters; Sonny and Cher, Ann-Margret, Phyllis Diller, Jack Jones, Minsky's Burlesque, George Carlin, Lily Tomlin, Diahann Carrol, Tony Martin and others.

Our showroom maître d'hôtel, Jerry Pawlak, told me that one night, during Jack Jones' engagement, Jones was in the kitchen with a brandy snifter in his hand waiting to be introduced when Henri Lorenzi walked through. Lorenzi mistakenly thought he was one of our busboys hanging around after his shift and began to chastise him for loitering on property This only ended when he was informed Jones was our headlining entertainer that week. At the end of his show, Jones said, "...and I want to thank all the staff from the busboys *down* to the general manager."

The booking of our entertainment was handled out of our corporate offices by Billy Rizzo, but once the act was on property, it was my responsibility to see that our side of the contract was fulfilled. It was in our best interest to take good care of the entertainers. I learned very quickly if they were treated well, they invariably gave 110% on stage. Our, on-property director of entertainment, Sam Distefano, was a talented pianist and the leader of our permanent house trio. He was also responsible for augmenting the trio with additional musicians as required by the performers from time to time. In addition, Sam worked closely with Gaylen Hayes who was our staff member responsible for the various sound and lighting requirements; usually different for each engagement. Gaylen also handled the introductions before the shows.

Sometimes, timing is everything, as it turned out to be with our booking of Sonny and Cher. Earlier that year they had produced a six-week series to be shown on CBS during the summer. They began their nine-day engagement with us between the second and third week of the show's broadcast. They had received rave reviews and there is no doubt that we were the beneficiary of the highly complimentary media coverage. They did two shows a night, except for Sunday when they did just one, and every one was sold out. They stayed in the hotel and mingled with our staff and other guests during the day. One day Sonny came to tell me that several of the bunnies had approached him about coming to see one of the shows. I told him that I was afraid we couldn't do that, as every one of their shows was already sold out; otherwise we would have been glad to accommodate them. Sonny thought for a moment and then said, "You know, Sunday night we are only scheduled for one show. What if we did a second show just for your employees?"

Raising my eyebrows, I said, "Would you really do that?"

"Sure, if you can get the orchestra to stay, we'd be happy to do it."

I told Sam Distefano what Sonny had said and that night Sam got the other musicians to agree to do it. Word spread like wildfire and that night every possible seat was filled with employees, parents, grandparents and friends. What a treat! It was a fabulous performance, looser than their normal show, but in no way sloppy. Their back and forth banter was hilarious, and I really think they enjoyed it as much as their audience. They deservedly received a huge standing ovation.

Then, to top that, Cher came to me and said, "Do you think I could work as a bunny in the Playmate Lounge for a little while one evening?"

I said, "Are you serious?"

"Certainly! I'd like to see if anybody would recognize me."

"Are you kidding?" I replied "Well, I have to get Hefner's approval, as all Playboy's trademarked products are so carefully protected, but let me see what I can do."

Once I received approval from our corporate office, Cher was fitted with her own bunny costume by our seamstress. We also got permission to have a tiny version made for their young daughter, Chastity, who was traveling with them. (See photo in Appendix II). When Cher appeared in the lounge, she was, of course, immediately recognized and enjoyed it so much she didn't want to quit. The room was in shambles but no one seemed to care; both the staff and the guests were getting a real kick out of it. In the end, I had to go and ask her to leave, not only because of all the disruption but she also had to get ready for their show.

We also benefited from another piece of fortunate timing for Ann-Margret's engagement which coincided with LIFE magazine's cover story, *"ANN-MARGRET: After ten years, big success for the 'Sex Kitten'."* I am sure that helped to fill the seats in the Penthouse showroom. (See Appendix II for photo).

One of the nicest headliners we had was Phyllis Diller. She was a class act in every sense of the word, both on stage and off. My boss from The Colony Hotel in Palm Beach, Led Gardner and his wife Bobbie, were staying with us during one of her engagements and they were thrilled to get to meet her. She passed away in 2012

With Sonny and Cher

at the age of 95 but her fabulous one-liners will no doubt live on forever. Lines like:

"Housework can't kill you, but why take the chance?"

"A bachelor is a guy who never made the same mistake once."

"Tranquilizers only work if you follow the advice on the bottle. Keep away from children."

"Burt Reynolds once asked me out. I was in his room." ...and many, many others.

A much less pleasant experience was an incident with George Carlin in 1970. He opened on Friday, November 27th. He was scheduled to do one show that first night, two on Saturday and, after taking two days off, he would be performing the rest of the week through Saturday night. As many will remember, Carlin was known for his cutting edge, coarse form of humor. On opening night, his act contained negative comments related to our country's involvement in Vietnam, among other topics, and it did not go over well. After the show, Sam talked to him and suggested he lighten up a bit. He didn't take this excellent advice, and he continued in this same mode for his first show on Saturday and really 'laid an egg.' To say he wasn't happy about this would be an understatement, he was mad. Again, Sam explained that his routine was just too strong for this particular audience.

It was the height of the winter season and the room was jammed for the second show. At the break, following the opening act, I left the Penthouse and went to check on the VIP Room. I had barely arrived at the maître d'hôtel desk when I was beeped and asked to return to the Penthouse because they were having some problems. I turned around and as I walked back along the second

Bill Pullen
is a dream
+ a scholar

Phyllis
Diller

With Phyllis Diller

floor concourse I saw people streaming out, all fuming and enraged. What could have happened? The show had just started barely minutes before. I worked my way through the crowd like a salmon swimming upstream and arrived at the podium where John Reed, our showroom manager, and Jerry Pawlak, his assistant, were surrounded by guests and trying to handle numerous complaints.

I said, "John, what happened?"

"You won't believe it," he answered, "I'll tell you once we get this mess sorted out."

And a mess it was! John, Jerry and I spent more than an hour apologizing, refunding, giving rain checks and responding to our outraged guests. Finally, everyone was gone. We ordered a drink, sat down to catch our collective breath, and John told me what had happened. Evidently, still hot because he had 'bombed' during the first show, Carlin came out, gave his usual opening and then held up two fingers explaining it was the sign meaning 'peace'. He then extended his middle finger, graphically explained what it meant, told the entire audience that is what they were doing and walked off the front of the stage, through the tables of guests and out the front door.

Three young American Marines were in the audience, and they were perhaps even more furious than Carlin, *and* now they were looking for him. I mean *really* looking for him – and not just for light conversation and an autograph. Carlin had a suite in the hotel and we advised our front desk and telephone operators that under no circumstances were they to give out any information whatsoever, nor put any calls through to his room. Our security officer was put on full alert.

Somewhere between one and two o'clock in the morning Sam Distefano and I were in the executive offices debating what to do next. Obviously, Carlin was through, we couldn't have him go on again even though it would not be until Tuesday night. We decided to call him down to the office, escorted by our security officer.

When he walked in I said, "What a disaster! George, I'm afraid that's it. You're through."

"You can't do that. I have a contract signed by Billy Rizzo, not you."

"George, there's a word in your contract that says 'comedian'", I answered, showing him the contract. "Comedians make people laugh. You were singularly unsuccessful at doing that. Trust me, you're through."

"I don't accept that. I'll speak to Billy on Monday. I'm staying on 'til the end of next week as I agreed."

"You can do what you want but you're not working here. We'll give you a ride back to O'Hare but that's it. From now on you're here on a cash basis. Just call the front desk when you're ready to leave."

Muttering something under his breath, he stomped out and was escorted back up to his suite.

I worked all day Sunday and by the time I went home late in the afternoon, we had not heard from him. However, around six o'clock I got a call from the hotel saying that Carlin was ready to leave for the airport. We put in a call to Herb Welch, our limousine driver, and the rest is history. The following week Variety magazine came out with the story on their front page, but it was strictly his version of the events. Many years later I happened to catch one of his television interviews. He referenced the time that he was fired from Playboy, but was now wearing it as a badge of honor. Oh well!

OK, so now what were we going to do? We still had the rest of his engagement to fill. His unknown opening singer was still here, but we needed a main attraction. I called Billy Rizzo first thing Monday morning, told him what had happened and he put the wheels in motion. He did wonders and secured the talented French personality, Jean-Paul Vignon, who had a television show on one of the Chicago TV stations. Billy could not have done better, even though he could not have known why. Sunday was often a heavy arrival day for the hotel with corporate and association groups checking out and checking in. We had a large contingency of General Electric people arriving that week, many of whom were from their French and Belgian offices. Jean-Paul, of course, spoke their language and it just could not have been any better, plus we still had our opening act. Who do you think that was? Bette Midler! As we now know, she went on to be much more than an opening act!

****

We also had issues with Lily Tomlin and her English traveling companion and manager who was a rather unpleasant person with whom to work. I had to step in when she stopped John Reed from seating some guests after Tomlin's show had started. I escorted her from the showroom so we could discuss this outside, and told her, in no uncertain terms, who was running the show here. She said she *never* misses Miss Tomlin's shows and I told her to enjoy the break!

I said, "We have big name stars play this room. Who on earth is this Lily Tomlin?"

She seemed to shake violently. "Don't say that to me!" She was almost screaming. Our conversation became quite animated and I felt myself losing control. Everyone was seated and the show went on. I drove myself down to the ski chalet and walked around for several minutes to put myself back together. I needed to stay calm and professional. We also had trouble with both of them and their rudeness to other guests on the tennis court so we were all quite pleased when they left.

****

Another incident concerned Tony Martin. On the last day of his appearance, he came to see me and said, "Can we move the second show up half an hour tonight? I need to catch a flight out of O'Hare and I will be running tight for time."

"I'm sorry, but we can't do that, Tony." I told him. "For one thing we need the time to clean and re-set the room after the first show and then serve dinner to the second seating. Anyway, the show is sold out and there is no way we would be able to advise our guests with reservations. Also, if we just moved the show up, we would still be in the middle of serving dinner."

He became irate and said. "What's a show?"

I said, "What do you mean?"

"What do you call a show?"

"You know what a show is. That's what you do."

"How many numbers do you want in a show? Twelve numbers? Fifteen?"

"Tony, I want you to do your usual show like you've been doing."

I answered.

"I'll do twelve songs, that's it!" and he walked away. Time came for the second show and, after his introduction, he came out and sang one song after another, hardly taking a breath in between. He plowed straight on through any applause, which quickly dissipated when everyone saw what he was doing. It was appalling and I just stood in the back of the room shaking my head and preparing myself for all the complaints we would receive. Finally, it was over and he left the stage. Sam Distefano was just able to grab him back stage to tell him that an avid fan had specifically asked for a front table and planned to present a valuable clarinet to him after the show. Martin came back on stage, grabbed the ornate box containing the clarinet out of the fan's hands and disappeared. I don't think he even said thank you. What a nightmare. I hope he missed his flight!

****

Arnold Morton was my boss's boss and Hugh Hefner's right-hand man in matters related to things other than the magazine. He spoke his mind and could be quite intimidating, so whenever he came to the resort you had better believe I was paying attention. One evening, when the resort was packed, he asked me to go with him to review our buffet offerings in the Living Room. He proceeded to look at every item on the buffet and commented critically on our selections. He had no problem with the overall presentation, just the individual items we had prepared.

Walking outside, so as not to be discussing these things in front of the guests, he asked, "Who on earth put this menu together? There's absolutely no imagination."

"I'm sorry, Mr. Morton. We're just following the instructions we were given." I replied.

"Whose instructions?" he barked.

Pulling a memo from my pocket, which, thank goodness, I had been smart enough to take out of my files beforehand, I replied, "You did, Mr. Morton!" and gave him his memo. Nothing more was said.

Tom Burrows, our golf course superintendent, had a similar experience. Every year, at the start of the summer season, he and Morton would ride around the two golf courses and discuss changes or upgrades to the Brute and Briar Patch. At one point, they were looking at the tee box on the Briar Patch that was situated close to the parking lot of the ski chalet. Morton was telling Tom that it needed some upgrading and additional landscaping. Tom was a little surprised and said, "Don't you remember? Last year I specifically asked you if we could do exactly what you are now telling me to do."

"Ok then, remind me. What did I say about it?" Morton replied.

"Well, Mr. Morton'" Tom answered, "You said 'Fuck it, let God take care of it!'."

Yep, that was Arnold Morton.

However, he was a genius in his own right and later was the founder and developer of the now famous Morton's Steak Houses and the then popular disco, Zorine's, in Chicago, named after his wife.

****

Our golf pro, Ken Judd, was a stand-up guy; everyone liked him. He was low key and to a great extent marched to his own drummer – and he was kind of a sacred cow. He had a great relationship with many of the people in our corporate offices, as he had been there from the start. I arrived at the pro shop one morning to speak to him but he wasn't there. I asked the other golf shop employees, and nobody had any idea where he was. They hadn't seen him all morning and that was unusual. Then one of them spoke up and said, "You know, he may have gone to the Masters but I'm not sure." Well, she was probably right. Ken did not show up all week and I was quite upset about it. He hadn't told his staff, he hadn't told any of his fellow department heads, and he hadn't even *told me*, let alone ask.

The following Monday morning, bright and early, I told the crew in the pro shop that when, and *if*, Ken came in, I would like to see him in my office as soon as possible. That worked, as soon Ken arrived. He sat down and I closed the door, all quite theatrical! When asked about his absence, he said he *had* gone to the Masters and had taken off without telling a soul. I explained that if I am supposed to be running the resort, I couldn't allow key staff members to disappear without *even* telling me, let alone without asking my permission. We discussed it some more and I am sure somewhere along the line he apologized and told me that he understood. Still, I told him that it was totally unacceptable and that he had given me no alternative but to let him go. Yes, he was fired.

It didn't take long for my phone to ring. "It's Arnold Morton for you," called out Marylou Krause, my secretary.

I picked up the phone and said, "Hello Mr. Morton," as cheerfully and as confidently as I could.

"Pullen, I hope you know what you are doing!" He was almost shouting. He wasn't happy!

I explained what had happened and the way I felt about it and he somewhat understood my point of view. Still he wasn't happy about it, and we discussed it for several minutes before we hung up. Wow! I wasn't overruled. To me that was *very* important. However, I knew that, in the long run, it would probably be better to work something out with Ken than to start recruiting a new golf pro. While this was considered a high profile and coveted position; a prime job for any golf professional, I felt that if we could come to terms on how situations like this would be handled in the future, it would be best for all concerned. I called the pro shop to be sure Ken was there and went down to see him. We went for a walk around the course and, after both stating our cases, agreed that he would stay on. At least I had made my point and, looking back on it today, I know it was the right outcome. In fact, we became good friends.

****

In the summer of 1971, Jack Nicklaus, one of the designers of the Briar Patch, came to participate in the Chicagoland Pontiac Dealers' golf tournament. It was the Monday following his win at the PGA Byron Nelson Classic in Texas. He played one hole with each foursome so, after each hole, he stayed back until the next foursome came through. Then he played the next hole with them, and so on. This was a long day for him as he was out there for about seven hours. Naturally, I was interested to see him play, and I left the office for a little while to follow him on a couple of holes on the back nine. Playing off one elevated tee, he drove his ball way down the middle of the fairway, as expected. One of the members of this foursome was left-handed and, after they had all hit, Jack said to him, "Give me that!", referring to the man's driver. He then proceeded to drive a second ball off the tee right handed but with the left-handed club. Once again, his ball went straight down the middle of the fairway, albeit about 30 yards shorter than his first one. Remarkable! Some years later, I was relating this story to a small group and one of the gentlemen spoke up and said "Yes, that's true. That left-hander was me." What were the odds of that happening?

****

I was fortunate to be involved with many high-profile events while at Playboy. One such event, in April 1971, was a televised boxing smoker, featuring well-established fighters George Foreman, Ernie Terrell, Stanford Harris and others. There were to be three-round exhibition bouts but Foreman and Terrell would not be fighting each other. A boxing ring had to be built in the middle of our new convention center, with huge lights installed overhead in addition to special lighting for television. On top of all that, we had to serve 1,100 dinner guests. It was an interesting event and it went off successfully. After we tore everything down, we were left with the nine huge lamps, which had been installed over the ring. Corporate had ordered them and arranged for their installation and I assumed that they would coordinate the dismantling and removal. Several weeks later I called my contact at the Chicago office to remind him that the lights were still there only to be told, "They're yours. You paid for them." So much for my budget!

Just a few weeks later, I was advised by our corporate office that our convention center was going to be needed for a week to film "The Best of Bowling", a pro-celebrity series to run on ABC. I was subsequently contacted by representatives of the Brunswick Corporation, to coordinate the construction of two bowling alleys from scratch. Miraculously, they accomplished this in just two days and by Monday morning everything was ready to go. While I was checking out their set up, I had the opportunity to meet two

With Jack Nicklaus and Ken Judd

of the celebrities who were getting ready to bowl, the famous western movie star Roy Rogers, and Greg Morris of CBS's "Mission Impossible" fame. Unlike the situation I had with 'buying' the boxing ring lights, this time Brunswick came back in and dismantled everything when it was over.

****

There was always a certain amount of mystique about Playboy and much of this naturally pertained to the bunnies and what was referred to as the 'bunny image'. While the Playboy dynasty was largely based around the sexual revolution, especially through the magazine, the club and hotel operations were strictly business, professionally run and monitored accordingly. There was no room for any nonsense of any kind.

To maintain the bunny image, it was critical that we hired the most beautiful girls to wear the bunny costume. We had a grading scale from '1 to 4', with '1' being an absolutely gorgeous girl. The goal was to hire all '1's; a '2' would be acceptable. A girl who was graded a '3' by the 'Bunny Mother', Ann Hamilton, would be an existing bunny who had been put on notice to correct a specific physical issue, such as her weight or hair. Falling to a '4' would be unacceptable and would result in termination. Ann was responsible for constantly interviewing applicants. Any girl that she graded a '1' or a '2' would be called back for a second interview and every Saturday, part of my job was to partner with Ann on the grading. If we both graded a girl a '1' or a '2', then she was eligible to be hired. If Ann had graded a girl a '2' and I gave her a '3', then she would not be considered.

Many of the applicants thought that being a bunny was a nice, glamorous job. They did not realize that it was indeed a difficult, tiring position requiring long hours in tight costumes and high heeled shoes. A certain amount of turnover was to be expected.

Another part of the Playboy mystique was Hugh Hefner's Chicago Playboy Mansion. I had a couple of opportunities to go there, usually tied into a general manager's meeting at the corporate offices. These visits involved cocktail receptions, hosted by Hefner, after the day's events. It was interesting to see it, complete with the fireman's pole for launching oneself into the indoor swimming pool on a lower level, something, thankfully, I did not get to do. When Anita and I were invited for a pre-Christmas gathering, we found the environment extremely uncomfortable. The main oak-paneled room was large and featured a high ceiling and a huge fireplace at one end. A group of musicians was playing loud heavily amplified music and the photographers were using synchronized flash bulbs high around the ceiling. Between the noise and the constant flashes, it was practically impossible to carry on any kind of a meaningful conversation with other guests. Frankly, we were quite happy when we finally could take our leave. Still, it was interesting to have been there.

****

My job at Playboy provided many proud and happy memories but it also gave me the most embarrassing experience of my entire career. Brian Piccolo, an outstanding young football player, played professionally as a Chicago Bears running back. Regrettably, cancer ended his brief four-year career, and he passed away at the age of 26. His life and career were immortalized in the movie "Brian's Song" based on his friend Gayle Sayers' autobiography. In 1971, our Playboy resort was selected as the venue for the first annual golf tournament to raise money for the Brian Piccolo Cancer Research Fund. Anyone who was anyone in the sporting world was coming. The hotel would be at capacity with many well-known people including athletes, team owners, media, vendors, etc. The details were being worked out by Bill Hickey, in our corporate sales office, and were being coordinated with our own sales department and golf staff. There would be two shotgun starts, 7:30 am and 1:00 pm on Saturday and Sunday.

However, this caused a potential logistics problem for the hotel on Sunday afternoon. In addition to a hotel full of departing guests from the golf event, we would be welcoming the Wisconsin Soft Drink Bottlers Association and the Admiral Corporation for their meetings the following week. This had been discussed with Hickey well in advance. It was decided the best course of action would be to have the morning golfers check out after their round, and the afternoon golfers before they teed off. This would minimize traffic at the reception desk and allow enough time to clean the rooms for arriving guests. It should work fine – right? It should.

The seven-building hotel was perched in a prime location, on top of the hill overlooking the 18th hole of the Brute golf course. The center building housed the arrival lobby, restaurants, lounges and meeting rooms. The six buildings containing the guest rooms were split evenly, with three on each side of the main building. The golf course wound around a central lake and the views were spectacular. Our reservations department, under the watchful eye of Jackie Rossmiller, had carefully assigned rooms for the two incoming groups. With few exceptions, each group would be accommodated evenly in guest rooms on each side. The numbers in each group were about the same. Suites had been blocked for the VIP's and guest speakers and, from an operational standpoint, we were ready to go and fully prepared.

However, come Sunday, things didn't quite work out that way. Some early arrivals started coming in late morning and the incoming flow continued all day. Intermingled with these new guests were some of the VIP's and guest speakers. The two meeting planners, with whom our sales department had been working, had arrived a day or so early to assist us in seeing that we delivered everything we had promised. By midday they were beginning to get a little nervous. So were we! Our housekeeping department had all hands on deck waiting for the check-outs, but there were hardly any. I sensed I had the probability of a real disaster on my hands and everything seemed totally out of my control. We needed rooms, clean rooms.

As you can imagine, most of those playing in the golf tournament were, in their own sphere of influence, VIPs. They were not used to being pushed around or regimented in any way. They were enjoying their stay and would check out at their leisure, but we needed clean rooms – and fast. I met with Jackie, got a list of those who were supposed to have already checked out, attached it to my clipboard and started running around the corridors to check the status of these rooms. In one case, calling out "housekeeping", I knocked on the door of a room that should have been vacated and on hearing "Come in" I opened the door with my passkey only to see five huge football players sitting around talking and drinking beer.

"Is one of you Gayle Sayers?" I am sure the nervousness in my voice was showing.

"No, he's playing golf," one of them replied.

"This *is* his room though, isn't it?" I asked.

"Yes, it is. Is there a problem?"

"W-w-w-well. He was supposed to have checked out," I stuttered.

"It's OK, he'll check out when he gets through."

I knew immediately that this wouldn't be until early evening at best, as it's normal for a little socializing after playing golf. I backed out of the room muttering "Thank you" under my breath. Oh dear! This is getting worse!

I returned to the office, making my way through the throng of people milling around in the lobby waiting for their rooms. I could distinguish murmurs in the same tone the captain of a ship must hear before the mutiny. I got behind the front desk to try to soothe our desk clerks who were being harassed by the guests and the meeting planners. It seemed they were all looking for me! Where were my sales people? Oh, yes, it was Sunday and many of them would not be at the hotel today.

Eventually, we did get the rooms back and our stellar housekeeping crew stayed as long as was necessary to clean them and release them to the front desk. Of course, the rooms that Jackie had so carefully assigned were now occupied by whomever had needed them on a first come first served basis. This meant, for instance, that an Admiral VIP, who perhaps had been waiting three or four hours, was put in the first room that became available instead of the suite that had been blocked for him. He may also be in the Bottlers Association building mixed in with attendees of that group. The VIP's were not happy, the meeting planners were not happy, my employees were not happy and I was going nuts! This was a day *not* to be wearing your nametag. I didn't think it would *ever* end – but it did. Tomorrow is another day.

I now had to face another difficult and uncomfortable situation. Not all groups are the same and there is a great deal of difference between corporate and association groups. In the case of a corporate group there is a natural pecking order of authority, so the company's meeting planner can assist the hotel in deciding who is to be accommodated on a priority basis before another attendee. Also, the company picks up the tab. Attendees of an association event are separate entities, paying their own expenses, so, except for board members and guest speakers, without a priority list, it can be a bit of a fight to see who gets the next room.

Unfortunately, many months before, while our sales department was finalizing the intricate details for the Wisconsin Soft Drink Bottlers Association, I was asked if I would give a brief welcoming speech before their first morning general session. There I stood, on the stage of the Penthouse showroom, facing the crowd that had been so intimately involved in the calamity of the day before. I am afraid this was another "Oh dear!" moment. I have no idea what I said. I just know that every single one of those people I was looking at from the stage was either someone we had personally "pissed off" in a big, big way or, at the least, had heard all about the previous day's disaster. To say I was nervous would be a gross understatement. I was never so happy to step out of the spotlight and back to the quiet sanctity of my office.

Despite all the aggravation and frustration of the check-in disaster, there was a small incident, which provided a sliver of a silver lining. While I had been behind the front desk on Sunday, a gentleman had elbowed his way through the maddening crowd and caught my eye. I remember it well. He said, "We are Mr. and Mrs. Maxwell from Indianapolis. I have to admit we are nobody important but we *do* have a reservation."

They had obviously been in the melee in the lobby for a while and had heard what was happening. I apologized profusely and checked with Jackie to see if there was anything that had been cleared for occupancy. Just *anything*. Luckily, our head housekeeper had just called in a few available rooms, so I took possession of one of them and went back to the desk to check them in.

"I don't suppose you have a bellman available, do you?" he asked hopefully. I knew, without even checking, that we did not.

What else could I say but, "I'd be happy to help you".

They were parked right outside the main entrance and Maxwell invited me to get in their car. Giving him directions, we drove off to the building where their room was located. We parked, unloaded their suitcases, and were just about to enter the building when one of our bellmen came out with a luggage cart. Seeing me carrying two of the Maxwell's suitcases, he said, "I'll take care of these Mr. Pullen. Leave it to me." Once again, I apologized to the Maxwells and he graciously thanked me for assisting them. Then he offered me a tip! Of course, I declined but he insisted. Again, I declined. He was most persistent and again insisted that he tip me. Finally, I said, "Mr. Maxwell, I am terribly embarrassed to admit this but, I am the Managing Director here and the disaster you saw in the hotel lobby is all my responsibility."

Unexpectedly, that little incident did bring about a 'warm and fuzzy'. At that time, Playboy magazine published a monthly member's magazine quite different from Playboy. It contained the various happenings around the clubs, plus one or two feature articles. It was called VIP Magazine and it was mailed out to the keycard holders. John Maxwell had kindly taken the trouble to send in a letter about their experience with us. The magazine printed it under the heading, "Beyond the Call of Duty".

"My wife and I took a brief holiday as guests at the Playboy Club-Hotel at Lake Geneva, Wisconsin. When we arrived on Sunday afternoon, there was a line of conventioneers waiting to register. I saw a young man behind the bell captain's window and asked whether or not he could help us avoid the delay. He found our reservations and explained that there were no bellboys available because of the conventioneers, but that he would take us to our room himself. After he assisted me in carrying our luggage and other paraphernalia to the door, I naturally offered him a gratuity, but he refused with the shy explanation that he was the Managing Director, Mr. L. William Pullen. Mr. Pullen's attentiveness to us was highly appreciated. In my opinion, he is a great asset to your organization."

John E. Maxwell"

And it doesn't end there; a few weeks later I received a letter dated December 9, 1971.

"Dear Bill,

I was idly thumbing through this magazine and saw the enclosed. (Mr. Maxwell's letter). I am delighted indeed that you are not only in such a significant post but that you are still a warm, friendly, accommodating Bill Pullen.

My best wishes to you for continued success.

Sincerely,

S. Joseph Tankoos, Jr."

Talk about the icing on the cake. I was only there because of him and our meeting in Paris at the Plaza Athénée in 1959. His letter with the attachment from VIP magazine is among some of my most treasured possessions. Was it all worth it?

You bet it was.

****

There was one more interesting incident that took place that weekend. On the Saturday morning of the golf tournament, the switchboard received a telephone call from the White House; President Nixon wanted to speak with Martin Casario. Casario, President and general manager of the Pontiac Division of General Motors, was out on the golf course with his foursome of Bart Starr, quarterback for the Green Bay Packers, John Baker, President of Fisher Body Division of G.M. and Chuck Coleman, President of Maritz Travel Corporation, whose company had been retained as the organizer of the event. There were several bunnies involved with hosting the tournament so we asked one of them to take a golf cart and try to find him. After some time, we see her returning but she was still by herself.

"Didn't you find him?" we asked.

"Yes, he said, 'Thank you. I'll call him after I get through.'"

Now that's class!!

I had occasion to recall this incident with Casario and his wife many years later when they were dining at the Jensen Beach hotel I was managing. He was retired and they had a home nearby.

****

With the additional rooms we had built, along with the new conference center, it was not unusual for us to have multiple groups in the hotel at the same time. Such was the case when we hosted the Wisconsin Student Nurses Association and the

Chicago-based Alexander Grant accounting firm. With over 300 partners, they were one of the largest accounting firms in the U.S. After all the events were over, on the day of departure, the meeting planners came to sit with the respective sales manager, with whom they had worked, a common practice, to review the entire meeting agenda of the past week. They would critique the event, often add additional gratuities for deserving staff members and discuss the possibility of holding other meetings at the resort in the future. In this case, the association executive with the Wisconsin Student Nurses Association followed this routine and made a tentative future booking for the following year. Not long after, the meeting planner for the Alexander Grant firm came to the sales office to do that same thing. They too had been extremely happy with their meetings, meal functions and sports activities and they too wanted to make plans for setting up dates for their next annual meeting. However, they had one stipulation – that it be over the same dates as the nurses.

Hmm? Yes, we wondered about that too! I guess we'll never know.

As I stated previously, I had felt under qualified for the position Playboy had given me. I always felt I had to overcome that. I did so with hard work and long hours and, if she were still here, Anita would confirm that. I was with the company for less than two years before we decided to return to Arizona and I had reported for work every single day I was there. For me, a day off was when I had to drive to Chicago for a managers' meeting. But what a priceless experience it was!

(Special Note: This wonderful resort is now known as The Grand Geneva Resort and Spa and it is owned and managed by the

Marcus Corporation based in Milwaukee. It is in excellent hands and even better than ever).

It Started at The Savoy

Key to Success #10

Be Specific: *When requesting references, clearly describe the responsibilities the candidate will be expected to assume. Even though a candidate was exemplary in a previous position, the job you are trying to fill may require very different skills.*

10. Return to the Desert (1972-1976)

Out of the blue, I received a call from the developers of a new community in the Arizona foothills, just north of Scottsdale, in Carefree. Although I was not considering moving at the time, I realized that one could pursue an interesting and fulfilling career without the cold and snow inherent to Wisconsin. There were times when I could not get the car up the hill to our home and I would have to leave it and trudge the rest of the way through the snow. My job with Playboy had been the most challenging and enlightening of my career. And while I did not have total control over the operating results, due to the many promotional events orchestrated by our corporate office, it did provide me exposure and experience with the most comprehensive resort with which I was ever involved.

The Carefree Inn was a little jewel of a hotel with just 125 rooms, tennis courts, and a location directly across the street from the highly-acclaimed Desert Forest Golf Club, once rated by Golf Digest as one of the top 100 courses in the U.S. The hotel purchased 60 annual memberships so that their guests could have playing privileges. The hotel could then use this excellent amenity for advertising and marketing purposes.

The hotel was owned by Carefree Developers, Inc, and operated by Western International Hotels out of their corporate offices in Seattle.

Carefree Inn

The founders of Carefree Developers, Tom Darlington and K.T. Palmer, knew of my involvement in the hotel business, and were looking for a general manager. Because it was a relatively small property, Western International had been using the hotel as a training ground for developing management personnel, resulting in a change of general managers on a regular basis. This policy conflicted with what Darlington and Palmer were trying to do. Carefree was being promoted as a high-end residential community, and the hotel was to be the center of activity with an excellent restaurant and a lounge featuring live entertainment. They intended that the local residents would treat it as if it was their country club and, in turn, the hotel would benefit from their food and beverage business. Carefree Developers felt that canceling the Western International contract and hiring their own general manager would be more consistent with their vision for the community.

Arriving in Phoenix for my interview during the winter accentuated the sharp difference in climate. The Arizona weather was beautiful – just beautiful. I went through my interview, took a close look at the property and was offered the position. Anita and I were well acquainted with Carefree, having purchased a residential lot there during my tenure at Camelback Inn. We discussed it and, although it was certainly a much lower profile position than I had at Playboy, we both agreed that we should take them up on their offer. Consequently, we moved, along with Wendy, Diana, Candy and Favorite, back to the sunshine.

Our flight from Chicago to Phoenix was uneventful but while we were waiting at the baggage claim carousel we heard an announcement. "Would the passenger with the cats please come to the American Airlines information desk, thank you."

I looked at Anita and said, "That's us. What could it be?"

We went straight to the counter and the first thing the agent said was, "Well, we got one of them!"

It seems that the container carrying Candy and Favorite had opened somehow during or after the flight. They had Candy but Favorite was nowhere to be found. I was invited to go back out to the plane and get into the belly area where the luggage is carried and see if I could coax him to come out. I have rarely felt so stupid as I did crawling around the mechanical workings of the baggage hold area calling out "Favorite, Favorite" as if he would come to me in that environment, or for that matter, any environment. He doesn't *even* know his name is Favorite for goodness sake. Still, the airline personnel thought this exercise would show that they were trying to do *something*. As you might expect, it was futile.

Eventually, Candy was put into another carrying container and we left Favorite wherever he was and went on our way. The airlines assured us they would keep an eye out for him and promised to call when they got him. They also gave us a phone number in case we wanted to follow up. Hearing nothing that night, the following morning I called and was advised that unfortunately he had not been found during the overnight stay. That plane had already left that morning for Los Angeles, but not to worry! "We've advised our ground personnel in L. A. to be on the lookout and when they get him, they will ship him back to Phoenix. We'll call you." Again, we heard nothing. Where was the flight going next? Boston! I guess the good news was that Favorite was racking up some frequent flyer miles if nothing else! I just hoped they weren't charging us for it.

"Don't worry. We've advised our people in Boston and we are sure they'll find him for you", we were told.

"Gee, thanks." That hadn't worked so far but what else could they do. We could see the headlines, *"Missing cat holds up 17 flights."*

Well, no luck in Boston either. Next stop Los Angeles - again. American Airlines was going to give the ground crew there a second chance. And, what do you know? They found him. Finally! They placed him in a container and put him on a flight back to Phoenix. We knew this had to have been a frightening experience for poor old Favorite and that he would be thrilled to see us when we went to get him. Wrong! Nothing! Just ho hum, yawn. We got him home and there was absolutely no reaction. He didn't even look thinner! Still, he was back with the family after his adventurous interlude, and we were all together again. The only follow-up was a column written by my friend Larry Rummel in the Arizona Republic about Favorite's ordeal. Why didn't the kids give him a more appropriate name than Favorite? Too late now. End of story.

****

The Carefree Inn was indeed a beautiful hotel with both Mobil Four Star and AAA Four Diamond ratings. The guest rooms, surrounding a spacious and attractive pool area amid the desert landscape, were large and beautifully furnished. This, combined with two restaurants, a lounge and excellent golf and tennis facilities gave me a property of which to be proud. In addition, several of the employees had been there for quite some time and not only were capable and knowledgeable of the operations, but were also well acquainted with many people in the surrounding area.

Even though Carefree was a relatively new and growing community, it was already home to several well-healed homeowners; three of our neighbors were Paul Harvey of 'The Rest of the Story' radio news program, Hugh Downs, known as Jack Paar's sidekick on The Jack Paar Tonight Show, and comedic actor Dick Van Dyke, who lived in Cave Creek. The nearby, newly developed Southwestern Studios and their sound stages were the base for several movie productions under the guiding hand of Fred Graham, a former Hollywood stunt man. Since it was also used for taping The Dick Van Dyke Show episodes, several of the actors and actresses who made guest appearances on the show stayed with us.

****

I was well supported by my new bosses and became actively involved in developing a new 72-room addition adjacent to the tennis courts and an extension to the main hotel with expanded meeting space. Both had been urgently needed. One of the first uses of this new area was a surprise 52nd birthday party for Hugh Downs on Valentine's Day in February 1973. All the guests had congregated in one of our new rooms and he had been invited to the hotel on some pretext. I was to meet him in the lobby to keep him occupied for a few minutes and then take him to where the guests were waiting.

****

Carefree was somewhat isolated although it was a 15 mile straight run north from Scottsdale. It was in the foothills across raw desert, not like it is today, and the road had a fair number of arroyos (deep gullies in the roadway that carried runoff in times of rainfall). Unlike many parts of the country, water did not soak into the ground here; instead it ran over the surface taking the path of least resistance. It was not a frequent occurrence, but when we did get heavy rains, these arroyos were quite dangerous, as they often washed out. If you were in a car, it was almost impossible to know how deep the water might be. It was on one of these occasions I had another one of my memorable experiences.

Because of unusually heavy rains that day, many of my evening restaurant and kitchen staff could not get to work. Rather than post an apology notice outside the entry to the restaurant and close, as I would if it were to happen today, I decided to proceed as if everything was normal. I hoped that some of them would still show up, even though they would be late. I had one line-cook in the kitchen, one busboy in the restaurant, and me. I was the headwaiter, the waiter and almost anything else that required hands on. Luckily, because of the weather, we were not especially busy but having come from Lake Geneva with a staff of 650, my restaurant skills were rusty, to say the least. I can still feel the hot flashes and cold chills, combining with a knot in my stomach, as I tried to go on as if nothing was wrong. We got by but I sure learned from that mistake.

We hosted some high-powered meetings; of particular note, two separate Regional Conference Board meetings and the Conquistadores del Cielo (translated "Conquerors of the Sky"). The latter was an exclusive and somewhat secretive elite aviation industry group founded by TWA President Jack Frye and V.P. Paul Richter. The group was limited, by their own rules, to no more than 100 members. At that time, they held two meetings a year; the summer meeting, held at a dude ranch in Wyoming, and a winter get-together, held at various resorts. One evening, as I was heading from the hotel to check on the group's barbecue at our nearby cookout area, I was accompanied by one of their attendees and we chatted amiably on our way. Once we got there, in the light of the flaming torches, I could read his nametag, "Charles Tillinghast." Once back in my office, I looked on my rooming list and found that he was the chairman and CEO of TWA. All the others in their group were senior executives of that same level. Not bad for our little hotel (see Appendix II letter from General J. B. Montgomery dated April 24, 1972).

The Conference Board meetings brought together the chief operating officers of major industries in specific regions of the country, usually with the appropriate senators and/or congressmen. They had an interesting format. The attendees would sit in a big circle in our meeting room and, one by one, they would be called upon by a chairman to speak on a topic that would hold the attention of the entire assembly. None of them knew when they would be called upon so it could be a bit stressful, particularly if one of the earlier speakers had already spoken on their intended topic.

Prior to arriving in Carefree, my new bosses informed me of their concern regarding a corporate booking with Ray-O-Vac Corporation. It seemed the Ray-O-Vac meeting planners were concerned that the change of hotel management might negatively affect their conference plans. It was too late for them to change venues, although I am sure they had considered it. I decided the best way to allay their fears was to meet with them in person. Fortunately, Ray-O-Vac's corporate headquarters were in Madison, not too far from Lake Geneva. I drove over there one cold, snowy morning to introduce myself and went over the details with them. As a result, when they arrived in Carefree, I had already established a good relationship with the key players and their meetings went off without a hitch. Ray-O-Vac became one of our best references (see letter in Appendix II).

****

Before we had added the new meeting room facilities, we had some smaller meeting rooms leading from our Sunset Dining Room but there was just one set of rest rooms to service both areas. We had a rather amusing situation one day when a group of ladies had booked one of these rooms. When they broke for lunch, many of them headed straight for the ladies' rest room, creating a waiting line outside. Evidently, one of them, not wanting to wait, and seeing no apparent activity in or out of the men's room, took the initiative and went in. She was immediately followed by several others. It was about that time we noticed that one of our busboys was missing. Upon enquiring if anyone knew where he was, one of the waitresses said, "I think he went to the restroom."

The doors to both restrooms were visible from most areas and word quickly spread throughout the dining room. There was great anticipation for a grand finale of some kind as the lines outside the restrooms gradually diminished. Finally, after the ladies had all gone back to their luncheon, the men's room door opened and out came our missing and blushing busboy. He had stayed locked in, just waiting for all the ladies to leave. I bet it was the only time he got a standing ovation for just doing what comes naturally! At least everyone had a cute story to tell that evening over their cocktails.

****

I had been there for just over a year when Carefree Developers decided they were not really in the hotel business. We had turned a profit at the hotel for the first time in its operating history, and I had been made a vice president but I think they felt it wiser to just focus on the real estate side of the business. Thus, the hotel was sold and the new owners, the Carefree Ranch Partnership, brought in their own general manager. It became a bit awkward because I was never let go. I knew the new fellow, Dick Osgood, as we both belonged to the Valley Innkeepers Association. We worked side by side for a while, a rather uncomfortable situation, until I eventually resigned.

Now what? Had it been a mistake to come back to Arizona?

Since returning to Arizona, I again became active with the

Arizona Hotel and Motel Association, the Valley Innkeepers Association and the Phoenix SKAL Club. I had reacquainted myself with many of my peers in the area and this helped greatly in leading to the next chapter in my career.

I was interviewed by some of the executives at the Ramada headquarters in Phoenix and was appointed to a new position as district director of the Arizona resorts reporting to Bob Francis, one of the vice presidents. The Arizona Resorts was a marketing name given to a collection of five resort-oriented properties in Scottsdale, four of which were formerly independent hotels that had been acquired by Ramada. There was already a well-established Ramada Inn in Scottsdale plus they added the Valley Ho, the Safari, the Casa Blanca Inn and the Scottsdale Inn and Country Club. Each had their distinct characteristics and having a golf course as a member of this small portfolio allowed us to offer golf packages to our guests at all five properties.

However, there was one aspect of my job which I found a bit difficult. My office was set up at the Valley Ho, and I had the additional title and duties as general manager of that hotel. It was an interesting time in my development, as I had never had responsibility for multiple properties before. While I enjoyed the challenges this presented, I sometimes felt that I was not able to keep all the balls in the air at the same time. I would find myself short changing one part of my responsibilities by focusing my efforts in one area and neglecting another. It was hard to give direction to four separate managers, having perhaps not fulfilled the same requirements at my own hotel.

The 200-room Valley Ho was situated on the corner of Indian School Road and 68th Street. It had been privately owned and operated for many years by Bobby and Evelyn Foehl before being acquired by Ramada. I knew the Foehls well and I had great respect for them as professional hoteliers and gracious hosts. As the representative of the new management, I worked hard to preserve the close relationships they had established with their guests. This included their long-standing association with Motorola and the company's most senior executives. There were many newer, fancier properties in Scottsdale at that time so it was vitally important to maintain this connection. The Foehls were also strong supporters of the Republican Party and good friends with Barry Goldwater, who lived close by in Paradise Valley. I had the opportunity of meeting and speaking with him when we hosted a fundraiser for his U.S. Senatorial campaign.

During the time I was managing the Carefree Inn, the Executive House was sold and Carl Devoe, president of Executive House, came from Chicago for a farewell celebration. He invited me to join him and several people who had been associated with the hotel over the years. It was an event with many mixed feelings but it did allow me the opportunity to bring Nadine Jansen and her trio over to the Valley Ho when the new owners made some operational changes. Jimmy Tattler, now seriously considering retirement, also came to join us on a limited basis. Our old crew was getting back together again!

****

In February 1974, Stan Kenton and his band were in Scottsdale doing a concert at a nearby venue. This was now high season in Arizona, and I made some generous concessions in our room rates to get them to stay with us. Hoping there would be the possibility of getting many of his musicians to sit in with Nadine's trio, I put the word out among her fans. I was not disappointed. After their scheduled concert, the band returned to the hotel and most of them came in to the lounge with their instruments. Roy Reynolds, a fellow Englishman and a baritone saxophone player, told me they rarely had a chance to sit in with such a quality group of musicians. He said they traveled almost daily, city-to-city, doing these concerts and just play their charts. Sitting in and improvising in this manner is what they *really* liked to do. While I was sitting with him, Kenton said to me, "You have a fabulous trio here. I hope you appreciate that. Do you know, there are not three cities in the United States where you would find a group as good as Nadine's? They're great and she's an amazing musician."

"Coming from you, that's a compliment indeed," I replied. "They have an avid and dedicated group of fans here in the Phoenix area, so I know she is fully appreciated. She has put on some incredible concerts."

With that said, he turned to his flugelhorn player sitting in the next booth, "Go and sit in with her."

The young fellow quickly declined the invitation saying, "I can't play as well with two hands as she can with one! I'm just sitting here enjoying it."

It was indeed a magical evening for everyone. After it was all over, I thanked them all and took them out for breakfast.

****

About that time, I was working with a British travel organizer, Ian Scarfe of the Flying Golfer, who promoted pro-am golf groups. We booked one of their events for January. The format was a typical one where a professional would be paired with an amateur threesome, who shared the full cost for his expenses. This way the professional got to spend a free winter vacation at a desirable venue during the off season and the amateurs could enjoy the company of a prominent pro. We scheduled this to coincide with the Phoenix and Tucson Opens during the two-week period when the PGA Tour was doing its Arizona swing.

Some of the professionals were Ryder Cup players from the U.K. and Ireland and one of them, John Garner, had an exemption to play in the Phoenix Open event. With this caliber of player coming, this also brought some of the U.K.'s primary golfing media, which, naturally, would benefit our hotel.

Karsten Solheim was making a name for himself in the golfing world with his development of the now famous Ping brand and his signature item, the Ping putter. He was a mechanical engineer and a genius in his own right and started this work in the garage of his home. By now he had a small manufacturing facility in Phoenix, and a U.K. representative who came over with the group. Scarfe approached me to see if it might be possible to get some sponsorship so that the pros would have something to play for among themselves. I made an appointment to meet with Karsten Solheim and his financial officer, Jack Monday. I told Solheim about the group that would be coming over and the names of the players participating, most of whom played the tour in the U.K. Some of these were Brian Waites, left-hander Peter Dawson, Christy O'Connor, Jr., Arnold O'Connor and John Garner. Although he didn't come over with this group, Tony Jacklin, a two-time major championship winner, was playing in the Phoenix Open and spent some time with his fellow professionals at the hotel that week. Solheim asked me what I was looking for and I responded by telling him that anything he could do would be appreciated but $5,000 would be a big help. I'd leave any decision up to him. After further discussion, he graciously offered to give us $9,500 to support our event. I was, of course, pleasantly surprised but I also thought it seemed an odd amount. Why not go to the $10,000? Anyway, it was more than I had asked for and Ian was delighted.

One of the amateur golfers, an Irishman by the name of Joe

Cuddy, was Ireland's most popular singer at that time. His No. 1 hit was Andrew Lloyd Webber's "Any Dream Will Do" from the highly acclaimed West End show "Joseph and the Amazing Technicolor Dreamcoat." He was a seven handicapper and part of one of the Irish teams. Having him here in the hotel along with Nadine had great potential for another magical evening, and again I was not disappointed. In fact, Joe sang with the group several evenings during their stay. This was all coming together!

With Jimmy Tattler at the hotel and, it being the week of the Phoenix Open, there was a good possibility that Bob Hope would stop by, as he so often did when he was in town. I told Cuddy that this *could* happen and, if so, it would not only be a great opportunity for him to meet Hope, but also perhaps perform while Hope was in the audience. I should mention also that Cuddy was the headliner for many years at the famous Jury's Irish Cabaret in Dublin and was a smooth deliverer of the wonderful Irish sense of humor, which combined with his fantastic voice, made him a most polished and entertaining performer.

The big evening arrived and, after a time, when it seemed Bob Hope would not show up, Joe and his friends decided to leave and go to a nearby lounge. They had not been gone long when Hope and a small group of his friends came in. Someone in the golfing group sent one of their members to tell him Hope had just arrived. That brought them back, but sadly Joe had already had a quick couple of drinks and, while not being badly affected, was just slightly off his timing. His singing was great, of course, but you can't top Bob Hope in storytelling. Hope was most cordial, as was always my experience with him, and I know Joe was thrilled to have had the chance to spend some time in his company.

****

When I was at the Executive House, Jack Stewart, former owner and 30-year operator of Camelback Inn, had used his well-established reputation to promote Phoenix and Scottsdale as an area able to host a major college football bowl game. At that time, there were just a few, like the Rose Bowl, Sugar Bowl, Orange Bowl, Cotton Bowl and so forth and it was his initiative that established the Fiesta Bowl. He approached all the hotels in the area and asked for just $100 from each of us to help get this proposal off the ground. This has been a huge success, and it is sad that he did not live to see it come to such prominence.

One of the hotels for which I was responsible became a direct beneficiary of this $100 investment. In 1974, the Fiesta Bowl hosted Oklahoma State and Brigham Young Universities, and we were successful in our bid to get the Oklahoma State team to stay at our Casa Blanca Inn. This property was relatively secluded and comprised a number of individual villas scattered around the grounds; about 120 total units. We worked closely with the team coordinators and had been apprised that one of their special requirements was to satisfy their appetites. Trust me, not an easy thing, as we soon found out.

By this point in my career, I had coordinated many varied and often complex banquet arrangements for diverse groups and, in terms of setup, this was no different than many, many others. But the first morning after their arrival, their buffet breakfast was unlike anything I had ever witnessed. Yes, we had been told that the normal food production would need to be adjusted upwards to account for these 300 lb., permanently hungry young men, but this was indeed not what we had expected. I had never seen 12 oz. New York sirloin steaks, scrambled eggs, breakfast potatoes and other buffet offerings disappear so rapidly. I was standing at the end of the line, as if I was taking the credit, and before half of the players, coaches and others had gotten anything to eat at all, we had nothing left but empty chafing dishes. "Chef?" "Help!"

It did get sorted out in the end and they all got some sustenance to start their day. I am sure they were late for their practice but I have never forgotten that morning, obviously. The best news to come out of that weekend was the result.

Oklahoma State 16 - Brigham Young 6!

Yeah!

Key to Success #11

Adapt: *A good manager must be like an orchestra conductor. Each person critical to the overall success of your operation will be different in many ways and will often respond to different styles of supervision. One may perform better when they receive constant encouragement and a pat on the back while another may respond better when pushed more under pressure. Be open to recognize these different personalities.*

11. Sandpiper Bay (1976-1982)

The hotel business in Arizona in the hot off-season, summer months was always a challenge. We would close the Casa Blanca Inn for several months, just staying open with minimal staffing for ongoing maintenance projects, sales and reservations activity. Because of this, our managers were often seasonal hires. In late 1975, when business picked up, rather than hire a new G.M., Frank Widmann, who oversaw our Arizona Resorts corporate marketing plan, was repositioned to perform both duties.

At the end of the 1975/76 winter season, we again closed the Inn and Frank accepted an attractive offer from General Development Corporation, a major Miami-based commercial and residential property developer. He was appointed vice president responsible for the company's hotel properties being developed in their communities to accommodate site visits for prospective home-buyers. At that time, the company owned and operated Sandpiper Bay, a 276-room resort in Port St. Lucie, about an hour's drive north of Palm Beach. It was attractively positioned on 1,000 acres on the banks of the north fork of the St. Lucie River, with two excellent 18-hole golf courses, the Saints and Sinners, the 9-hole Wilderness course plus a 9-hole par 3, an 11-court tennis center, a 66-slip marina and a conference center. It had previously done business as the St. Lucie Hilton Inn and

Country Club. Having a Hilton flag at that time did not produce the amount of business the parent company had hoped for, primarily because Hilton, in those days, was associated with hotels in more urban locations than resorts. A decision was made in early 1976 to break away from the Hilton franchise and, in May, General Development took over the management of the resort to run it as an independent property. They then re-named the hotel "Sandpiper Bay Resort – <u>The</u> Resort at Port St. Lucie".

A seasoned and well-respected hotel professional, Jim Bearce, was hired as the general manager but it did not take long for some friction to develop between him and the corporate offices. He tended to treat it as *his* hotel. He felt that General Development had hired him to run the property because they had no experience. Therefore, he did not respond well to any level of supervision. One of the primary purposes of the resort was to be a showpiece and a country club amenity to attract home buyers for the growing Port St. Lucie community. When, towards the end of 1976, Jim Bearce resigned, Frank called me. The offer sounded interesting so I flew to Miami for an interview, and was subsequently offered the position as general manager. The hotel was losing money at that time, with annual occupancy averaging around 45 percent. There would obviously need to be a heavy emphasis on sales and marketing. Fortunately, Ken Benjamin, an excellent sales and marketing director, had already been hired so, between us, we would have some challenges ahead. Leaving Anita at home in Arizona to spend Christmas with Wendy and Diana, I flew to Florida and took over on December 19th. Where do I start?

The resort had so many great amenities, it could host a large number of special events, and in many ways, was similar to the Lake Geneva Playboy property. During the six years I managed this resort, we hosted the PGA Florida Open for several years featuring many players who went on to make a name for themselves on the PGA Tour like Mark Calcavecchia, Paul Azinger, Bruce Fleisher, Mark McCumber, Donnie Hammond, and others. Julius Boros, a Hall of Famer and two time U.S. Open Champion, also participated on a regular basis. We also established the exclusive John Gardiner Tennis Clinics, opened with the help of John Gardiner himself and his touring professional, Grand Slam tennis champion Ken Rosewall. We presented the first annual Water Ski Show Championships in the bay of the St. Lucie River and we hosted Dinah Shore for a week when the property was used as the backdrop for the filming of several segments of the Dinah Shore Show. For four years before I arrived, the resort had hosted an LPGA tournament and in fact, Hall of Famer Mickey Wright, was one of our neighbors, living off the 14th fairway of the Sinners Course.

I had been there only a couple of days when I had a welcome surprise. Our primary restaurant overlooking the bay on the St. Lucie River was called the Brass Sandpiper and the adjacent lounge was the Pelican Perch. As I was doing my rounds early one evening, I stopped by to check the action in the lounge where I had been told some people had been asking for me. There, sitting at the bar, were two of my fellow employees from our Playboy days. No, they were not two of the bunnies – unfortunately. It was Tom Burrows, our golf course superintendent, and Bill Mangold, who ran our delivery dock in Lake Geneva. Tom had moved to Florida and was the golf course superintendent at Mariner Sands, a country club just south of the nearby town of Stuart, and Bill had taken a position on Tom's staff. Somehow, they had heard I was going to be taking over this property and had come to welcome me to the area and to wish me luck. I had no idea they were in the neighborhood and, this early in my new responsibilities, it was nice to visit with a couple of friends whom I had not seen since I left Lake Geneva almost five years before.

And they weren't the only familiar faces I saw in those early days. Sandpiper Bay was only about a 20-minute drive from Jensen Beach, across the Indian River lagoon to Hutchinson Island where there was a beachfront Holiday Inn. I found out that the general manager there was none other than Jim McManemon, whom I had known since 1962. We had first met when Led Gardner, my Colony Hotel boss, and I attended a West Palm Beach Chamber of Commerce breakfast at the lake front hotel that later became the West Palm Beach Holiday Inn. Jim had been the general manager. Again, it was great to know of another old friend in the area, especially a fellow hotelier.

Taking over a new property and inheriting an existing staff can be intimidating. Even though you may have come from a successful position where you had earned your stripes, the move wipes the slate clean. You have to start all over again to earn the respect of your new staff. These people could not care less about how much you were respected and appreciated in your previous job. They may have a certain amount of skepticism. As I would later learn, a couple of the department heads had already bet that I wouldn't last a year.

An excerpt from Nina Baranski's historical book "Port St. Lucie at 50 – A City for All People" reported: "Cain, (Ralph 'Cap' Cain) who was comptroller at the time, well remembers Pullen's arrival. *'I took a bet that he wouldn't be there a year, because we had had a new general manager every year.'* Cain couldn't have been more wrong. Pullen stayed with the resort until its sale to the Tollman Hundley hotel chain six years later." This opinion had some validity based on the resort's recent track record, but I am glad he lost that bet. Incidentally, Cap and I are *still* good friends.

I think it is a good thing to be a little nervous, as it makes the newcomer try just that much harder to get it right. One of the critical things to remember is to not change anything immediately but to keep notes regarding all your first impressions. I had learned some time ago, taking time to settle in during the first few months is most important.

Ken Benjamin was the finest hotel salesperson with whom I have ever had the pleasure of working. Despite my experience with both booking and servicing meetings and conferences, he taught me some very basic lessons. One of his more effective techniques was to set an alarm clock on his desk to go off five or ten minutes before a group's next coffee break or meal function. That way he was there when the meeting broke and he could check with the meeting planner to be sure everything was going the way we had promised. If there were any issues which needed to be addressed, he could immediately get them resolved. Usually, he was back at his desk within a few minutes but the meeting planner was comforted that the hotel was right on top of things. Even if a group had an early morning event scheduled on their day of recreation, Ken would be there at the crack of dawn to assure the food and beverage department had everything ready. This attention to detail had much to do with the repeat business he and his sales team generated, plus it enhanced the hotel's excellent reputation.

Another lesson I learned from Ken was the importance of knowing why a particular group was meeting, to understand their objectives for the event, and to share this information with the department heads. There is a big difference between a meeting held in appreciation having achieved record levels of success and a meeting to pump up enthusiasm to improve results. In the first case the meeting planner and the attendees would be relaxed and enjoy the scheduled golf and tennis tournaments, cocktail receptions and any other planned activities. In the second case, the meeting planner and the attendees would normally be more tense and business like.

Ken also understood the importance of knowing *who* was in the hotel. A perfect example of this was when we hosted the meeting of a major national corporation. Ken would be sure to attend their first cocktail reception so he could meet the key people in a relaxed environment. The meeting planner would typically introduce Ken to the most senior executives in attendance. In one instance, he learned there were five separate division presidents in attendance, each of whom held their own separate annual meetings. With this knowledge, he was able to follow-up and subsequently book two such future events just by being there in our own ballroom. Had he not taken the time and made the extra effort, he might not have known of this potential business. Learning of it later, he would most likely have to make individual solicitations either by phone or by incurring the expense of calling on them by way of an expensive sales trip. Then it would be on *their* time and certainly not in quite such a friendly and informal atmosphere.

Our greatest challenge was the issue of bringing the occupancy level up so that the resort would be a positive profit center for the company. Our local real estate people did a good job of bringing in guests to tour the area with a view to purchasing a home or home site, but this was at corporately established special rates and certainly not sufficient to meet our goals. Ken and his staff did an excellent job but group sales revenues are not immediate. The bigger, better revenue producing groups are usually booked

Ken Benjamin, Director of Sales and Marketing
Marilyn Wagener, Director of Travel Industry Sales
Bill Pullen, General Manager

a year or more out, so it takes a while to see the results on the bottom line. However, I feel we complemented each other. I was responsible to see that the service levels of the resort supported the groups he had booked and the promises that had been made to the meeting planners involved. Over the course of the next three years our reputation improved substantially, thanks to the increase in the resort's group and leisure bookings, and by the end of our third year the hotel breached the 70% occupancy level. The resort turned a profit for the first time. We were nationally recognized with meetings and travel industry awards and it was satisfying that we were now contributing to the company's combined results.

Unfortunately, it soon became apparent that our single-minded focus on the bottom line had drawn our attention away from the morale and motivation of our staff. This became painfully obvious when one of our recently hired maintenance department employees turned out to be a Teamsters Union member who began the process of trying to unionize our hotel. In some ways, we were ripe for our employees to consider representation as we had been neglecting the critically important things needed to recognize and stimulate the morale among the troops, particularly our hourly employees.

I contacted Bob Cullen, vice president of human resources, and apprised him of the situation. He then brought the company's human resources attorney into the picture and, between us we developed a plan to address the issues. Had we been part of a chain, rather than an independent hotel, these policies would have already been established by corporate.

Unions tend to be counterproductive in the hospitality business so it was decided the best way to combat the organizing attempt was to immediately address the issues affecting our employees.

We needed to institute policies and programs to effectively improve the areas we had been neglecting.

We had recently hired Jan Shelly as our public relations director and she was a huge help in developing policies to improve employee relations. These included the publication of a monthly employee newsletter, an employee of the month recognition program for both back-of-the-house and front-of-the-house employees, employee of the year awards, and other employee events and recognition programs. We also established a structured procedure for periodic evaluations and annual performance reviews.

Upon the recommendations of Cullen and our attorney, I started having small-group employee meetings and I admitted to the attendees that I had been remiss in not paying attention to this side of the resort's operations. However, I emphasized that there was no way a union could be more interested in the wellbeing of our employees than were I and our company. Thankfully, the Teamster's mailings that were sent to our hourly employees' homes on a regular basis were weak and poorly coordinated. They were just boilerplate mailings taken off the shelf and not at all directed to hotel employees. One of our employees, Sue Commerford, shared these communications with us.

On one hand, it was a painful time for me. These time-consuming meetings ran from November, right through the busy winter season, until the employees' vote was scheduled. On the other hand, it was fulfilling for me to get to know my employees on a much more personal level. I well remember the great anxiety I felt the afternoon when the votes of over 200 of our employees were counted under careful supervision. The 'YES' votes (for the union) were tallied at 99. Not knowing how many employees in the unit had voted, it seemed like it was going to be close. Then the 'NO' votes were tallied. The count passed 80, then 90, 100 and all the way up to 132. Management prevailed!

Thank you, employees! I felt a massive weight had been lifted off my shoulders. However, even with this win, it was still sobering to know that at least 100 of our employees felt that union representation would have been beneficial. This had been a valuable learning experience and we still had work to do to convince them that we really were all on the same side.

We were starting to be recognized nationally, both in the meetings market and in the tour and travel market. In 1977 and 1978 we were awarded the Mobil Four Star rating (see Appendix II) and this was soon followed by the AAA Four Diamond award. In the category of meetings, in 1979 we were recognized by Meetings and Conventions Magazine with their prestigious Gold Key Award and Successful Meetings Magazine gave us their highest national rating for conference resorts in the "under 300 room' category. The February 21, 1980 issue of Travel Weekly carried a banner front-page story:

"Sandpiper Bay in Port St. Lucie Enjoys Pattern of Growth with Concerted Drive:

Textbook Example of How to Turn a Property Around"

Early in 1980, we had the coup and great pleasure of hosting the Travel Weekly Tournament, which brought many top producing travel agents and tour operators to the resort. Shortly afterwards, we received a letter from Dick Friese, President of Ziff-Davis Publishing Company, telling us that the event was "...the best Travel Weekly Tournament to date. The entire event was conducted in the highest of professional standards and everyone enjoyed themselves immensely". This was soon followed by a letter from Travel Weekly Chairman, Irwin "Robbie" Robinson, a copy of which is included in Appendix II. Also, hosting this event brought about a flattering front page story in the February 21, 1980 issue of Travel Weekly carrying a banner story (also in Appendix II):

There is no doubt that these endorsements helped enormously in generating more premium business. I had hosted two regional conferences of the New York-based Conference Board while I was in Carefree and we hosted another one of their regional meetings at Sandpiper Bay. I believe there were no greater critics in the national meetings market in those days than Stu Clarkson and John Wisham and the fact that they were using our property was indeed a feather in our cap. After all, they were responsible for hosting groups of 60 to 65 chief executives and needed to be supported in every way at their selected venue. But you can't rest on your laurels; they have to be earned every single year, as our peers knew only too well.

****

I did make one rather embarrassing faux pas on the night of their first cocktail reception held on the outside terrace of the Brass Sandpiper restaurant. I was in conversation with a gentleman and talking about the interesting make up of their group. He was wearing a nametag, with no business affiliation, as they wanted it. I was telling him about my experience in Carefree where we had hosted two similar Conference Board meetings. I also described the meeting we had hosted for the Conquistadores del Cielo. I told him that it was an impressive group, and that they hold two get-togethers a year, a summer one regularly at a ranch in Texas and a winter one that they rotate among different resort venues. He let me ramble on a bit longer and finally said, "I think their summer meeting is at a ranch in Wyoming, not Texas." Oh, so he had heard of them! When I had an opportunity to excuse myself, I went back to my office and looked him up on our rooming list. There he was, the CEO of Grumman Aerospace. Yes, I guess he *would* know about the Conquistadores del Cielo. Oh well! Why do I keep doing this to myself?

****

Another interesting facet of managing this resort was that we were also a country club with an extensive membership of local homeowners. This could, and did, sometimes create areas of conflict, especially if one or both golf courses needed to be reserved for a meeting's golf event and it just happened to be on men's day or ladies' day. We worked hard to minimize these issues by forming a golf committee made up of members representing all interested parties, including the homeowners association; with our golf professional, greens superintendent and myself representing the resort. This allowed for good communication among all who had a stake in the use of our amenities and kept everyone advised of future events. Initially, there was some resistance to us hosting the PGA Florida Open but when our members understood the investment we were making in the golf courses, of which they would largely be the beneficiaries, they were content with losing the time the event took away from their play. In fact, they were quite excited about it and in the end helped us enormously by providing volunteer support. Still, it was always a bit of a balancing act.

One event which gained attention, was a pro-celebrity tournament put on by the Senior Professional Golfers Association, a prelude to what became the Senior Tour, now The Champions PGA Tour. In one of the foursomes, comedian Joey Bishop was paired with veteran golf professional Sam Snead. It was rather like combining oil and water. Bishop kept throwing out funny one-liners to the gallery following them, but Snead, clearly, was taking it all much more seriously. On one hole, a par 3, Joey Bishop hit a good drive, which landed on the green. Looking heavenwards, he yelled out "Thank you! I'll take care of it from here." Snead was not amused which confirmed his reputation for always being strictly business any time he picked up a golf club. Coming off the 15th green on the Sinners course, Snead banged his putter on the ground in a moment of frustration. It hit the cart path instead of the grass and snapped the blade. He putted the rest of the way with his one iron. He wasn't happy.

The Sinners golf course had opened in 1961 and was followed by the Saints course over the Thanksgiving weekend that same year. To celebrate that opening, Perry Como, who lived nearby in Jupiter just south of us, hosted the Perry Como Invitational along with Chick Harbert, the director of golf for all of the company's golf facilities. Chick, a member of the Golf Hall of Fame, was a former PGA Champion and the captain of the 1955 U.S. Ryder Cup Team. As Perry Como knew several of the celebrities and the professionals playing in this event, he had driven up to see them. I spotted him walking near to the first tee on the Sinners course and went over to introduce myself. I asked him if he would ever consider doing something similar in the future but he graciously declined. The day ended with a dinner that concluded with a "roast" and Leslie Nielson, Bobby Riggs, Claude Akins, Bob Newhart, Joey Bishop and others gave all in attendance a memorable and entertaining evening.

****

When the English movie actor, Roger Moore, came to town to film part *Moonraker*, the 007 James Bond thriller, it created a lot of local interest. The north fork of the St. Lucie River is unspoiled with no visible development, power lines or any signs of civilization. The scenes, which in the movie took place in the Amazon, had speedboats blowing up. While the scenes were performed by a stuntman, Moore was there to watch the filming. He met with several of the General Development executives down at the North Port Marina where the boats were based.

****

I was always aware of the need to provide functions and events for our members and local homeowners, as well focusing on our hotel guests. After all, Sandpiper Bay was also *their* country club and one event I thought would be a huge success was a dinner and show featuring the Tony Award winning actress and singer, Anna Maria Alberghetti. While we always featured nightly entertainment in our Pelican Perch Lounge, it was primarily patronized by our hotel guests.

This night, featuring a top named artist and an opening act comedian, would be strictly for our members and homeowners. Our main ballroom, with a full stage, a comprehensive lighting system and a projection room, where the sound and lighting could be controlled by Steve Finn, our excellent audiovisual technician, would be the perfect venue for something like this.

Success? Oh no! Disaster? Oh yes!

The dinner went well but when it came time for the comedian to start the entertainment, Alberghetti still had not arrived and I was getting a little nervous. We delayed the opening act for as long as we could but eventually it became time for him to be introduced; and on he went. Still, she was a no-show.

By this time, I was outside the convention center in the parking lot anticipating her arrival so that I could show her to her dressing room behind the stage. Cap Cain, who was now my assistant general manager, was with me. I was pacing up and down. Where the heck was she? What could we do? It was a terrible and completely helpless feeling. The comedian was great and continued his act as long as he could, but after what seemed ages, he finally dried up and had to take his final applause. *Still* no headliner. We apologized to the audience for the delay and re-opened the bars to provide complimentary drinks while we all waited. I was going nuts and went back to pacing up and down on the road leading to the parking lot as if this would get her to appear any sooner. It didn't, and eventually some of our guests started leaving. I certainly could not blame them. Such a well-intentioned evening was having the exact opposite effect of upsetting everyone. I was so angry!

Finally, yes finally, she pulled into the parking lot along with her agent. Thank goodness, he was there so I could tell him what I thought of him then, instead of having to wait until I cooled down. Do you think we would get an apology or a reason for their extreme tardiness? Couldn't they have called us? Not even that! Just as we were showing her where to get changed, she turned and said, "I need to get something to eat before I go on."

That did it. I don't ever remember being as upset and angry as I was that night. I had to get out of there and cool down. I turned to Cap and said, "You take care of it! I'm out of here before I do any damage."

What a night! And what an utter disappointment.

The next morning, after the dust had settled, I learned that the agent had double booked her on purpose, thinking that the time between her two appearances would be adequate to satisfy both events. Her earlier appearance was at a condominium develop-ment in Vero Beach, close to an hour's drive north of us. Naturally, that was the last booking that agent ever got from me.

All good things must come to an end and in 1982, City Investing Company, the parent company of General Development Corporation, decided to sell some of their assets to reduce some of the company's short-term debt. They had several holdings in their portfolio and a decision was made to sell our resort. This process took some time but, at the end of 1982, at a reported selling price of $16.8 million, the property was taken over by Tollman Hundley Hotels, which owned and operated a variety of hotel properties. Stanley Tollman of South Africa, served as chairman of the company, and Monty Hundley served as the chief operating officer.

By coincidence, before we became aware of the decision to sell, we had presented the resort for consideration to host the Association of Southern African Travel Agents (ASATA) annual convention. The selection process was being coordinated by the Florida Division of Tourism in Tallahassee. We were one of several Florida destination resorts being considered. We took our turn hosting the site inspection team to show off our facilities and after all the due diligence was completed, we were thrilled to learn that Sandpiper Bay had been selected. This was a significant feather in our cap, as several of the resorts competing for this impressive piece of business had a slightly higher profile than we did. Not only was it a good booking from an immediate economic standpoint but, by hosting these travel agents, we would be giving the property great exposure for future business originating from South Africa. Having been selected, we were invited, along with a representative from Florida's Tourism office, to attend ASATA's 1982 annual meeting in Torremolinos, Spain to do our respective presentations for their members.

As I was preparing for my departure, I was advised that indeed a contract for sale had been negotiated. It was necessary therefore that the principals of that company approve my attendance at the ASATA meeting, as this future business would mostly likely be managed by my replacement. It was mutually agreed that I should still go and, while I was not now going to be responsible for handling their meeting in Florida, I was quite looking forward to telling them that Sandpiper Bay would, by then, be under the management of a fellow South African. I felt sure they would be happy to know it would be in the hands of one of their countrymen.

Wrong! After our arrival, we were invited to meet with their site selection people, whom we knew from their Florida visit, along with some of the other members of their board. After introductions all around, it did not take me long to give them the news.

"Just so you all know," I started, "Sandpiper is being sold and will be under new ownership next year when you hold your meeting. However, I think you will be happy to know it is being sold to one of your countrymen."

John Bing, executive secretary of the association, looked a little disappointed and said, "Really? Who is that?"

"Stanley Tollman," I answered. I knew instantly that this was *not* good news.

"Stanley Tollman is buying Sandpiper Bay?" one of the others asked.

"Yes." I said. "Is that a problem?"

No one answered me. Instead, one of the other board members spoke up. "Well, it's too late now to change venues. What can we do?"

They huddled for a few minutes away from us and came back to me and said, "You're not going to mention this in your presentation in the morning, are you?"

"Well, I was planning to but I'll do whatever you think I should. What's the problem?"

"Well, Stanley Tollman owns and operates a half dozen hotels in South Africa, mostly in Johannesburg and Durban, and he doesn't have a particularly good reputation. We don't think you should mention it."

"Fine. I won't." I assured them.

They obviously had other information about this but were understandably hesitant to tell me much more. We adjourned for a pre-dinner and very welcome drink and the rest of the conversation took on a much more amenable and social tone.

At the general opening session the following morning, the presentations went well and I made no mention of the resort's impending sale. It really wasn't pertinent information for the general membership anyway. Unfortunately, when the morning session ended, I was surrounded by many of the attendees asking if I could confirm what they had already heard. The news had traveled fast. What could I say? I told them the truth without any bias and left it up to them to talk about it among themselves but I could tell it wasn't good news. Later that evening, a small group of us were enjoying cocktails in a corner of the lounge before the banquet, I happened to be sitting next to John Bing's secretary, Carmen. The sale of the resort was about the only topic of conversation. She said, "Bill, I can tell you this. I used to be Stanley Tollman's secretary and I can sum him up in one word, 'crook.' He *had* to leave South Africa, and if he ever sets foot in the country again, they'll lock him up!"

"Wow! I'm sure our corporate officers at General Development are not aware of this". *I suppose there is nothing much they can do about it now, anyway.*

Our part of this now over, we enjoyed a free day while we were there. It was a delightful beachfront property and we enjoyed a light lunch at the pool snack bar. Of particular note to us sheltered visitors from America, were the number of ladies all around the pool deck unabashedly topless and sunning themselves *almost* all over. Apparently, this was quite normal in Spain. Having been somewhat spoiled, because of my time with Playboy, I honestly thought most of them would have looked a lot better wearing the second part of the two-piece bikini.

Before I end this particular tale, on November 21, 2008, the New York Times published a story by Martin Espinoza, *"Exiled Hotel Executive Makes Plea Deal."* This did not pertain to Stanley Tollman's dealings in South Africa but to some of his other business involvement in the U.S. where he agreed to settle tax evasion charges and pay $60 million in back taxes, interest and fraud penalties plus an additional $40.7 million to settle a civil forfeiture suit.

I guess Carmen was right!

****

As expected, Tollman Hundley brought in their own management team. Vic Appleby, their marketing director, came on site quite quickly. However, as my bosses at General Development had requested, they did go through the motions of interviewing me. I flew to New York to meet with Hundley but he was obviously not treating it with any seriousness. After six exciting and successful years at Sandpiper Bay, the end was in sight. I had the most wonderful and supportive staff from the department heads down to the rank and file associates and it was a somewhat sad ending to a very satisfying tour of duty.

There was one silver lining. Just before my last day, I received a most complimentary letter from Irene Chapman, secretary of the Sandpiper Bay Homeowners Association, expressing their appreciation for my time as general manager – despite Anna Maria Alberghetti! (Her letter is included in Appendix II). To me, that was heartwarming and deeply appreciated. There had been some rough issues along the way but it was a great comfort that they knew I had tried my best to please both our guests and local homeowners. Now what?

Key to Success #12

Delegate: *Let department heads manage their own sphere of responsibility without undue supervision. They will be more inclined to make a success of their own ideas than having to implement an idea they feel they cannot support.*

12. Frances Langford's Outrigger Resort (1983-1986)

Initially, my departure from Sandpiper gave Anita and I some concern. Both Wendy and Diana were attending John Carroll High School in Fort Pierce and doing well in their studies. It would have been a big mistake to disrupt their progress as well as separating them from all their friends. Although there were similar, if not comparable, opportunities, both in Florida and nationally, these would have involved relocation or long commutes, neither of which were viable alternatives.

My friend Dick Campbell, owner and production editor of one of our local newspapers, was also a close friend of Frances Langford, the famous singer, stage, television and movie personality. She owned and operated a well-established resort in nearby Jensen Beach on the Indian River, the intracoastal waterway connecting to the St. Lucie River and the Atlantic Ocean a few miles to the south. The resort was best known for its fabulous Polynesian restaurant, The Outrigger, but it also had 27 villas and an excellent deep-water marina where she and her husband, Ralph Evinrude, kept their beautiful 110-foot private yacht, *The Chanticleer*. Dick kindly referred me to the Evinrudes, when Alan Holley, who had been managing the resort for several years, announced he would be leaving to take over another property. I was offered the position following an interview with

The Outrigger Resort

Frances Langford at 70

Evinrude and his long-time secretary, Ruth Penning. Quite understandably, the compensation was less than I had been earning at Sandpiper Bay but, at least, we would not have to move away from the area. He offered us one of their villas, which made the offer more attractive. I took over as general manager in March of 1983, reporting to Ruth Penning. She was a delightful, diminutive lady and easy to work with even though I often felt we were on different wavelengths. We had such completely different backgrounds. Still, it was a comfortable relationship.

The restaurant did well and the marina was always busy due to its excellent location, but I immediately saw opportunities to substantially improve the income from the rental units. They were quite dated and needed a considerable amount of renovation. I broached this issue with the Evinrudes and, although they did not see anything particularly wrong with the accommodations, they accepted my recommendations to bring them up to a much more competitive level. I really wanted to get them to be AAA approved, as this would certainly help to market this aspect of the resort. After the renovation work was completed, we received approval ratings from both AAA and the Mobil Travel Guide and within a couple of years we were able to double the income of the rooms department.

The transition from what I had been doing at Sandpiper Bay to this small privately-owned resort was interesting to say the least. In the kitchen, we had two talented Chinese cooks, Bill and Tangy, and they and their crew worked incessantly. However, every week we were racking up many hours of overtime costing us a small fortune. I approached them to see how we could resolve this and was told, "It's OK! You don' unnerstan' na Chinese peepo."

I replied, "Indeed, that true, but we are not in China. Here in the

U.S. the Chinese 'peepo' have to understand us!"

But I wasn't getting through to them. It was apparent I was going to have a few challenges. Eventually, after gradually massaging their schedules and hiring another couple of cooks, I was successful in correcting this problem but only with the two of them kicking and screaming! Sometimes change doesn't come easily. They had worked there a long time.

We had an excellent restaurant manager, Dan Burris, whose dry sense of humor was a delight, and a wonderful maître d'hôtel, Tom Odessa. Tom had come from a similar position in New York at the famed 21 Club and everyone, and I do mean *everyone*, knew Tom. The problem with that was, Tom didn't know *anyone*. That first season, I would often stand with him at his podium as patrons would come through the front door, throw their arms around him and scream, "Tom! How great to see you."

After he had taken them to their seats, I would say quietly, "Tom, who were they?" to which I got his standard reply, "I don't know. They come every year." Yes, this was going to be different.

This was a difficult time for Anita. While we were at Sandpiper Bay, she had gone into the real estate business with only modest success and had not really enjoyed it. At a friend's suggestion, she took the U.S. Postal Service exam and passed with flying colors. That was the good news; the not so good news was that in those early days she found herself unloading the 18-wheelers in the middle of the night at the Fort Pierce post office, a good 30-minute commute to the north. Often, I would come home late in the evening, open a beer and sit down to read the newspaper just as our automatic coffee pot would start percolating. Yes, Anita was getting up, and I was getting ready to go to bed. Much to her credit, she never complained about it and eventually applied for a much better administrative, daytime position, which she got, thanks to her proficiency in typing.

****

Frances Langford had a successful career and naturally had many friends and contacts in the entertainment industry. Some of my readers may remember her doing many of the Bob Hope USO Shows when he would visit the troops overseas. She also had a popular radio show, "The Bickersons", teaming up with Don Ameche. When she built the Outrigger restaurant, it was done in true Hawaiian style, complete with a palm frond roof. The famous Hollywood set designer, Ed Lawrence, was brought in to do the interior lighting, so important for this style of décor. He had a few movie successes, one of which was *"Around the World in 80 Days"*. The restaurant was built several years before I worked there but his modus operandi regarding lighting effects lived on. *"One must see the effects – but not the source."*

Even at 70, having Frances Langford's name on the restaurant had great appeal, especially among those of her generation. Though she seldom ventured down to the restaurant for dinner, when she did, she would be greeted by many of our guests and often with requests for her to sing. Ray Thompson and his trio were almost a permanent fixture in the lounge and very popular with the local community and with Frances. On the rare occasion when she would be willing to honor these requests, she would sing her signature melody, *"I'm in the Mood for Love."* Privately, she would admit that this was the only number in her extensive repertoire for which she still remembered the words.

****

I have been fortunate to have many interesting experiences in my career and one that was truly unique happened at the Outrigger in 1984. We had received notice that a life-sized replica of a

1,000-year old Norwegian Viking merchant ship was making a 35,000 mile around-the-world tour and that they would like to stay at our marina. If we so wished, we could make it available for public viewing while it was there for its three-day stop. The ship was a Viking knar and was built by an experienced boatwright, Sigurd Bjorkedal, in Bjorkedalen, Norway. It was modeled on the *Skuldelev*, which had been excavated in 1962 at the Roskilde Fjord in Denmark. It was called the *Saga Siglar* and was sailing under the experienced hand of Captain Ragnar Thorseth. Ragnar had started his dramatic career by rowing single handed from Norway to the Shetlands in Scotland. This worldwide expedition was receiving wide publicity back home in Norway where Ragnar was a well-known adventurer and explorer celebrity.

The *Saga Siglar* was launched in 1983 and had sailed to Newfoundland later that same year. In 1984, as part of its round-the-world tour, it visited New York City, where it had received a great deal of attention. It was now sailing down the eastern seaboard and the anticipation of its arrival in tiny Jensen Beach was exciting, to say the least.

The day it finally arrived, I think the first thing we noticed was how small it was considering the long trips its 1,000-year-old predecessor had made and which this unique vessel was now making. It was 52 feet long and had a crew of six to eight. Their quarters on board were, of necessity, tiny. The interesting thing was that the main part of the ship was actually a single box-shaped unit that, with a crane, could be removed entirely.

Ragnar and his crew elected to stay aboard rather than take advantage of our resort's accommodations. I contacted our beer distributors to see where the closest outlet would be for some imported Norwegian beer. Fortunately, the closest retail outlet was just a few miles south and I went and bought them out of all of the Hansa brand beer they had on hand. As I soon learned, that was a good move.

The local media had done a good job of covering this story both before and during their stay and we had a constant line of inquisitive visitors to see the ship. The three days passed all too quickly and as they were making their preparations to continue on their way, Ragnar approached me and said, "Would you like to come with us? We can let you off anywhere that would be convenient for you." Wow, what a great invitation. I wasn't ready for it but it would be a shame not to take advantage of his thoughtfulness and this one-of-a-kind opportunity to share at least a few miles with them on their historic trip.

"Well, yes, I'd love to," I was quick to reply. "If you could let me off in Jupiter."

"Absolutely. We can take you much further than that if you like."

"Thank you, but no. I really do have to get back as I would have to make arrangements to get back up here. If you can let me off in Jupiter, that would be great. I can have one of our staff drive down and pick me up."

Jupiter is only 20 miles south of Jensen Beach, so it was a quick trip down the intracoastal waterway. We attracted a great deal of attention along the way, especially from the drivers of the cars waiting on the several drawbridges, which are a long-established part of the south Florida transportation system. It was explained to me that the waterway always has precedence over road traffic, as it was there first! A reasonable explanation.

****

In May 1986, at the age of 78, Evinrude became ill and was admitted to Martin Memorial Hospital in nearby Stuart where he

Saga Siglar at the Outrigger Dock

passed away. A decision was made soon afterwards to sell off the restaurant, the villas and the marina and, for all intents and purposes, my job as manager came to an end.

During my time at The Outrigger, a good friend of mine, Preston Hicks, and I had purchased a nine-acre piece of property in Port St. Lucie on the southwest corner of Port St. Lucie Boulevard and Westmoreland. We had negotiated a purchase price in the low $300,000's and had approached a bank regarding the financing. Not only did the bank approve the loan but increased it by about $30,000 to allow for the initial servicing of it. The western portion of the property bordered on the eastern bank of the St. Lucie River immediately south of the boulevard bridge and would have provided great access for potential business from boat traffic. The "East Chop," a party boat operating out of Stuart, was a popular local attraction with which we had done business while I was at Sandpiper Bay, and they kindly made a trial run up to this location to confirm that it could be a possible venue for lunch and dinner tours. I wanted to develop a restaurant and pub on the western end of the property. It would have had a one thousand square foot boardwalk area on the river for docking, an outside deck area overlooking the river, a mid-level table service restaurant and bar inside, a banquet room on an upper level and an independent pub adjacent to the parking lot on the eastern end. It was an exciting dream. We would develop the balance of the property for commercial use. Port St. Lucie Boulevard traversed the river at this location where it divided naturally so that there was an island 'median' and two bridges, both 340 feet in length going east-west. I was going to name the restaurant *The Twin Bridges Inn* and I was already working with an artist on a logo. Yes, I was excited.

Preston worked for General Development out of the Port St.

Lucie office and was in an excellent position to know what was going on in the area. The company was primarily interested in developing residential housing and was working with third parties in developing commercial space. In the course of his duties he had received an inquiry from a developer who was looking for key sites in the area and had enquired about the land we had just acquired. Preston and I discussed it and we both felt that we did not want to sell it. When a follow up enquiry was made, jokingly, we put a price of $1,330,000 on it, being a million dollars more than we had paid for it. We wanted to keep it for our own project. But, if we were going to sell it, we wanted it to be worth it. Well, we were in for a surprise.

While real estate deals often end up in negotiations, the offer presented to us was a straight purchase price of $1,080,000 with the remaining $250,000 being satisfied through a percentage of the profits from other sales, rental revenue and/or re-financing. At that price, it didn't take us long to ditch our own plans and say, "OK, you've got a deal!" As it turned out, the deal covering the $250,000 part of it, did not work out the way we had hoped and anticipated. We had some disputes with the developer over this but he insisted he never generated enough to give us this distribution. We considered legal action but, after considering all the implications, we decided against it. However, the day came for the closing and Preston and I drove down to Palm Beach and each of us came back home with checks of $365,000 after simultaneously paying off the bank loan. That was the largest check I have ever received. If my dream had to go down the tubes, at least it was worth it.

Preston and I, now having had a taste for this real estate stuff, decided to purchase a ten-and-a-half-acre parcel in a prime location at the northeast corner of Port St. Lucie Boulevard and the entrance to the Florida Turnpike. I believed this would be an ideal location to put up an 80 or 120-room limited service hotel. Preston agreed. At that time, Sandpiper Bay had the only accommodations in town and being a Four Diamond, Four Star Resort, it was naturally in the upper price bracket. Port St. Lucie was a rapidly growing community and I felt the market was ripe for a project of this kind.

We apparently were not alone in this thought, and found ourselves in competition with a local businessman by the name of Bert Deluca. This was a new experience for us, as we would need to buy a couple of houses, which were already sitting on two of the residential lots. I volunteered to try to acquire one of them and one evening I walked up to the door and rang the bell. A man, probably in his early to mid-30's, came to the door and I asked if I could speak with him for a few minutes. He invited me in and I sat with him and his wife and their young family.

"I was just wondering if you were interested in selling your house." I started.

"No, not really, why?"

I explained that I was involved with a small group that was trying to acquire this piece of property with the purpose of developing it. He told me they had already been contacted by someone who had wanted the property for a fast food restaurant but he had never heard anything more about it. Anyway, we discussed it and I was quite relieved to find out that they would not be opposed to considering selling if the price was right. As development out west picked up, Port St. Lucie Boulevard became a very busy east-west corridor and it was no longer an ideal location for raising a young family. I left them to do their own research and to let me know whenever they had reached a decision. They finally came back to us with an asking price, which was understandably a little high but not totally unreasonable under the circumstances and we bought it.

Once the dust settled, it turned out that Bert Deluca had acquired about the same amount of the property as Preston and I had. After getting our heads together, we decided to join up and we became DHP Associates, representing our last names. A road, which split the property in two, dead-ended at the western end and, once we had acquired all the lots on both sides of it, we applied to the city to have that vacated so that we had one single contiguous site. We also applied for a change in zoning from 'Residential' to 'Commercial' and both requests were approved. Having the road vacated, also gave us an additional three quarters of an acre of land.

At this point, we found a general contractor in Palm Beach with whom we could joint venture the development phase. We told him of our plan to put a limited service hotel on the site with other supporting commercial businesses but it wasn't until after the ink was dry on our agreement, he said, "Do you guys *really* want to put a hotel in there? I primarily do shopping centers and I could probably bring several tenants to the site."

I was the only one who really wanted to do the hotel and now we all had a stake in the development's success, so I backed off the hotel idea and went along with everyone else. I hope I hid my disappointment. Still, we all wanted a profitable outcome, so that is what we did.

From there it became complicated. Preston, Bert and I found ourselves now dabbling in an area with which we were not familiar. DHP Associates put the property into the agreement and it was understood that the developer would obtain and secure the construction loan and that after the construction was complete, DHP Associates and the developer would have a 50/50 interest in the project. There were terms in our agreement, which allowed for action in the event of the default of a partner and, when Preston, Bert and I were informed by the bank, which had granted the loan to the developer, that he was delinquent in his payments, we discussed this issue with him. This brought accusations on both sides, as the developer tried to defend his delinquency, and we were eventually faced with either him buying us out or vice versa. We went to mediation and were encouraged to try to work things out without anyone filing a lawsuit, if at all possible. Then nobody wins. If he was already delinquent with his bank, we surmised the odds of being paid if he bought us out were slim, so we negotiated to buy him out, which we did at an elevated price. Now we had the site back in the hands of DHP Associates and we decided to put it on the market as-is. It was still a valuable piece of property but the timing was not so good at that point and we sold it for less than it was worth. By the time our banking obligations had been either settled or written off, we were about where we had started. Oh well. Lesson learned? I guess so.

All this had taken about a year and now I needed to go back to work.

Key to Success #13

Maintain Oversight: *Take time to thoroughly review invoices from all departments. You cannot be on top of all issues all the time but a large part of the story of your operation is told through your payables. Keep track of the pricing of your primary, regular, on-going commodities.*

13. Indian River Plantation (1987-1989)

It was early 1987 and the Indian River Plantation on Hutchinson Island, just across the Indian River from the Outrigger, was in the process of building a 200-room hotel addition. The resort already included 1900 condominiums, a first-class tennis facility, an 18-hole golf course and a large marina on the St. Lucie River. The ocean to river resort had many similarities with Sandpiper Bay, as there had to be harmonious interaction with residents of the condominiums and the club membership. When I heard they were recruiting for a general manager, I felt my experience was a perfect fit. The property was owned by Radnor Corporation, a division of the Sun Oil Company and I was interviewed by Steve Powers, vice president for hotel operations. My interview went well, but it seemed, perhaps, that Steve thought it was a bit too easy. Here was a highly qualified, unemployed candidate, who was immediately available, living just a few minutes down the road.

When my job at the Outrigger came to an end, so did our ability to live in the villa we had been given while I was working there. Fortunately, Anita and I owned a beachfront condominium nearby on Hutchinson Island, which we had been using as a rental property, so we stayed there while we considered our next move.

Doing his due diligence, Powers decided to put the position out to various hospitality employment search firms. Not being aware of this, I found it difficult and a bit perplexing waiting and waiting for a call. Things became clearer when I received a call from an old friend, Francisco Almeida. He had been the director of food and beverage for the Executive House chain in Chicago, and we had both worked in New York for Restaurant Associates. He now worked for a prominent search firm in California.

"I have the perfect job for you." he started, and immediately went on to give me a full description of the job opening at Indian River Plantation. When he had laid out all the details, I finally spoke.

"Frank, I've already interviewed for that and, you are right, I think I would indeed be a strong candidate. I don't know what they were waiting for." My interview had been several weeks prior and I was still waiting to hear something. Now I understood the delay, Powers was conducting a nationwide search.

I found myself in a quandary. Months passed as Powers was evidently interviewing other candidates. I needed to get back to work but we still did not want to relocate. Somehow, I felt confident the Indian River Plantation position was eventually going to be offered to me. Having heard nothing, I flew out to Springfield, Missouri to be interviewed by Johnny Morris, owner and developer of Bass Pro Shops. He had a unique little resort, Big Cedar Lodge on Table Rock Lake about 65 miles south of Springfield, near Branson, and it was a fascinating prospect. Morris had started out by selling his fishing lures at the back of his father's liquor store in Springfield and, as they say, the rest is history. Bass Pro Shops now has over 90 magnificent stores, both in the U.S. and Canada. The day after my dinner meeting with him at the lodge, I drove back to Springfield and met with one of my former Playboy colleagues who was now the chef and manager of Hemingway's Blue Water Café, the restaurant on the upper floor of the store. Again, it was a while before I heard anything but finally I was advised that they had hired the marketing director of Silver Dollar City, a prominent attraction in Branson.

Finally, my patience was rewarded. I was invited back to meet with Powers, and was subsequently offered the position as vice president and general manager of the resort. It was a high compliment that I had emerged as the best candidate after an exhaustive nationwide search. I took over the position in June and initially worked out of a conference room in a corporate office across the street from where the new hotel was in the final stages of completion. This was not ideal, because when the conference room was needed for a meeting, I had to pick up my papers and move out temporarily. However, this was only until I could move into a proper office in the new hotel. One of my first responsibilities was to fill a few department head positions. A sales and marketing director was already on board, and here again it was someone whom I had first met through Playboy, where he had been the sales and marketing director of the new 700-room resort in Great Gorge, New Jersey, a similar project to the Lake Geneva property. Bob Samuels was highly regarded in the industry and an excellent choice to help get our new hotel and conference center off the ground.

The resort already had several oceanfront condominiums in a rental pool from two 40-unit buildings on the beach, Pelican and Spoonbill. About 55 units were in this program, so a reservation department and a small sales staff were already on site. Also, the resort had two small food outlets, the Porch and the Inlet overlooking the pro tennis court. The Porch essentially served as

Indian River Plantation

the coffee shop and the Inlet was a more up-market, intimate, gourmet restaurant only open in the evenings. They shared a small kitchen situated between the two and were under the direction of a talented chef, Greg Scott. Every November, the resort would do a large "Welcome Back" homeowner's party and, with a tent over the tennis court, would put on a fabulous reception and a sit-down dinner for several hundred people. What Greg produced out of that tiny kitchen was absolutely miraculous, and it was always received with huge accolades.

It was exciting to see the final touches of the hotel come together. Opening a new property was a first for me and being an independent resort, I had to be mindful of so many of the small details that, in a chain operation, are part of the established pre-opening procedures. Chef Scott continued as our executive chef. We hired Frank Winter as food and beverage director and a wonderful fellow Brit, Bob Davis, as maître d'hôtel for our new, beautiful, top floor restaurant and lounge overlooking the marina and the river. Bob had held similar positions with the Cunard Lines on many of their finest ships including the Queen Mary and the QE II, so he was familiar with high quality restaurant service. It was an exciting morning when our first guest, a single gentleman, arrived at our reception desk. As Bob Davis would say, "We're under way."

One of the resort's assets, which I believed could be used as another great amenity, was our marina. Several similar resort properties offered river sightseeing cruises, and I thought it would be a great draw to have cruises tied into weekend and other types of packages. We already had excellent golf and tennis amenities and, with our marketing and promotion through the hotel, a leased cruise concession operator could be well supported. Initially, I put the word out to several companies providing these services. However, no one would agree to operate year-round at our location. I felt this was important, as I believed one of the key things a seasonal resort should offer is consistent services, certainly as much as possible. Almost all those with whom I spoke, operated in Florida in the winter and moved their vessels to northern venues for the summer months.

Stuart, known as the Sailfish Capital of the World, had several boat building enterprises, marinas and marine accessory outlets. One day Bob Samuels and I visited one of them to talk about building a vessel to our specifications. The boat would have to be equipped with large ice bins and facilities for holding and serving both hot and cold food items. As luck would have it, they had one such vessel partially built and they believed the customer who had ordered it could be persuaded to wait a little longer. It seemed almost perfect, as the required food and beverage support facilities could be located on a lower deck. The main deck would be glass enclosed with a bar at one end and fitted out with tables and chairs. There would be an upper open-air, partially shaded deck around the captain's cabin. It was never intended for the resort to own and operate this ourselves so all we had to do now was find a qualified owner-operator who would be willing to buy the boat and operate it out of our marina.

A local entrepreneur, Hans Hammer, expressed an interest, and after he did his due diligence, we entered an agreement to add this amenity. He named the ship *The Island Princess* and we provided both premium dock space and dedicated parking to support local and hotel-generated business. It was an amenable and successful partnership. Also, this new amenity gave our sales department an important added feature to offer to our regular hotel guests and the group business we were soliciting.

It was an interesting first year as we went through the various operational adjustments and we took great satisfaction when I was invited to Orlando to receive the AAA Four Diamond Award after only being open for 11 months. At that time, this was the fastest that AAA had ever presented this award. Happily, this was followed soon after by being awarded the Mobil Four Star Award. We were off to a great start.

****

Soon after I had the great pleasure of meeting Victor Borge again. His "Comedy in Music" show never got old and he had been booked to appear at the Redeemer Lutheran Church in nearby Stuart for a single engagement and was staying at our resort. I greeted him upon his arrival and reminded him that we had met back in 1962 at The Colony Hotel in Palm Beach where he had stayed when he appeared at the Royal Poinciana Playhouse.

While he did not remember me, he did remember that engagement. I asked him what arrangements we could make for him for dinner, as I was not sure whether his preference would be to dine before or after his performance. Typical of his Danish background, he requested some open-faced sandwiches and fruit after the show. I assured him this would be brought to his suite when he returned to the hotel. I had purchased tickets for Anita and me and, as I would be going straight from work, I arranged to meet her at the church. As always, his show was terrific and he got his usual standing ovation. His timing and his facial expressions were priceless.

When the show was over, I told Anita that she should go home. I was going back to the hotel ahead of him, just to be sure that the

With Victor Borge

room service staff had delivered his dinner, as arranged. Room service had done everything correctly and the order was on the table waiting for him. I checked the bedroom and seeing that the maid had not performed the turn down service, proceeded to do it myself. It would only take a moment. I had almost completed it when I heard a key in the living room door and in walked Borge. I felt a little stupid standing there, folding the bed cover as I tried to explain what I was doing and why. I won't repeat what he said but it was typical of his incredible sense of humor! Blushing and laughing, I bid him good night and went home.

****

As any hotel manager can tell you, there are situations which come up where no amount of training helps. One of these happened to me on a quiet summer Saturday morning. I usually used this time for catching up on administrative work, reviewing invoices, signing checks, responding to correspondence and so forth. I always felt that the resort's invoices gave me a real feel for all aspects of the operation, as I could not possibly be on top of everything that was going on week in and week out. There was so much information to be gleaned from this exercise. A little before noon, I received a call from our switchboard operator saying that she had a gentleman on the line saying that his wife was staying at the hotel with another man and that he knew their room number and he was coming over to "take care of the situation", whatever that meant. I told her to put the call through to me. He was angry, as I could well understand. He told me the man's name and I assured him I would look into it. We hung up with his threat still ringing in my ears. Was this a hoax? It didn't sound like it but what do I do about it? If what he was saying was true, the hotel had no control over the situation, but I certainly didn't want this kind of conflict playing itself out here.

I double-checked the name he had given me and called the room. There was no answer. The guests could be anywhere. I scanned the pool area, packed with guests, and saw no one whose behavior indicated they might be engaged in a tryst of some kind. I went to the pool bar and asked if there had been any room charges for the guest I was looking for. Bingo! Yes, there had been a bar charge. I asked our two bartenders if they thought they could see the person around the pool. This was difficult since some people were in the pool, some were sunning themselves, several were lying on their stomachs making them difficult to recognize, some were reading and some were just chatting. With the number of people already served, it was a challenge for the bartenders to remember the person we were trying to find. By a simple process of elimination and trying not to be obvious, we determined that a couple at the far end of the pool *could* be them, but they couldn't be sure.

I took the bull by the horns and walked over to them. The man was sitting up reading while his companion was lying face down sunning herself. I was quite nervous as I said, "Excuse me, are you Mr. Jones?"

"Yes?" he said, with a question in his voice.

"I'm Bill Pullen, the general manager. May I speak with you for a moment?"

"Yes," he repeated, remaining seated.

I had to get him away from his companion, as I still could not be sure the call wasn't a prank. If this was a married couple, I certainly did not wish to be discussing all this in front of both of them with other guests nearby. I motioned for him to follow me.

Somewhat reluctantly he put his book down, got up and we walked to a corner of the pool area away from others in earshot.

"I am really sorry to trouble you, but a little while ago I received a call from someone claiming you were here with his wife and that he was coming to the hotel. He was quite angry. I am not asking you to comment, one way or the other. I just wanted to make you aware of the call; I leave any decision up to you. Of course, I would like to avoid an unpleasant scene, if possible."

He looked down, thought for a moment and looked back up again. "Thank you," he muttered and returned to his companion, still sunning herself, seemingly unaware that he had left her for a moment. I immediately returned to my office and called the pool bar to ask if there had been any reaction.

"Yes," I was told. The couple had talked, gotten up, taken their things and gone back into the hotel. They checked out shortly after. End of story.

Thankfully, there was no confrontation at the hotel, but the incident had certainly spiced up my usually quiet catch-up Saturday morning.

****

In the course of a hotel management career, you can expect to confront situations, which catch you totally by surprise. That is the case here and, unfortunately, I had no plan to handle it.

It was a Thursday morning and things were pretty routine up to that point. We had a meeting booked in the hotel and the attendees were in their late morning sessions in the conference rooms. Everything was going as planned.

I was in my office when Susan Hall, my secretary, put a call through to me from the switchboard operator. "Mr. Pullen, I just had a call claiming there was a bomb somewhere on the property and before I could say anything, they hung up. What should I do?"

What should *she* do? More to the point. What should *I* do?

We immediately called 911 and quickly had representatives of the sheriff's department arrive along with the local fire station personnel, including Fire Chief, Cliff Appe. Our Hutchinson Island Fire Department was just about a quarter mile down the road from the resort.

Our telephone operator was asked to repeat exactly what she could remember from the conversation and we all congregated out in the parking lot to discuss this totally unexpected threat. We had no knowledge of any disgruntled former employee or any other suspect for something like this. To complicate matters, Indian River Plantation was on 192 acres, comprising our 200-room hotel, golf and tennis facilities, the marina and the 1900 condominiums. Where do we start?

Immediately, we enlisted our maintenance and housekeeping personnel to do a thorough search of the entire hotel and all our related facilities. While this was under way, Cliff Appe said to me, "What do you want to do? Do you want to evacuate?"

I said, "You tell me! You guys are the ones running this thing."

"Oh no," he replied, "You represent the property owner, and this is your call."

This was another "oh-oh" moment for me. "Gosh darn it. What *do* we do?"

We discussed it further and I was only mildly comforted when they told me the majority of these calls are just a hoax. But we couldn't be sure. After laboring over this decision for way too long, I made the call.

"No, I don't want to evacuate. In any event, I could evacuate the hotel but how on earth are we going to evacuate all the condos? We have no idea where this thing could be."

At that point, the first responders assisted us in doing a thorough walk through of all public areas on the property. After a couple of hours or so, the only thing that turned up was an unidentified suitcase in a condo laundry room. This was carefully removed to a parking lot and the hazardous material team, in their space suit type of protective uniforms, was called in. Tension! As we watched from a safe distance, the suitcase was very carefully opened. Finally, a member of the team came to tell us what was in it. Dirty clothes! Who would have guessed? ...and it was left in a laundry room!

Phew! Believe me, I was sweating over my decision, as it *could* have gone the other way and my mind could hardly get around the potential consequences. I gave a huge sigh of relief. It was over. Back in my office, I found it almost impossible to settle down again and certainly could not concentrate on anything I had been doing when this started. I needed a beer!

****

Opening a new operation always requires a shake down period. Operating systems, physical layouts, and employee responsibilities all need to be reviewed and tested to assure that the property will function as designed. Even with pre-opening and systems training, hiccups can easily occur. There can often be personality conflicts of one kind or another, as there is usually a certain amount of stress associated with the necessary adjustments that need to be made. I and one or two of the department heads had such a situation with Steve Powers. He tended to be more critical than supportive. Steve Osburn, was responsible for this geographic area on behalf of Radnor and, while he was mostly involved with the real estate side of the company, the chain of command went on up to him.

One day, as I was heading off to our weekly department head meeting, I bumped into Osburn. He said, "Can I talk to you for a moment? I understand from one of your department heads that some of you are having a bit of a problem with Steve."

I said, "Yes, that's so but I think we can work around it. It's just not as smooth as it could be."

"Would it work better if you reported to me instead of Powers?"

"That's not my call," I replied, "That's up to you."

We talked about it a little more and finally he said, "Well, from now on you will report to me. I'll speak with Steve about it."

"Is that final?" I asked.

"Yes," Steve Osburn replied.

"Then I'll comment. I think it will work better. Thank you."

And it was better – at least for a while.

Several months later, Radnor promoted Osburn to another position and, guess what? I ended up reporting to Steve Powers again. I had never had a conversation with him about the change in my line of reporting, but I could understand him not being happy about it. I assumed he thought that I was the one who requested the change. It was an uncomfortable situation for me and it came to a head one Thursday, the day of our weekly afternoon department head meeting.

Just before the meeting, Tony, our Controller, called me and said,

"Steve Powers wants to see Betsy at two o'clock. Do you know what that's about?"

A chill ran down my spine. Betsy was our payroll clerk and two o'clock is when we start our staff meeting. I knew as sure as I am writing these words, he was getting her to cut my final paycheck while we would all be in our meeting. As the reader knows, this would not be the first time I had lost my job involuntarily but this would be the first time it would have happened by being summarily fired. I felt terrible running the staff meeting but the show must go on. The rest of the day ran normally and I discussed the situation with Anita when I got home that evening. We knew what to expect.

The next morning, Powers called to see if I was available to meet. I knew what was coming. We sat down at a table in my office, and he told me he was making a change in general manager and he had two checks for me. One was my regular salary up to that day and the other one was a severance settlement that came along with a legal separation document for my signature. It is a fairly standard procedure that when a senior management or sales and marketing position is terminated, that it is done immediately. This is prudent business practice and does not necessarily mean there was any specific negative reason for the termination.

I said, "Steve you obviously had this document drawn up by an attorney and, before I sign it, I will have my attorney take a look at it, OK?" In all honesty, I assumed it was a boilerplate document used in these situations but I wanted to have time to settle down, have it reviewed and certainly not sign it there and then in the office.

"Yes, that's fine. Just understand that I cannot release the check until you do."

"Yes, I know. As soon as I get feedback from him, I'll let you know."

As this was now a done deal, I took the opportunity to express my feelings about the difficulties I had working with him. I stated my case calmly, with no animosity, and I felt better about it. There are always two sides to an issue and I was glad for the chance to speak my mind.

I told Susan Hall, my secretary, and immediately started putting my personal items together. I met briefly with the department heads so that they would hear it directly from me, and I don't think there were many surprises. We had all had some issues with Powers of one kind or another and there was definitely some uneasiness all around.

It was still early enough for me to speak with my attorney, Rickey Farrell, and, as I expected, he felt it was pretty standard and that I had nothing to be concerned about.

The following week, I signed the document, got my check and said "Goodbye."

Key to Success #14

Research: *When servicing group business, take time to determine the overall objective of your client. Is it a pep talk session requiring a more serious meeting environment or more of a fun occasion, a reward for achieving record results?*

14. My Final Assignment (1990-2005)

First Sandpiper Bay, then the Outrigger and now Indian River Plantation. Oh boy, I'm running out of hotels in this town. Once again, I find myself looking for a job.

Our front office and reservations manager at Sandpiper Bay, Millie Carmack, was now the front office manager at the 180-room Jensen Beach Holiday Inn Oceanside, which was located on the beach almost halfway between our condominium and Indian River Plantation. This was the hotel that was previously managed by my friend Jim McManemon when we had returned to Florida in 1976. He had passed away in 1985 and the hotel had been managed by Jas Ahlualia since then. Evidently there had been some issues recently and Jas had been terminated. The owners were looking for a new general manager, and Millie knew that I was available.

The owners were members of the Walter Duncan and Joe O'Neill families, the patriarchs of which had been friends since their college days at Notre Dame University. The Duncans lived in Oklahoma City and the O'Neills in Midland, Texas. As an interesting aside, O'Neill's son Joey and Joey's wife had introduced librarian Laura (now Bush) to former President George W. Bush at a barbecue at their home. When the former president visited The Villages for a book signing event in 2013 for

Jensen Beach Holiday Inn Oceanside

his new publication, 'Decision Points', he had mentioned this in his public remarks. Anita and I joined the throng going through the line to shake his hand and we had a brief opportunity to speak with him.

"It's great to meet you, Mr. President. Thank you for coming to The Villages. Before I retired I used to work for Joe O'Neill and his partner, Walter Duncan, running their hotels." I told him.

He smiled and reacted to their names. "Great people. I bet you were the only person out there (where he had just spoken from the bandstand at Market Square in Lake Sumter Landing) who knew who I was talking about."

I had the highest regard for President Bush and felt the media treated him unfairly much of the time. He is a fine man regardless of which side of the political divide you're on.

Walter Duncan was responsible for this beachfront Holiday Inn and also for a sister property they owned located on U.S.1 in Stuart, the 120-room Holiday Inn Downtown, about a 25-minute drive to the south. I was asked to fly out to Oklahoma City for my interview, and I was met at the airport by Duncan's daughter, Lynn Leedy. The interview went well and I was offered the position as general manager of the Holiday Inn Oceanside and I was given the additional responsibility of overseeing the operations of the Holiday Inn Downtown. In the past, these hotels had two independent managers and, on occasion, there had been some personality conflict, which had prevented the maximum amount of cooperation between the two. Having one person responsible for both properties would eliminate this potential problem. I was to report to Leedy regarding daily operating matters although I was directly responsible to Duncan on all matters pertaining to the budgets and financial results. Our downtown property already had an excellent manager, Charles Calvert.

This was my second experience working for a brand franchise and, in many respects, it is quite different from managing an independent hotel. In a sense, one has two bosses, the property owner and the franchise company. Naturally, the brand has many services to offer and certain required standards, as it should, but it took a bit of getting used to, especially when a young and, sometimes, inexperienced career person arrived unannounced on property to do a standards inspection. We had an excellent property with a friendly staff to match, and I am proud to say we were often recognized with the annual Holiday Inn Quality Excellence Award. In fact, in 1993, we were one of a very small number of hotels honored with the brand's highest recognition, the Torchbearer Award. For a 20-year old property, we had much to be proud of and we exhibited the impressive award in our lobby for all to admire.

Duncan was a wonderful boss and usually I would see him only once a year when he and the family would come to Jensen Beach for a vacation. He would take this opportunity to meet with our auditors and go over the annual reports for both hotels. He also did not communicate that often. I learned my first lesson shortly after I joined the company when his secretary, Cheryl Millard, called me and said that he would like me to come to Oklahoma City to meet with him. I flew out the day he wanted to see me and met him in his office where we sat around a boardroom table with his accountant, Ken Fry. I was waiting to see what he wanted to see me about when he said, "OK, Bill. Go ahead."

"What do you mean, Mr. Duncan? You said you wanted to see

me."

"Yes. I want you to give me a report on the hotels."

"Oh. I'm so sorry." I was flustered and totally unprepared. "I didn't realize that was what you wanted. I'm afraid I didn't come prepared, but I can give you a general outline of what's going on."

That was the last time I made that mistake. The next time I was overly prepared and we discussed all aspects of both hotel operations. While I felt he was satisfied, I really got no reaction one way or the other.

The next day, back at the hotel, I got a call from Cheryl. She said, "Bill, I thought you would like to know Mr. Duncan was very pleased with your report yesterday. I know you will never hear that from him!" Thank you, Cheryl. She certainly knew him a lot better than I did.

A similar situation took place during one of his visits to Jensen Beach. He and I met in my office and discussed a number of subjects. When he was ready to leave, I said to him, "Mr. Duncan, am I doing what you want here?"

"Bill, if you weren't, you'd see me more often." and he left.

We were walking past my secretary, Susan Jensen, when he said this. When he was out of earshot, Susan said to me, "That was a compliment!"

Yes, he was a man of few words but very kind, and a shrewd business man. He was the first owner of the New Jersey Generals football team when the new U.S. Football League was being formed. He had recruited Herschel Walker, the University of Georgia Heisman Trophy winner, for the team, which he ultimately sold to Donald Trump. I got to know him a lot better as time went by and I have always had the highest regard for him.

There is just one other point along these lines that was interesting. The salary they hired me at was very fair; however, there was never any suggestion that this should be reviewed occasionally. After seven years, I finally said, "You know, Mr. Duncan, we review all our employees and their compensation levels at least annually and I just wondered, if some time you would consider reviewing mine."

"Of course, Bill. What do you think it should be?"

They were so hands off they just never thought about mundane issues like that. Overall, it was a very fulfilling experience, as I essentially ran the hotels with the philosophy of "If this was mine, what would I do" and I followed that ideal accordingly. I don't think I made too many mistakes.

In my 15 years at this hotel, one date particularly stands out. Saturday April 4, 1992. And except for the people involved, it had nothing to do with the hotel business. We won the lottery! And it was all thanks to Katie.

At that time, the Florida Lottery was fairly new and, it seemed, almost everyone was getting involved to some extent. It was sometime in January 1992, when the lottery had a rollover and Katie Moorman, our poolside bartender, thought it would be a good idea for us to get in on the action. We wouldn't play every week, after all a payout of a mere six to seven million dollars would be too insignificant to bother with, at least in Katie's opinion. When there had been no winner on March 28th, and the rollover pot was raised to $17.3 million, Katie started hitting on some of our regular bar customers and fellow employees to become a part of the pool. When she asked me for my $20, despite our 'no solicitation' rule, I only had a ten in my wallet. I told her she could take the other ten out of my winnings – but that didn't seem to work! Fortunately, I came up with the other ten. In the end, there were twelve shares; eleven full partners plus one share split between a waitress and our night auditor.

Saturday night came along and I was in bed in the early stages of deep sleep when our phone rang. I groped for it and croaked, "Hello."

"Mr. Pullen. This is Drew. We hit six of six!"

Drew Nicholson was our excellent young food and beverage director, and it was he who nearly always was our manager on duty Saturday nights due to the usually busy restaurant and lounge, plus we often had banquets going on downstairs in our function rooms. His calls would seldom be good news, either somebody had drowned in the pool, some drunks had gotten into a fight and the police wanted to see me, there was a fire, or other similar mini disasters.

"What are you talking about?"

"We hit six of six!" he repeated.

"Drew, what *are* you talking about." I was still half asleep.

"We've hit the lottery," he insisted.

"Oh, come on Drew, leave me alone. I'm not in the mood for jokes right now."

"No. Really. Our six numbers have come up." He read them off, 2-3-8-22-24-27.

At this point, I *was* awake and I went to where I had written them down and, sure enough, those were our numbers – but he can't be serious.

"Drew, are you pulling my leg?"

The winning ticket

"No, I'm not. Check the newspapers in the morning."

"OK, I'll see you tomorrow. Thanks. Good night."

Of course, at this point Anita was also awake and I related what Drew had said. There was really nothing to be done at this point so I turned off the light and said, "Good night."

After about ten minutes, Anita whispered. "Are you still awake?"

"You bet your sweet life, I'm still awake!" I was almost shouting.

I turned the light on again. I did not recall the estimated amount of the rollover, but I knew it had to be in the region of at least $14 to $15 million. Of course, there could be more than one winning ticket so I started breaking it down if there were multiple winners and then dividing it by twelve. Whatever it was, it was still all good news! We did finally go to sleep.

It was all the talk at the hotel the following morning with so many employees mad at themselves for not coming across with their $20. We did confirm the numbers published in the newspapers and found out there were actually four tickets matching the winning combination, so our ticket was worth just over $4.3 million before taxes. Divided by twelve, this would be around $360,000 for each share. Does this figure sound familiar? It was very close to what Preston Hicks and I had received from our first real estate endeavor and what we had lost on our second one. Could it be that someone 'upstairs' was giving me a second chance? Maybe. Well, now what do we do?

Our group was diverse, however, there was never any dispute of any kind. There was no shortage of ideas on what to do first. Many wanted to head straight to Tallahassee and collect the cash. Of course, it doesn't quite work that way. Everyone agreed to have a meeting on Tuesday to talk about it and it was suggested that we hire an attorney to draw up an agreement with everyone's share properly documented. Also, the ticket needed to be protected and we should probably meet with a bank to handle the various transactions that would be necessary.

Our primary local bank, with which the hotels did business, was the First National Bank of the Treasure Coast (now Seacoast National Bank). I called and made an appointment with one of their senior trust officers. This was interesting. We arrived at the bank at the duly appointed time and were shown into a formal oak-paneled boardroom. Our group, a mixture of off duty employees, beach bar regulars and I sat around the table. I am sure I was the only one wearing a jacket and tie. Katie was sitting immediately on my left attired casually in shorts, flip-flops and a baseball hat hanging off the back of her head. The trust officer came in and introduced himself and there was a general round table conversation. It seems their trust department had never handled a situation like this before, as it was their usual duty to manage financial portfolios. In this case, they would be the agent receiving the funds from the lottery agency and then almost immediately disbursing them to all of us. Many of us already had accounts with the bank, but they did require those who did not to open an account for the purpose of depositing the disbursements. Other than that, there was not much they had to do other than file an annual tax report and notify all of us about the distributions. At one point the trust officer said, "I have a silly question. I guess you all have the ticket, right? I hope it is in a safe place."

Everyone looked at Katie. "Yes, I have it" she said. "I'm sure it's quite safe."

"May I ask where it is?" The trust officer inquired.

"Yes, I have it right here." Katie answered as she took off her baseball hat and pulled the ticket out from its 'safe' place inside.

I exploded! "Katie! That's $4.3 million dollars you're holding and it's *not* all yours; that's *not* a safe place. On top of that, you drive a convertible!"

Be assured, its next *home* was a safe deposit box. Time for another "phew!"

The details did eventually get finalized and a legal document identifying all the interested parties and their proportionate share was signed. In those early days of the lottery, lump sums were not an option so the distribution would be made annually starting on May 15th for a period of 20 years. This was just over $18,000 annually per share (around $13,000 net after the taxes were withheld). This did not seem enough for anyone to go completely crazy but certainly a nice little annuity for the next 20 years.

The local media covered the story and I received a call from Steve Powers at Indian River Plantation who said, "What are you going to do now? Give all your guests lottery tickets?" That made me think. I knew he was joking, but it gave me an idea. I had a die cut card made up to hold a single $1 lottery ticket, which said *"Thank you for staying with the winners!"* and we gave one out to every check-in for the next month. It didn't cost us that much and we got a lot of mileage out of it.

****

My 65th birthday was to be another significant date, September 11, 2001. I arrived at the hotel just before 9 a.m. and greeted the front desk staff with, "Yippee. Today I go on the government's payroll!"

I was met with stares and, "Have you seen what's happened in New York? Go into the bar, it's on the TV. Everyone's in there."

I walked in just as the second plane hit the south tower of the World Trade Center. My birthday would never be the same. But that's not important. May we never, never forget.

****

Having a beautiful beachfront location is certainly a great asset. However, there is also a downside. Florida is hit with strong summer tropical storms and hurricanes from time to time and being located on a barrier island made us especially vulnerable. Wind, rain, storm surge, beach erosion and flooding were all possible hazards and during my fifteen years there we had our share of evacuations. We maintained specific hurricane procedures that went into effect at the earliest indications and we evacuated when directed to do so by the local authorities. There were two major storms in September 2004, just three weeks apart, which hastened my subsequent retirement. The first one, Hurricane Frances, hit the coast less than five miles south of the oceanside hotel on the Saturday of Labor Day weekend. Hurricane Jeanne arrived almost at the same location exactly three weeks later.

We suffered considerable damage at our home, just a few miles inland, with Hurricane Frances tearing off several of our roof shingles and destroying our aluminum enclosed and screened patio. We had watched it flap in the wind and then it seemed to disappear with a grinding noise. When it was safe to go out, we saw it was still largely attached to the soffit on the roof but completely folded back over the house. The storm also created an early and premature 'harvest' of our healthy and prolific grapefruit tree; grapefruit were everywhere. Still, we were OK and, happily, we had no water leaks. Naturally, our electricity was cut off and the hot and humid weather, so typical of Florida in early September, really made things uncomfortable. We had wonderful neighbors, Carolyn and Terry Shores, and they very kindly let us tap into their generator periodically so that we could at least make a cup of coffee and do a few more important things.

One rather amusing by-product of losing our screened patio was a cute performance by our lovable cat, Eddie. The concrete slab that was the base for the patio was still covered by the indoor/outdoor carpet and this area had always been one of his favorite places. He could see the birds and the many squirrels in our oak tree, which would often taunt him by hanging on the screen. Now there was absolutely nothing to stop him from going out anywhere he pleased. We were trying to keep him inside, but one morning, we unintentionally left the door slightly ajar. He went out and immediately saw one of the teasing squirrels at the base of the oak tree. He headed off in determined pursuit; but as he came to the edge of the carpet, he screeched to an immediate halt as if he was auditioning for one of the ever-popular Roadrunner cartoons. There was nothing there to stop him but, evidently, he was so used to not going any further that he had not realized that he could! Fortunately, he didn't get the part – or the squirrel!

Over the next few days, we listened to the local weather and road condition reports and as soon as it seemed I could get out on the island to view any damage the hotel may have suffered, I decided to try. The roads were covered with debris from trees and aluminum siding and the police were controlling the limited traffic leading from our area to U.S.1, the major north-south highway from Key West to Canada. I was allowed access to U.S.1 and I drove carefully over to Jensen Beach. Some power lines were down and no traffic lights were working. I had a permit, previously issued by the Hutchinson Island Fire Department, to go on to the island in cases of emergency but, at this point, the local authorities were not permitting any access at all until the roads had been properly cleared and were considered safe. I turned around to go back home but when I got to where I should turn off U.S.1 to go into our development, the police would not let me in. I was stuck. I couldn't get to the hotel and I couldn't get home. I drove to the local Lowe's home improvement store, closed by the storm, and parked under the covered entryway. Thankfully, I had my phone and could call Anita and tell her where I was and what had happened. After a good hour or so, I decided to try again and this time, the officer did allow me to at least get home.

The following day, when I heard the authorities were allowing limited access to Hutchinson Island for homeowners and business owners, I tried again and this time I was allowed to proceed. Wow, what a mess. From the outside, the hotel appeared to be all right but the parking lot was full of sand and debris. It is not often a hotel has to lock the front door. Our attempt to do so during evacuation failed and we had to jerry-rig a bar and padlock. I entered and proceeded to do a quick walkthrough of the building. A closed hotel is surprisingly eerie. Our chief engineer, Ed Genter, arrived right behind me and a few others got there within the next couple of hours. The building itself, built with concrete and solid block construction, appeared to be fine but the interior water damage was extensive. The hotel had four floors of guest rooms where the bathrooms backed up to each other with eight bathrooms being vented by one extractor fan on the flat roof. We went up to the roof and saw that the hurricane-force winds had torn off several fans leaving a square hole in the roof where they had been. The roof had a parapet, so the heavy rain had created a mini swimming pool which had then drained through the gaping holes and down into the hotel. The fierce winds had also forced the rain through several of our sliding glass doors and many of the rooms, especially on the ocean side were soaked. In one room, I pushed my hand into the mattress and water went up to between my wrist and my forearm. Looking outside, there had been severe beach erosion and our swimming pool was full of sand and seawater. All in all, it was a desolate scene.

✳✳✳✳✳✳✳✳✳✳✳✳✳✳✳✳✳✳✳✳✳✳✳✳✳✳✳✳

Not long before Hurricane Frances put us out of business, we had one rather comical situation develop. Two ladies had a four-night reservation and after their second night they had complained about the mattresses and asked to be moved to another room. We were happy to accommodate them and this seemed to satisfy their complaint at the time. It was normal for us to replace our box springs and mattresses on a routine basis and, as it turned out, the room that they first were assigned had box springs and mattresses that were less than a year old. Curious, we checked our records, and sure enough, the box springs and mattresses in the room to which they were moved were also replaced at the same time. Despite all of this, not long after they had checked out, we received a letter complaining about their stay. I responded with an apology and offered a complimentary two-night return visit.

My office had been located on the lower floor before the hurricane and it had suffered considerable water damage. We moved our desks up to the lounge while we regrouped, so that we could have a place to operate from even though the hotel was closed. One day, my secretary, Susan Jensen, received a telephone call from the guest saying that she had misplaced my complimentary offer letter and could we send another one, as they would like to accept my invitation. In our apology letters, we would ask the recipient to bring the letter with them, as the original had a value and a specific expiration date. Susan politely explained that the hotel was closed due to storm damage and, at this point, we did not know if or when we would be able to re-open. Still the guest said she would like to leave the option of a return open.

This happened to be at a time when we were stripping the hotel completely and our box springs and mattresses were being thrown out into the street-side parking lot; piled almost up to the level of the second floor. I had taken photographs of this and, with tongue in cheek, had enclosed one of these photographs in my letter saying that we had taken her past complaint so seriously we were replacing everything in the hotel. I also asked her to stay in touch with us and if and when we were able to reopen, I would be happy to accommodate them. As far as I know, we never heard from her again.

****

Three weeks after Hurricane Frances had passed through, we braced ourselves for Hurricane Jeanne. This one made landfall almost exactly at the same place as Frances, just south of us at Stuart. During the first storm, Anita and I took shelter in the small hallway between our second and third bedroom along with our pillows, bottled water, a flashlight and a battery-operated portable radio. A bathroom separated the two bedrooms so this was easily available to us as well. For Hurricane Jeanne, a single lady, recently widowed and living directly across the street, invited us and another neighborhood couple to ride out the storm with her. Being good friends, being together, provided comfort for all of us.

Again, our area took practically a direct hit. When the eye of the storm passed through, and we had a momentary calm, I ran across the street in the rain to assess any additional damage we might have incurred. Our roof had lost more shingles but, using my flashlight, I was relieved that I could not see any water damage. We had been most fortunate to engage an aluminum contractor to remove the wrecked patio just a couple of days before Jeanne arrived. As you can imagine, house contractors were in high demand. Anyway, we were safe and the damage could have been much worse. As it was, we were without power for 18 of the 30 days in the month.

Out on the island, Jeanne had not done much more physical damage to the hotel than Frances had. The problem was that we had spent the previous three weeks doing extensive cleanup work not knowing that we would be hit again. Now we had to start all over again. One of the most interesting things I noticed when I first arrived back at the hotel, was a huge mound of live land crabs mingled with sand piled up against the two doors leading to the banquet rooms on the lower level. They were quite scary as they only have one huge claw and they appeared quite hostile.

At the request of our insurance company, we made arrangements to have the two roofs on our guest room buildings replaced (at a cost of $260,000). Of course, roofers were at a premium then but, thankfully, we contracted with one who did an excellent job for us. Our downtown property had survived relatively unscathed and was actually completely full of local residents who had left their homes seeking shelter. There had been a loss of power in the area but it was restored quickly. I think the cooked breakfast I had there one morning was the best I had ever enjoyed. There was a lot going on.

Back out at Oceanside, we were focused on a massive cleanup in all departments. I spent a lot of time with the insurance adjusters preparing to re-open at some point. They recommended a restoration company to assist our local contractor in drying out the hotel and we proceeded with their recommendation. It was a painful time, as it became more and more apparent that, if we were going to re-open, it would take a long time. We had to let most of our employees go, many of whom had been there longer than the 14 years I was there. My secretary, Susan Jensen, and I continued to operate out of the lounge; Carol Appel, our controller continued to operate out of her office on the lower level; and Genter and a few others stayed on in the maintenance department to help with the cleanup.

Personally, I had hoped we would be able to do a complete restoration and apply for a designation as a Holiday Inn Hotel and Suites. We already had three suites which had been closed off to create a small foyer with a separate living room and bedroom. These could connect to a second bedroom if needed. I would have used the same format on the other five corridors and converted all the top floor rooms into suites. If these units could have been then sold as condominiums, I believed, with that income plus a considerable insurance settlement, we could probably reopen without any further outlay of funds. It would still have given us total control of almost 75% of our existing inventory, even if the condominiums were not all turned over into our rental pool. Still, this concept was not seriously investigated and no pro forma was developed. Mr. Duncan was not in the best of health and I felt the company had no appetite for pursuing their interest in the hospitality business.

Finally, about a year after Hurricane Jeanne, the oceanside hotel was sold 'as is' in a completely stripped down condition. All framed interior walls were removed, as was all electrical and plumbing so that only the concrete and block walls remained. We had transferred all linens, china, glass, supplies and silverware to our downtown location as well as our beer, wine and liquor inventory and non-perishable food items. It was indeed a sad ending after 30 wonderful years as one of Martin County's primary lodging facilities. So many area residents and local business people had used us when relocating and we had hosted numerous local meetings, wedding receptions and other events.

The Holiday Inn Downtown had long been threatened with being dropped from the Holiday Inn system. While we had regularly received high guest comment scores and had been recognized with the annual Quality Excellence Award on several occasions, it was an older exterior corridor property which the brand was trying to discontinue. Once this was confirmed, I set about looking at other potential brands and determined that, if we would be accepted, the Best Western flag would be the most beneficial. There was no other Best Western hotel in our immediate market area and being a membership association rather than a brand franchise, I estimated that we could save approximately $250,000 a year by not having to pay royalty fees. The brand still offered all the essential reservations, marketing and support services we would need. Ultimately, overseeing this conversion was the last major influence I had as director of operations.

It was during this last year of my being gainfully employed, that I toyed with the idea of spending a few more years in circulation as a consultant. I am certainly not the first person to do this to bridge the gap before becoming fully retired. A local developer, Marty Tabor, whom I had met previously, discussed with me the possibility of developing a hotel on a prime site he owned at the Stuart exit off Interstate 95. I felt it was an ideal location for a limited service property and after evaluating other existing brands in the immediate area, we determined that a Hampton Inn would be the preferred flag for the site.

I contacted their franchise department and we met with the company's representative for this area of Florida who agreed with our evaluation. Tabor completed the franchise application, in which I was included as the selected management entity, and with a $50,000 application fee, it was submitted to the Hampton Inn head office. This would be an exciting project and a perfect activity at this stage of my life.

I spoke with our attorney, Buddy Googe, about my involvement with this project and he recommended that I become a limited liability corporation (LLC) so that I would have some legal status in the event I was to take on any future projects. He filed this application with the state on my behalf.

The site included considerably more land than the hotel would need and Marty had an overall commercial master plan conceived for the balance of the acreage. However, shortly after we had put the wheels in motion, representatives of a New England based hotel company met with the Martin County Economic Development staff inquiring about opportunities for the development of a hotel site. Obviously, the staff knew Marty Tabor and his ownership of this piece of property and they put these representatives in touch with him. I was not privy to any discussions they had but the result was that Marty sold them the site that we were planning to develop as the Hampton Inn and they subsequently developed a Courtyard by Marriott there. That concluded my involvement. At this point I was approaching 70 and felt it was time to start enjoying retirement.

The Duncan family was wonderful to me and I finally retired from their employment on November 30, 2005, 52 years and three months after I first set foot in the Westminster College Hotel School in Vincent Square to begin the hotel operations course in September 1953.

Looking back on my 52 years in this business, I don't think I appreciated all the many and varied experiences I had at the time they were happening. As challenges came into view, we tackled them the best we could, whether they were business related or family decisions. It is really only now, as I look back, that I fully appreciate the tremendous opportunities I have been given, the wonderful life I have been so privileged to live and the many, many friends I have made along the way. To have had the opportunity to live and work in London, Paris, New York, South America and many parts of the United States has given me countless happy and priceless memories. And my association with SKAL International, has allowed me to travel to parts of the world about which one can only dream. I have been truly blessed, and I sincerely believe that merely being in the right place at the right time is not a fluke. All these things don't just happen. We may not understand it all, but I truly believe there is a plan that is made for us. I think I would have enjoyed the challenge of getting into the development side of the hotel business when Preston Hicks, Bert Deluca and I had successfully acquired the site in Port St. Lucie and maybe there is a twinge of regret that I never really had the chance to do this. However, when I consider that, indeed, I did have a certain amount of uncertainty when I chose this career, if I was to ask myself, "Would I do it all over again?" Absolutely, without any hesitation.

Key to Success #15

Network: *Be involved in your local community, such as the Convention and Visitors Bureau, Chamber of Commerce, Rotary, etc. This is very important. You cannot move the hotel or restaurant-but locals almost always have an alternative. Your property should be their first choice.*

15. A Look Back: Associations and Community Involvement

During my career, I was a member of several industry related associations. While I was in Arizona, I was active in both the statewide Arizona Hotel and Motel Association and the Valley Innkeepers Association, the members of the latter being limited to hotels and resorts operating in the immediate Phoenix metropolitan area. I served on the boards of both. In December 1974, I was fortunate enough to be invited by Phoenix Mayor Tim Barrow to serve on a select Ad Hoc Interim Executive Committee with several of my peers to do a complete review of the Phoenix Convention Bureau. This was done based on a report conducted by the International Association of Convention and Visitors Bureaus. It meant putting everything together from scratch, including a comprehensive review of the existing by-laws and scope of the organization, as it would relate to the surrounding cities. This required a critical review of the roles and responsibilities of the board of directors and administrative staff, analysis of the composition and industry representation of the board, and a review of compensation levels for the administrative personnel. We were also asked to put together the financial plan including revenue sources, membership fee structure and a budget. In addition, we were charged with recruiting an executive director. This whole process was not only a huge privilege but also a priceless learning experience.

When I returned to Florida in 1976, I was invited to join the board of the Florida Hotel and Motel Association at the tail end of the Board's lobbying for the Local Option Tourist Development Tax Act. This Act was originally intended to create a vehicle for individual counties to generate revenue for marketing and promotion for tourism development. This passed the state legislature with specific guidelines and, while the aim was to regenerate tourism, as we now know, most counties which adopted this tax, have misused it. Many have since lobbied for amendments to the Act to permit spending for numerous other causes, which do not necessarily accomplish the original goal. I guess that's what they call politics.

Martin County, where I was situated with the two Holiday properties, did not have a tourist development, or 'bed' tax as it is often called, and I got myself into a compromising and difficult situation.

I was president of the Martin County Hotel and Motel Association and, because we could see how other counties were abusing the original intent of the tax, we decided to create our own funding source for promoting tourism for Martin County. This would allow us total control regarding how these funds were spent. All primary accommodations facilities would need to agree and, after extensive discussions, we decided we would add a $1.00 per night per room charge to every arrival. It would be a voluntary fee and a lot less than a 'bed tax' would have been. A guest checking in to one of our hotels would be told of this fee and advised of their option to decline it. If the guest agreed, the fee would be applied when the room rate and applicable taxes were posted. Appropriate notices were printed and placed at the front desks and in all guest rooms. It seemed like a good idea.

It started out well but it would take a year to accumulate adequate funds to put a marketing plan into action. After several months, with a high acceptance rate, we had collected just over $160,000. Just about the time we had reached that level, a guest staying at one of the county's resorts, questioned the $3.00 charge on his bill as he checked out following his three-night stay. He was given the proper explanation and the hotel had the signage posted, as we had agreed. It turned out that he was an attorney with the Medicare Fraud Division of the state attorney's office and he took exception to what we were doing. I will not take you through the whole process but, as president of the association and a full participant, I was served to appear at the state attorney's office in Tallahassee. Faced with this new development, I needed legal advice and consulted our own Stuart-based attorney, Buddy Googe.

It was an interesting day, to say the least. Buddy and I appeared at the appointed time and spoke with three representatives of the state's attorney's office. I explained my background, what we were doing, and how our actions were, in fact, more honest than the abused Florida Tourist Development Tax. It was to no avail. They didn't give an inch. The key sticking point was that a potential guest had to be notified of this optional fee when they made their reservation. That, of course, would have been practically impossible given the large number of available reservations sources. They threatened to levy a six-figure fine on me personally. How they ever came to a figure like that, I have no idea.

After the meeting, we went immediately to Hospitality Square, headquarters of the Florida Hotel and Motel Association, to advise our president, Tom Waits, of this development. It had been a rough morning and Tom's suggestion to treat us to lunch in Doak Campbell Stadium's private dining room didn't help. That was Florida State University's storied football field and Buddy was an avid University of Florida "Gator", their in-state archrival. At the most recent meeting of their football teams, Florida State had beaten the University of Florida. If that wasn't bad enough for Buddy, this beautiful tiered restaurant was looking down field straight at the scoreboard and the score was still up there. This wasn't a good day for either one of us.

Fortunately, we had a good friend in government in Tallahassee, State Senator Ken Pruitt. He was highly respected and became president of the Florida senate in 2006. While we were waiting for our connecting flight in Orlando, we called Ken and explained our situation. Thankfully, he understood our predicament and assured us he would do what he could. That was the call that helped us – or I should say helped me. It took a few days but eventually Ken came back to us and said we had to immediately cease the practice, if indeed we were still doing it. He advised us the penalties would be waived but we had to divest ourselves of the funds we had acquired. He told us half of what we had, just over $80,000, should go to the local YMCA to support the building of a new swimming pool in Indiantown and the other half to another local charity. What we thought was a great creative idea to develop tourism for Martin County came to naught. It was worth a try and it did at least bring the county-wide hotel community together.

****

During the fifteen years I spent at the Holiday Inn Oceanside, I was involved in a number of organizations. One of these was the

Martin County Chapter of the Tallahassee-based Florida Shore and Beach Preservation Association. Obviously, because of our location, maintaining a good clean, attractive beach was absolutely critical. With the passage of time, there had been significant beach erosion, much of which was caused by the various tropical storms and hurricanes to which Florida is most vulnerable. This problem also affected the property values of the many condominiums on the island so we had a small but active committee to work at protecting this vital asset. It was not a simple matter, as the federal government, Florida and Martin County all played a role in accomplishing any beach re-nourishment project. Funding was a critical issue and permitting from the U.S. Army Corps of Engineers was always a long and drawn-out process. I got to know the principle players important to getting these projects accomplished and during my time there we were successful in getting two beach re-nourishment projects completed. In 2002, I was honored by the state association with the Member of the Year Award, having been nominated by Ann Decker, district manager for Congressman Mark Foley (see letter in Appendix II).

****

In the early 1990's, the only tourism marketing being done in Martin County was on an individual hotel/resort basis. A few of us got together and formed the Hutchinson Island Tourism Development Committee (HITDC) to develop various cooperative marketing efforts. While the hotels and condo rentals would be the primary beneficiaries of any successful effort; the restaurants, bars, retail outlets, banks, water-related attractions and others would also benefit. The group grew to almost fifty members and collectively produced and distributed a four-color brochure, a billboard campaign for some key locations on the Florida Turnpike, and some travel agent familiarization (fam) trips. With several participants sharing the costs, this was generally affordable and fairly effective. After Martin County passed the bed tax and established the Martin County Convention and Visitors Bureau (CVB), our small association was disbanded. I was involved with the creation of the new CVB and, serving as treasurer, made many appearances before our county commission.

One of our HITDC members brought to our attention a sports festival that was being promoted by a destination like ours on the west coast of Florida. After looking at what they were doing, we decided to develop a similar event on Hutchinson Island, but primarily based on water sports. After all, we had the great expanse of the Indian River Lagoon, the St. Lucie River and easy access to the Atlantic Ocean. We decided to develop and promote an Annual Hutchinson Island Water Sports Festival during the mid-season in October. This is typically one of the best weather-related times of the year with lower temperatures and humidity, and a diminished threat of storms. Hotels needed more occupancy and restaurants too could use additional business. We contacted the operators of various water sports related attractions in the area and they were enthusiastic to participate.

However, as it turned out, the water sports festival concept never became reality, because our efforts eventually morphed into a full-fledged sports commission. During this time, we were being contacted by operators of other sports activities and this brought Tom Colucci to the table. Tom was an avid sports enthusiast and very heavily involved in basketball tournaments. His input was invaluable and helped enormously in taking our original plan to a much higher level.

Many meetings were taking place and as the ideas grew, it was felt that we could make this a much more effective effort by collaborating with St. Lucie and Indian River counties to the north of us. Martin County was working towards a referendum on a Tourist Development Tax but the other counties already had this established with a staffed tourism office and a budget for tourism development.

As part of our planning process we contacted Jimmy Carnes, executive director of the Florida Governor's Council on Physical Fitness and Sports. He met with us and offered many good suggestions and the support of his office (see letter in Appendix II) This all led to the creation of the Treasure Coast Sports Commission charged with the responsibility of attracting sporting events to the tri-county area. It was a bit of a struggle at first but eventually became established with Tom Colucci as our first executive director. I sat on the board up until the time I retired.

During this period, I also took on the creation of the Tri-County Holiday Inn Scholarship to assist in supporting our local college. The Indian River State College had its primary campus in Fort Pierce in St. Lucie County with satellite facilities in Martin, Indian River and Okeechobee counties. There were six franchised Holiday Inn brand hotels in the four-county area with a total of 777 rooms. I contacted all the general managers and suggested that we divide the number of rooms into the cost of a year's tuition and books and share the cost accordingly. The idea was well received and while we preferred the recipient to be a hospitality industry student, we always accepted the college's recommendations. The letters we received every year from the recipients expressing their appreciation were our reward. Overall, this was a great return on a very modest investment.

****

Among my longest affiliations, dating from 1968 to the present, was with SKAL International. When I was transferred from Suriname to take over as general manager of the Executive House in Scottsdale, I was invited to 'inherit' the membership of Joe McGovern, my predecessor at the hotel. Hal Gamble, a club member and co-owner of Halabill Travel Agency, called me and suggested I become a member. I was not familiar with SKAL but was advised it was an international association of travel industry executives, with a worldwide membership. The international headquarters at that time was in Brussels and, even today, it is the only association of its kind, which brings together executives from all segments of the tourism and travel industry. Several years ago, the headquarters was moved to Torremolinos, Spain. I later learned that each prospective member is supposed to present certain travel industry qualifications and be vetted before being invited. This procedure was not followed in my case. However, I did qualify as general manager of a hotel, so this was no real issue.

My first meeting was in September 1968 at Dale Anderson's, one of the most popular restaurants in Scottsdale. We were in a small private room, thank goodness, and the attendees were quite boisterous, to say the least. At one point, they were throwing bread rolls at one another and constantly calling on each other to say the SKAL toast, whatever that was. If a member could not do it correctly, they were immediately shouted down and fined. It all seemed uncivilized and unprofessional to me. I immediately wrote it off as an organization in which I would have any interest in belonging. Little did I know then, that 21 years later, I would be elected the national president.

Despite this dismal first impression, I continued to attend the monthly meetings. I got to know many of my Arizona tourism peers based in the Phoenix and Scottsdale area and many became good friends. In 1974, I was appointed as vice president of the Phoenix club and then was elected President for the 1975/76 administrative year. The members really were a terrific bunch of guys and, because we all came from different segments of the travel and tourism industry, our friendships led to many excellent business partnerships and often some personal perks, frequently on a reciprocal basis. One of our fun events was a joint meeting with the members of the Tucson Club. When we went there, our member Bobby Cox of Tanner Gray Lines generously provided a bus and, furnished with appropriately stocked ice coolers in the back, we merrily proceeded on the road trip south. When it was our turn to return the hospitality, I hosted the event while I was at the Carefree Inn. We always tried to outdo one another with the dinner menus and overall presentations so, once again, I suffered some light-hearted humiliation when a little field mouse started running around our banquet room during the meal. The Tucson bunch never let me forget it, and the following year when we re-visited them, they presented our club with a unique 'mouse' award trophy dutifully acknowledging our club's excellence in providing the unscheduled entertainment.

In December 1976, we moved back to Florida when I took over as general manager of Sandpiper Bay. At that point, I was anxious to continue my affiliation, if possible. I was happy to learn that a club was being formed in Palm Beach under the guiding hand of

Charlie Matthews of Eastern Airlines, who had been a member of SKAL for many years. I contacted him, and was welcomed into the group while the club went through the required formation procedures. We soon received our charter, and officially became Club No. 427 on March 4, 1977. Having shepherded our club through the development phase, Charlie turned the presidency over to Paul Bell of National Airlines who would serve for our first two years. Our formal installation banquet, with spouses, was a beautiful black tie affair held at the magnificent Breakers Hotel in Palm Beach on May 28th, 1977.

Because I had been a member of SKAL for almost nine years and had recently gone through the chairs of the Phoenix Club, I was elected to succeed Paul and served as president for the 1979/80 year. I was also asked to represent the club at the 1979 Annual International SKAL Congress being hosted in Germany by the Berlin Club. This was my first exposure to the impressive international presence of SKAL. With the worldwide association having membership in well over 80 countries, the official languages used in our meetings were English, Spanish and French. We used simultaneous translations in all general assembly meetings, rather like a mini United Nations. It was a unique experience indeed, as it facilitated meeting many travel professionals from all parts of the world. I developed many close friendships along the way.

The event was held in the huge Berlin Congress Center and had close to 2,000 participants. Following one morning session, the photographs taken at earlier sessions were posted in a reception area prior to the planned luncheon, in a similar way as they are on cruise ships. There were many to look at and I got carried away looking for the ones of Anita and me. At some point, I looked around and everyone was gone and it was completely quiet. I knew they must have gone to where the lunch was scheduled, but where was that? I went up and down a series of escalators and along several wide corridors, but no luck. How could I lose 2,000 people? There should be a noise from somewhere. There was not even anyone around to ask. I did find them, eventually, but must have wandered aimlessly for at least 20 minutes. They were about half way through their lunch by the time I found a place to sit down.

I went on to serve as our club's national representative in 1981, 1982 and 1983 when I was then encouraged to run for vice president of Region IV. This region represented clubs in the southeastern part of the United States. Puerto Rico, St. Thomas and St. Croix. I won the election and I will return to this a little later.

****

With our new Palm Beach club emerging, we were always looking for suitable venues to host our monthly dinner meetings. Sandpiper Bay Resort had a lot to offer but we were a good hour's drive from many of the members' locations. So instead of offering to host one of the monthly mid-week meetings, I suggested we host the June 1978 meeting over a weekend to allow spouses and children to attend. Our club was quite small, having just 23 members, and I offered everyone complimentary rooms with free golf and tennis. We had 276 rooms and, at the time I made the invitation, very little business was booked in the hotel.

I thought it might be fun to have a golf tournament. However, with our small membership and only a handful of those being golfers, there would not be sufficient players to make it a 'tournament'. I thought, *why not invite some of the Miami members to play?* This seemed like a good idea, so I called Karl Pfistner, the executive secretary-treasurer of their club and extended the invitation. He too thought it would be good to bring several members of both clubs together for a weekend. He then put out the invitation to his club, which at that time had over 130 members. As it turned out, this was received with enthusiasm and I responded to many telephone calls asking about the arrangements. Having already offered complimentary rooms for our own club members, it would be difficult to charge the Miami members, so I confirmed that I would be happy to offer the same deal to them. This made it even more attractive and it generated even more interest. No problem; we still had plenty of open rooms available.

One morning, as this was taking shape, I received a call from Bill Graves, district sales manager for Delta Airlines in Central Florida. He was an avid golfer and a member of the Orlando club. "Pullen, I hear you have a golf tournament coming up soon. Can anyone join in?"

"Yes, Bill," I said. "We'd love to have you."

"What about other golfers in our club? I know we have a few who would be interested."

What was I going to say? "Of course, put out the word and see how many would be interested."

"What's the deal? I know they will ask." He inquired.

"Well, I am offering comp rooms, free golf and tennis and, because it's over a weekend, families are invited. I have a great activities director who will put together some fun stuff for the kids. We've already invited the Miami Club." More comp rooms. I was beginning to wonder where this was going.

There were two other Florida-based SKAL clubs, one in Jacksonville and one in the Tampa area. Together they had about 100 members. What the heck! I might just as well throw it open to them as well and make it a statewide event. I called the clubs' presidents, Gene Wieneke of Eastern Airlines in Jacksonville and Finley Myers of the St. Petersburg Motor Club, and told them what we were doing. They both thought it was a great idea and said they would pass the information along to their members.

If you ever want to spur on your sales department, start giving the rooms away. As luck would have it, they started booking some small summer groups, mostly social events, and we were beginning to fill up. I was becoming a little concerned, not quite knowing how my boss, Frank Widmann at the corporate office in Miami, would react if we started to turn away paying customers because I had given away so many rooms.

It turned out to be an outstanding weekend for all our SKAL members and their families. We had about 250 people attending our awards banquet on Saturday evening and I ended up comping 96 rooms. We came within less than ten rooms of selling out. At the banquet, Bill Perry, the president of the Miami Club, stood up and said, "This has been so great, we'll host this event next year in Miami." He got a huge round of applause. We had started something.

Widmann was an old-school sales and marketing hotel man. Thank goodness. Our daily summary reports for the weekend were sent in on Monday and I knew I would be hearing from him. As I expected, Tuesday morning my phone rang.

"Pullen, I guess it's not too difficult to get 100% occupancy when you give 100 rooms away!"

"Yes, Frank. It was a good weekend," I said confidently. "I know I comped a lot of rooms but they were all industry people and having changed the name of the resort from the Hilton to Sandpiper Bay, we need to get the word out as soon as we can. It was really no different than having a fam trip." (I knew he would appreciate that.) Nothing more was said.

However, not surprisingly, Bill Perry and the boys in Miami couldn't find a resort to match what we had done, when it came their turn. In a difficult spot, he called me to see what I thought about them acting as hosts, but holding it again at Sandpiper. I said I would, but I would have to charge for rooms this time if I wanted to keep my job. I put a $25 rate on the rooms for the 1979 event, so nothing showed up in the 'complimentary' column on the daily report. Again, it was successful and it continued as an annual summer event in Florida for 35 years, with the different clubs hosting it on a rotating basis. The original golf club team trophy kept getting bigger and bigger as more bases were added to it over the years. The event also attracted several national and international officers on many occasions.

By now SKAL was well and truly in my blood and as vice president for Region IV, I maintained contact with many of the regional members. When possible, I would visit them, usually once a year to install the club's new officers. There were also a few occasions when a club visit was needed to address a specific issue. One of these concerned the club of St. Croix.

One of my duties was to be sure that the clubs in my region filed their monthly reports. These reports provided insight as to whether the club was functioning properly; and would often signal possible need for follow-up and assistance. In the case of the St. Croix Club, I was having a very difficult time getting their officers to fulfill this simple requirement and it eventually became necessary to place the club on suspension. This formally established the issues involved and put the club on notice. To return to good standing, they would have to make the required corrections. Our national president, Schuy Lininger of the Tucson club, and I scheduled a meeting with the club's officers at Club Comanche on the picturesque waterfront in Christiansted.

This wasn't my first visit to the St. Croix club. During my annual visit the previous year they had scheduled a joint dinner meeting with the St. Thomas SKAL Club at the St. Thomas Yacht Club. The new president of the St. Croix Club, Tony Collins, was a gregarious British fellow whose business was running coral reef tours to the Buck Island Reef National Monument from his 42-foot catamaran, the Jolly Roger. He had invited their members to join him, and a young man he had lined up to be the crew, for the sail over to St. Thomas. I had arrived the day before and had performed the function of installing the new officers the previous evening. We were to depart from the Christiansted dock at noon.

This annual visit to the Caribbean covered the clubs in Puerto Rico, St. Thomas and St. Croix. They would try to schedule these events back-to-back so that my travel expenses could be minimized. Even though these venues were known for their great vacation amenities, I was there on business, and my expenses were being paid for by our national committee. I, along with my suitcase, was at the dock a good fifteen minutes early, waiting for whoever was coming with us. The first to arrive was the young man whom Tony had hired to crew the Jolly Roger, along with two young ladies. He did not introduce them but it seemed they were coming with us. Soon other members of the club arrived and just after noon, we set sail for St. Thomas. For me this was a special treat.

"About how long does this usually take?" I asked Tony.

"It shouldn't be more than about four hours but it will depend a bit on the wind," he answered. "Help yourself to a beer or soda from the coolers. We also have some good Cruzan rum."

This was going to be fun. It was somewhere around two o'clock when St. Croix disappeared below the horizon and no other land was in sight. Everyone was relaxing, taking in the sun and enjoying the libations. The two girls, still not properly introduced, had removed the tops of their bikinis, getting the full benefit of the sun. Three o'clock came and I guessed we would soon be able to see St. Thomas, but no land was visible yet. Everyone was having a good time and there were many photographs being taken. The drinks were beginning to have some effect.

"Who are the girls?" I asked Tony.

"The fellow I asked to come along as my crew told me he met them in a bar in town last evening. He told them we would be making this trip and invited them to come along. I think they came in on your flight. They're here on vacation."

"Shouldn't we be seeing St. Thomas about now?" I asked. I was just beginning to be a little concerned.

"Soon," he said. "There's not much wind so we are going to be a little later than I expected. We are going to have to tack and see if we can speed up a bit."

At this point, the crew was not 'crewing' but engaged in socializing with members of the St. Croix club. I was standing next to Tony and, not really having a nautical bone in my body, I asked him what he meant by 'tacking'. We were standing near the stern, or as I called it, 'the blunt end', and Tony was holding the long metal bar, which was attached to the two rudders of the twin hulls.

"You kind of zigzag into the breeze to pick up as much of the wind as you can." he answered. As he went off to get another beer. I took over the tiller.

This was all new territory for me but what the heck. After all, I was the only person on the boat who was *supposed* to be working! I zigzagged, as I thought I should, and no one seemed to even notice. I must be doing a great job, I thought to myself.

Four o'clock, and still there was no land in sight. I was the only one on board who seemed to care. *Weren't we supposed to be there by now?* Still topless, the girls were now up and happily being photographed with the passengers. Someone dropped a bucket on a rope over the side and threw the contents over whoever was close by. Great fun! Someone else thought this was a good idea and followed suit, fortunately still holding on to the bucket.

Wind, wind, where are you? Finally, land ho! Over to the right. I turned the rudders to this new direction. I was beginning to feel a bit better now. After about twenty minutes, Tony came over and said, "I don't think that's St. Thomas."

"If it's not St. Thomas, where is it?" I pleaded.

"It must be St. John. We need to go back that way." he answered, pointing to the left.

I yanked the bar which I was *still* holding tightly and pointed the catamaran in the direction he had indicated. By around six o'clock St. Thomas, thankfully, came into view. The wind had picked up a little so we were going a bit faster.

"We won't have time to go around to Charlotte Amalie", Tony said. "We'll probably have to go in to Red Hook." That didn't mean much to me but at least he seemed to know where we were. Sure enough, around seven o'clock we pulled into a marina at Red Hook. It was completely full and the only space we could find was at the gas dock. In the meantime, the crew had returned to work, did the final maneuvering and we tied up. Phew! Our next challenge was to get to the St. Thomas Yacht Club. The cocktail reception had already begun and I am sure the St. Thomas members wondered if their St. Croix colleagues were ever going to show up. There were no cell phones in those days.

Fortunately, there were a couple of small Volkswagen busses close by and with instructions to go to the yacht club, off we went. I was staying in St. Thomas overnight before leaving for Puerto Rico the next day but I had no idea how the others had planned to get back to St. Croix. Maybe they planned to sail back in the dark?

Even though this annual ritual of installing the new officers was considered one of the more important annual club occasions, here it was by no means a formal affair. We were, after all, in the islands. Our group must have been quite a sight, having the alcohol in our insides and the salt water on our outsides as we dragged ourselves into the reception. I was able to change into something more appropriate for the occasion. The 'crew' and his lady friends headed off into town and were never seen again.

Now back to the important, serious stuff.

Schuy and I were now seated at a long table in a small private room of the Club Comanche. I was at one end, Collins, now representing the St. Croix Club at the other end, with Schuy in the center of one side. He opened the meeting by stating the reasons for our visit and emphasizing the importance of keeping a proper record of the club's activities. This was by no means an adversarial meeting. After all, one could not know a nicer group of tourism colleagues than this close-knit group in St. Croix. Still, business is business and they needed to do a better job. Tony spoke up. "OK, I understand that Bill and the other national board officers feel that we don't keep a record of our meetings. Is that right?"

"Yes." Schuy answered. "We are not asking much but we do need you to follow the basic criteria for running a club."

"I understand," said Tony. "Would you mind passing this envelope down to Bill?"

A manila envelope was passed down the table until it reached me. I opened it and immediately saw a contact sheet containing several photographs immortalizing our infamous travels to the joint meeting the year before. These included a few shots of our two topless companions in a variety of poses and I was in a few of them.

"Bill," Tony went on, grinning broadly. "Those are only prints. We still have the negatives. How can you come all this way, sit there and have the nerve to tell us we don't keep a record of our meetings?" He had made his point!

With a great deal of hilarity and promises from the club to do better, Schuy and I took our leave. At least, we had made our point. But so had they!

****

Our national committee held quarterly board meetings at venues around the country hosted by the local clubs. We would be expected to attend our North American congresses, which rotated between venues in Canada, Mexico, the U.S. and what were known as the Affiliated clubs in our geographic area. This provided the opportunity to visit places I would probably not have visited otherwise. While most of our time was spent in meetings, the hosts always made every effort to show off their destination in a true tourism-marketing manner. Spousal programs allowed for even more exposure in this regard.

It was the opportunity to attend the annual international congresses, which gave birth to a completely unexpected turn of events in my life. I attended ten of these, which included the one in Berlin, plus those held in Johannesburg, Las Vegas, Paris, Jerusalem, Puerto Rico, Vienna, Vancouver, Colombo, and Munich. I also attended mid-year meetings of the international council in Mar del Plata, Southern Argentina, and in Panama City, Panama.

However, it was the congress in Colombo, Sri Lanka in October 1990, which added a totally new and unanticipated dimension to my life.

It Started at The Savoy

Key to Success #16

Evaluate: *Using the rooming list, try to evaluate those attending a group booking. A potential client may already be staying at your hotel. As an example: One time our resort was hosting a national brand company and those attending included presidents of five different divisions. By being attentive to who was already in our hotel, we booked future meetings of two of these divisions without doing potentially expensive sales calls.*

16. An Unexpected Turn: Sri Lanka

My dear wife, Anita, was Roman Catholic and while we were in Arizona, she became familiar with the work of the Secular Order of Discalced Carmelites (OCDS). She was both an active supporter of their mission and an OCDS lay person right up until the time she passed away. The word "discalced" is derived from Latin, meaning "without shoes". These nuns live in cloistered convents and dedicate themselves to a life of prayer and poverty.

In February 1990, Anita attended a meeting in Port St. Lucie where she and other members of her community were learning how to make rosaries. It was there she met Jesse Benedict, a lady who, indirectly, was going to change my life. Jesse was from Trincomalee, on the northeastern coast of Sri Lanka, which has one of the finest natural deep-water harbors in the world. Unfortunately, it was also an area that was heavily involved in what became a 25-year civil war (1983–2009) between government forces and the Tamil Tigers.

During their initial conversation, Anita told her that I would be going to Sri Lanka later in the year to attend a meeting in Colombo.

"Do you think your husband would mind taking a package over there for me?" Jesse asked.

"I'm sure he'd be only too pleased," Anita replied. "The only thing is he won't be going until the end of October and this is February. Wouldn't it be better and faster for you to mail it?"

"No, it is really important to me that it gets there but there is no hurry. The package will contain several rosaries and some rosary making kits. If he could deliver it to a Carmelite convent in Colombo, the sisters will be able to get it to St. Joseph Convent in Trincomalee. Some of the sisters there are friends of mine."

"Well, let's stay in touch and when you are ready, get the package to me, and I'll see that he takes it. He will need the address of the convent."

I was certainly happy to help her with this mission, and when October came around, I secured her package carefully in my luggage.

Sri Lanka, formerly known as Ceylon when it was under the British, is the teardrop-shaped island off the southern tip of India. It is almost half way around the world from the east coast of the United States. The local time there is ten and a half hours ahead of Florida. I flew from Florida to London and took a Sri Lankan Airways flight from London to Colombo with a refueling stop in Dubai. We did not have a long wait there and the time passed all too quickly as I was in awe of the airport's duty-free shop. I had never seen automobiles in an airport shop before and, if I had had room in my luggage, I might have been tempted to buy a Mercedes!

The flight was enjoyable, as several SKAL members, all bound for Colombo, met up in London from various originating cities and were seated in the same area on the plane. We arrived in Colombo in the pre-dawn hours and were met by several members of the Colombo club and efficiently whisked away to the Colombo Hilton Hotel, the headquarters hotel for the Congress. Everyone was tired from the long journey and, thankfully, our rooms were ready. (It was somewhere between 6 and 7 am.) After getting settled, I took the Colombo phone book out of the bedside table and found the number for the convent but it was still too early to call. I resisted the temptation to lie down, afraid I might fall into a deep sleep. Instead, I busied myself organizing my papers for the upcoming meetings and reading the in-room material about this fascinating country. Around nine o'clock I dialed the number. The phone was answered promptly but the first two ladies I spoke with did not understand English. However, the third person did and she turned out to be Sister Constantia, the provincial superior. I explained who I was and why I was calling, but she was naturally rather suspicious. As we continued to speak, she appeared less uneasy and suggested I meet with her at the convent at two o'clock that afternoon.

In Colombo, all the major hotels had dedicated cars and drivers and, well before my appointment time, I took one of those to the convent. The driver was fluent in English and navigated through the crazy traffic with exceptional skill. He pointed out the Colombo cricket ground as we went by. In years past I had listened to radio broadcasts from there when England played Sri Lanka in one of the international test matches, never imagining that I would ever be anywhere near there. A little less than half an hour later, we entered the Borella district and arrived at the convent on Ananda Rajakaruna Mawatha, a rather narrow street. The gates were open and, as we pulled up to the entrance, I was met by two of the sisters. I am sure they were curious to see this foreigner and to learn more about the nature of my visit. Sister Constantia had brought along Sister Stella Maria, the principal of the school on the adjacent property next to the All Saints Church. They courteously escorted me into a small comfortable reception area. I had never been inside a convent before.

I handed Jesse Benedict's package to Sister Constantia with a full explanation of how it all came to pass and how Anita was a dedicated secular Discalced Carmelite. At this point, any suspicion about my visit dissipated, and they were absolutely charming. Sister Constantia assured me the package would be safely delivered to the St. Joseph Convent in Trincomalee. They asked me to express their sincere gratitude to Jesse for her concern and thoughtfulness.

The sisters offered me some good Sri Lankan tea, and small cookies and then went on to explain the work done by their order. They are essentially a teaching order and work among poor and marginalized children in over 30 communities around the island. They asked me if I would like to see one of these facilities, a small daycare center in an extremely poor neighborhood about a mile or so away from the convent. The driver was still waiting for me and, as I had nothing else scheduled for the rest of the day, I said I would be most interested. The two sisters got in the car with me and gave directions to the driver. We passed through a desperate slum area and arrived at a gated campus with the name Carmel Piyuma in a part of Colombo called Wanathamulla.

We were met by Sister Suzanne, the sister-in-charge, who took us to see the children. The facility was called the Bethlehem Crèche and they were taking care of between 70 and 80 children from as young as three months up to the age of five, all coming from homes, if they could be called "homes", from the local area.

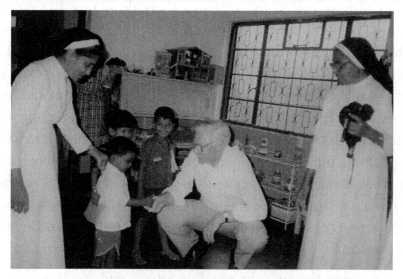

*Sister Suzanne introducing me to some of
the children at the Bethlehem Crèche
daycare facility in Colombo, 1990*

Children of the Bethlehem Crèche

The children were as cute as could be, and their wonderful wide smiles almost belied the truth of their desperate life circumstances. They came from broken homes where the usually absent fathers were mostly drunkards, drug addicts or convicts, and the children were left in the care of the mother, a relative or even just a friend or neighbor. On a typical day, the caregiver would bring the children to the crèche early in the morning and pick them up again later in the afternoon. The sisters and their helpers would bathe them, put them in clean clothes, and spend the day watching over them. The three to five year olds had some nursery school activities. Each child would be given two small cups of milk, one in the morning, one in the afternoon, and a little lunch of some kind.

After walking through the small, spotless and modest facilities and meeting several of the children, we sat and talked. I asked who sponsored this spot of heaven in the middle of this squalid neighborhood. I was told that neither the local nor state government gave them any help and that support from the diocese was minimal. They were almost solely dependent on donations from benefactors. The sisters would also visit the local markets and beg for whatever food items they could get to provide the children's lunch. It made me think of how quickly I spend $5 on a beer without a thought in the world, and yet here that would buy enough powered milk to give all these children their two cups a day. That alone would solve a problem for these sisters. It was indeed a humbling and eye-opening experience.

I should mention that while this is a Roman Catholic order, the children they care for come from all backgrounds. Most are Buddhist but others are Muslim, Hindu and Christian. The latter make up about 8% of the population, of which only a portion are

Catholic.

At the time of my visit, a building was under construction on the same campus which would become a pre-school. It would also serve as an education center where some of the area teenagers would learn English and sewing skills to help them gain future employment. It was being funded by a grant from Norad, a Norwegian agency providing assistance in third world countries. When Ceylon was under the British, English was widely taught and spoken. However, when Sri Lanka became independent, the government decided to make Sinhala their official language, and English was no longer taught in the government schools. Of course, by making this decision, they were essentially shooting themselves in the foot, as English, being the international language that it is, could be critical for those seeking employment. I believe the sisters taught English in all their facilities around the island.

After a while, I bade farewell to Sister Suzanne and returned with Sisters Constantia and Stella Maria to the convent in Borella, again passing through the slum. It was difficult to fully comprehend what I was seeing. It was like something from the pages of National Geographic, but like nothing I had ever seen before. Being so close to this extreme poverty was certainly one of the most emotional experiences of my life. I was still tired from the long travel, the time changes and far from the comforts of the United States. Within just a few hours of my arrival in this strange land, I was in the slum of a country half way around the world. I will never forget the way I felt at that moment. It was as if I was in a dream.

Arriving back at the convent, Sister Constantia turned to me and said, "If you still have time, would you like to see our church? We are very proud of it."

"Yes, I'd be most interested." I replied, as she escorted me over to the main entrance.

"You'll notice the beautiful statues of the saints", she said, pointing towards the ceiling as we entered.

Looking up, I could see the colorful statues positioned all around the walls. The church had large side panels, which secured the building, but when opened, would give the impression of it being an open-air facility.

"And look at this," she went on, as we walked down the center aisle towards the pulpit. "That beautiful picture of our Blessed Mother is made up of many precious and semi-precious stones given by our parishioners. Our country is well known for mining these stones. Many people in our parish are quite poor and often, if they don't have money to put into our collection plates, they give us these instead. From here, you may not realize it but, if you look closer, you can see the colorful jewels." It was indeed a beautiful, unique picture of the Virgin Mary and so precisely made.

"Why don't we take a minute and say a little prayer", she suggested as she knelt in one of the pews.

As I knelt beside her, my brain was totally scrambled. I could hardly think, let alone pray. I simply could not get over where I was, just a few hours after my arrival.

I was raised in the Anglican Church of England, the Episcopal Church in the United States, and for most of my life had been a regular Sunday churchgoer. Still, I would never have considered myself particularly ardent in my faith, albeit always a loyal believer. Without intending to be overly dramatic, I firmly believe I received a divine tap on the shoulder at that moment. On my knees, on the verge of bursting into tears, I distinctly remember saying, *I want to help - I can help - I will help.* I was clearly given those powerful ten words, as I was not able to gather any intelligible thoughts on my own. I could not have foreseen what has taken place since.

****

As the Immediate Past President of the National SKAL Committee of the United States, I was scheduled to attend the Congress. It would have been my last official role at one of these annual meetings. My immediate predecessor, Joe Neary, was a wonderful man and a good friend. He was a member of the New York Club, of which he was a past president. He was now serving as our International Councillor, the official U.S. delegate on the International SKAL Council. This is a body of 51 people representing the worldwide membership. He was active in the car rental industry, and was a marketing executive with Budget Rent-a-Car.

On October 8, 1990, Joe suffered a fatal stroke while raking leaves at his home in Peekskill, north of New York City. His eight-year old niece, Cecilia, was with him when this occurred. She is now one of our trustees. It was just 18 days before he would have left for Sri Lanka to attend the Colombo congress. My role had been to be his deputy, but I was now there to serve in his place on the international council and to serve out the remainder of his two-year term of office. I decided, at that point, that whatever I did to help these children, I was going to dedicate it to Joe's memory. Even my own personal support could be of significant help to Sister Suzanne and her mission.

Two of my friends on the national committee were Liam Sexton and Gene Leonard. Liam was from the Boston club and ran his own travel agency (the Milton Travel Bureau in Milton, Massachusetts). Gene, a member of the Chicago club, was the area manager for Northwest Airlines in Chicago. Both were past presidents of their respective clubs and, not that this was critical in any way, both were Catholic. I felt they would not only be interested in sharing the experience I had, but would perhaps also be a witness to my emotions and my exposure to this extreme poverty. I also wanted to go back a second time after a full night's sleep, to experience it again in a more unemotional way, being better prepared.

Our first official SKAL meeting would not be until the afternoon the day after our arrival, and I suggested we spend the morning essentially the same way I had done the day before. Thankfully, they agreed, and I called Sister Constantia to be sure she would be able to meet with us. It was a repeat of what I had done the day before, but I was able to see it all in a more objective light. Liam and Gene were amazed at the poverty they saw and both agreed we should solicit help from others in our association, and that it was most appropriate to dedicate these efforts to the memory of our recently departed friend, Joe.

As we were leaving the sisters later that morning and saying our 'goodbyes', Sister Constantia pulled me to one side and said, "Thank you, Mr. Pullen. You are truly God-sent."

During the five days of the congress, we talked up our visit to the daycare center, and there was a general feeling of support. One of our members, Bill Hughes from the Vancouver Club in Canada, had a long-running 15-minute travel radio talk show. When he learned of our experience in Colombo, he taped a 15-

minute interview with us and then solicited financial support from his regular listeners. This effort raised $2,584 and by the end of January 1991, we had raised almost $5,000 with only word of mouth solicitation. Other than the three of us, the first donation we received was from an admirable fellow, Omur Caglar, who was there as the international councillor representing the SKAL Clubs of Turkey. He later sent us another donation from the Turkish clubs.

At international congresses, it is customary for attendees to be given gifts; usually items native to the hosting country. In Colombo, the ladies were thrilled to receive a piece of beautiful silk fabric, from which a sari, typical dress in Sri Lanka, could be made. However, after word spread about the sisters teaching sewing skills to the girls in the neighborhood, many decided to donate the silk to the sisters in Wanathamulla. We checked with Sister Suzanne and she was overjoyed with the donation. On our day of departure, the fabric was collected, and our good friend, Cyril Lawrence, congress chairman for the host committee, saw to it that it was delivered. He had been a close friend of Joe Neary, and was tremendously grateful to Joe for the support he had given on behalf of the U.S. clubs, when Colombo was going through the often tough and competitive bidding process for the congress.

While Anita often came with me to these congresses, on this occasion, she had stayed home. I was naturally impatient to tell her about my meeting with the sisters and my amazing experience, so I called her early the following morning, allowing for the time difference. As soon as she answered, I burst into uncontrollable tears. It took me a few minutes to collect myself but I still had a difficult time getting the words out.

"It's OK. Take it slowly." Anita's voice was soothing.

"Well, I delivered Jessie's rosaries as she requested. But I wasn't ready for what happened after that. The sisters took me to a wonderful daycare facility, which they run, but it's in the most unbelievable slum you could imagine. There's about seventy children and they are gorgeous little ones but they come from desperate homes. It's just amazing what the sisters do with so little resources. I'm sure we can help them somehow. I went by myself right after I got here and then Liam and Gene came with me again yesterday. I think we're going to try to get some of the SKAL people to help us and maybe dedicate it to Joe. Even just a little help can go a long way here."

"That sounds unbelievable," Anita said. "Maybe you were meant to be exposed to that. So often these things don't happen by accident. Did you take any pictures?"

"Oh yes, I took quite a few. I can't wait for you to see them. I'll be able to give you a better account of all this when I get back."

Upon returning home, we set up a meeting with Jesse Benedict to assure her that her package had been safely delivered and to show her the photographs I had taken. She was so happy and interested to hear of my visit to the daycare center.

As I write this, it is now over twenty-five years since the first trip to Sri Lanka, and I could never had imagined, in those early days, what this would have become. Without any long-range plan, it seemed, to a great degree, to take on a life of its own.

One of the first things I did was to visit with Father Thomas Rynne, the Pastor of St. Martin de Porres Catholic Church in Jensen Beach. As I started to tell him about my experience, he stopped me abruptly and said, "Come with me, Bill." He took me to a nearby office and introduced me to David Deci, the parish treasurer. Father Rynne had me repeat the reason for my visit, and he immediately approved the parish giving me a quarterly donation. This continued for the next three years. Try as I might, I could not thank him enough. He would often tease me in his strong Irish brogue and say, "You're doing a wonderful thing, Bill. You'll be the first Episcopal pope!"

I then contacted a number of SKAL Clubs, especially those who knew Joe Neary well, and many of the larger U.S. Clubs continue to help us to this day. I approached several local parishes to see if they would put a small announcement in their weekly bulletins and this too generated some welcome donations. A front-page story in the Palm Beach Diocese edition of the Florida Catholic in 1992 was particularly helpful and another in the Palm Beach Post helped enormously to give us some much-needed credibility. As I never wanted to handle donations directly, it was important that they be sent, in their entirety, directly to the sisters in Colombo. This also alleviated the requirement to become a registered charity. There were never any hard-hitting solicitations, and one of the things of which I wanted to be sensitive, especially with the SKAL Clubs, was that we have the Florimond Volckaert Fund, a long-established charity, named after our founding president and supported by all clubs internationally. I certainly did not want to do anything, which could have undermined or even diluted that particular effort.

If I ever doubted that there are indeed guardian angels in our lives, an incident happened shortly after my return from Sri Lanka, which removed all doubt. I had been in touch with the young Carmelite priest who was the spiritual director for the St. Jude Parish High School in Boca Raton in the hope that a freshman class might adopt the children at the Bethlehem Crèche as their charitable project as they go through to their senior year. This was not to be, but he offered an extremely interesting alternative. A good friend of his, Father Matthew Faulkner, was the procurator for the Carmelite Missions of the St. Elias Province in New York. Father Matthew would be coming down to visit them in the near future and he suggested that perhaps we could get together for dinner one evening. The Carmelite missions support many worthy Carmelite projects around the world and he thought Father Matthew might add the sisters in the Sri Lankan Province to the mission's annual distribution of support. Naturally, I was thrilled at this wonderful opportunity and I set a date for Anita and I to go down together.

We left our home in Port St. Lucie in plenty of time and were driving south on Interstate 95. We were almost halfway between Jupiter and West Palm Beach when the car was slowing down even as I was trying to accelerate. I eased over to the emergency lane and stopped. I had no idea what could be wrong and I thought what a terrible time it was for me to have this happen when we had such a promising evening ahead. We had a motor club membership and I called their toll-free number, told them about our problem and gave them our location. The operator put me on hold while she tried to find a towing service in our area.

I was still on hold when a white Ford Pinto station wagon passed us and pulled up just ahead. A youngish fellow got out and walked towards us. His vehicle did not appear to be in particularly good condition, and he looked like he may have come from a construction site. We were a bit apprehensive and felt quite vulnerable sitting where we were. Anita locked her door but put her window down a little as he approached and asked if we needed any help. At this point I hung up, not having heard anything yet from the operator with whom I had been speaking. We told him what had happened and he suggested I open the hood so that he could take a look. As I mentioned earlier when my mother had visited in 1962, when it comes to automobiles, I haven't got a clue except for filling it up with gas, putting air in the tires and checking the oil.

I released the latch and almost immediately he said, "It's your transmission. I can smell it. You should be able to drive it slowly in the inside lane. If you want to follow me, we can take it to the Sears store in the mall on Palm Beach Lakes Boulevard. They have an automotive department and they can probably help you. Be sure to put your emergency lights on."

What do we do? Should I try to get hold of the motor club people again or do what he suggested. He was waiting for an answer. "Thank you, "I said. "Let's give it a try. I really appreciate your help." I wasn't sure he was right about being able to go slowly but what were our options at this point?

With him leading the way we finally arrived at the Sears automotive department. We thanked our good Samaritan for his help and prepared to go inside to explain our problem.

"That's OK. I'll stay until you know that they can help you."

After describing our predicament to the Sears service agent, he apologetically explained they were currently only doing basic services, such as oil changes, tire rotations, etc. It seemed Sears was under investigation for allegedly performing unnecessary service work to pad their revenues. So our problem was not solved and, if we were to make our dinner appointment, we would have to rent a car. Our new friend spoke up.

"Why don't we go on to the airport? It's not that far and I am sure you can get a rental there. Leave your car here. I am sure it will be OK. I'll take you."

Why is he being so kind to us? What's in it for him? We were still feeling very uncomfortable. Again, what were our options? "Are you sure? We hate to put you out. You've been very kind." I said.

We got into his car, Anita in the front and me in the back along with his tools and some pieces of sheet rock. It turns out he was a dry wall installer and had just come from his job up near Vero Beach, a long commute from his home south of Palm Beach. We arrived at the airport in less than ten minutes and pulled into the Budget Rent-a-Car lot. Again, we thanked him for all his help but, still, he wouldn't leave. "No, that's OK. I'll wait until you're sure they can take care of you."

They had a car available for us and he stayed until we were ready to leave.

"We really don't know how to thank you. We were on our way to a rather important dinner appointment in Boca Raton and, thanks to you, I'm sure we can still make it." I reached for my wallet to at least give him something.

"Don't even think about it. I'm happy I could help.'

When I asked his name, he responded "Bill".

"That's funny. That's mine too. Can't I give you just something for a couple of beers at least?"

"No, no. That's fine. I just hope the rest of your evening is trouble free." And he waved as he drove away.

We had already called our priest friend and told him we were having some problems and that we might be a bit late. Now we could call him and tell him we were on our way.

Are there *really* guardian angels? You bet there are, and we had just met ours!

When it was all over I was sorry that I never got his last name or a phone number so that I could tell him again, how much we appreciated his help. Unfortunately, between our initial suspicions, our concern about our appointment and what to do about our car, neither Anita nor I were thinking clearly. As it turned out, we were not that late and we had a great evening. The bottom line was that Father Matthew did include the Sri Lankan sisters in the Mission's annual distribution. I think he approved something around $2,000 but it was handled directly, so I was never exactly sure nor do I know if it was done on a regular basis. Whatever it was, it was an enormous help to the sisters and the children under their care. Father Matthew eventually went on to other responsibilities and Father Sean Harlow became procurator. I have remained in constant touch with Father Sean to keep him apprised of the Joe Neary Foundation's activities. Also, he has continued to support us by serving as the U.S. distribution agency for any approved grants made on behalf of the Carmelite sisters contingent on requiring an official U.S. based agency to receive funds.

****

In Matthew 13:3, the Bible tells the story of the farmer who went out to sow his seed. Some fell on rocky ground and died and some fell among thorns, which came up and choked the seedling. Still, *'some seed fell on rich soil and produced fruit, a hundred or sixty or thirty-fold.'* This has also been so true in our efforts. One parish may have all they can do to support their own community while another may offer significant assistance. We have been fortunate to have a few such gifts but one that just blew me away occurred here in Florida.

A Catholic parish located about 45 minutes from our home had a wonderful Irish pastor. Anita and I attended mass there one weekend and after the service, I asked him if I could make an appointment to see him. He said, "Certainly, just call me. I make my own appointments."

We met in his office on the appointed day as we had agreed. I had not quite finished my presentation on the Carmelite sisters and how I had become involved when he interrupted and asked, "Well Bill, how can I help you?"

"Well, Father," I said, "I wanted to ask if you would consider putting a brief announcement in your weekly parish bulletin any time you might have space. Other parishes have been willing to do this from time to time and I have brought a few examples and some proposed copy for you to look at."

I had hardly got those last words out when he said, "Bill, I won't do it! I won't. I'm sorry, but I won't do it." He was emphatic. Then he added, "I don't like to nickel and dime my parishioners."

"That's fine, Father, I quite understand."

"No, I won't", he repeated. "But Bill. You wait here just a minute." He walked out of the office and returned with a large leather-bound checkbook. He sat back down at his desk and asked, "If I give you a check, how do I make it out?"

I said, "You can make it out to Carmel Piyuma Convent and put Joe Neary Charity in the memo portion."

He made out the check, signed it, tore it out of the book and handed it to me. It was for $10,000! I started to cry. "But Father, you don't even know me. I've only be in here for ten minutes." I didn't know what to say.

"Oh, Bill. God is good! The sisters will appreciate it!" His Irish brogue seemed more pronounced than ever.

I thanked him over and over again. I returned to my car and called Anita, "You won't believe it. The pastor just gave me $10,000." And I started to cry again.

****

Now, as I write this in 2016, the Joe Neary Memorial Foundation has raised just under $200,000 over the last 26 years. One hundred percent of all the donations are sent to the sister with whom I coordinate these activities. She then purchases certificates of deposit with interest paid monthly. Through these investments, we now support five projects in Sri Lanka to which we distributed approximately $15,000 this year. Interest rates in Sri Lanka are typically higher than in the U.S. and, since we began this effort in 1990, they have averaged well over ten percent. They naturally vary but the highest we ever received was 19.75%. Each project account is established to operate like an endowment, as there are always carry-over balances after the monthly distribution is made. These accumulate for the purchase of additional investments in the future. The five projects are:

- The Bethlehem Crèche Daycare Center, Carmel Piyuma Convent, Wanathamulla, Colombo, with about 80 children from three months to five years old.
- The Apostolic Carmel School, St. Mary's Convent, Maharagama, with 100 high school age girl students, of which just over half are boarded at the school.

- The Carmel Girls' Home, Carmel Arunodaym Convent, Akkaraipattu housing nearly 40 girls.
- The St. Joseph's Girls' Home, St. Joseph Convent, Trincomalee, approximately 40 girls.
- The Joseph Vaz Children's Home, Nainamadama, with about 40 girls.

Over the years, we have also raised funding to furnish a new convent, provide emergency aid following the tragic tsunami in December 2004 and other specific projects. Our primary focus, however, has been to establish permanent investments, which are structured to grow on their own in perpetuity even without additional donations. Should anyone have any interest in supporting these efforts, the contact information can be found on the SKAL International website at www.skal.org under "links" or by Googling the Joe Neary Memorial Foundation.

You can tell this goodwill mission which, unexpectedly sprung out of my hotel career, is very close to my heart and still keeps me active today.

Joe Neary

Key to Success #17

Accommodate: *When handling a guest complaint in person or over the phone, listen attentively, take notes but wait until the guest has finished what they have to say. Do not interrupt or give excuses. Then make a sincere apology and offer appropriate restitution. If the offer is complimentary accommodations for a return visit or a dining invitation, always ask the guest to respond through your office so that you can ensure the original complaint is not repeated (i.e. guest room location). This way you are also in a position to personally follow up with the guest.*

Appendix I. The Family

I was born Leonard William (Bill) Pullen in the morning hours of September 11, 1936 in Blackheath, Kent, just a little south of London. My parents were Dorothy Muriel Faulkner (Dorothy) and Leonard Albert (Len) Pullen. My brother, Brian James (Jim) Pullen was five years older, born June 26, 1931. I don't know why both Jim and I were called by our second names but I assume, in my case, it was to distinguish my name from my dad's.

My mother was born on April 29, 1904 in Finchley, a northern suburb of London and her parents were Alfred Faulkner and Lizzie Woodcock who lived in Croydon, south of London, at the time of my early youth. She was blind in one eye, a wonderful diminutive lady who we lovingly knew as "little Granny." My mother had two sisters, Phyllis, who was married to Arthur Young and they had two boys, John and Tony. Her older sister, Nora, was married to George Rowland and they lived in Newry, Northern Ireland where Uncle George had a BMC car dealership. They had one son, Hugh.

My father was born on March 15, 1902 to William James Pullen and Elizabeth Willett. The Pullen/Willett marriage was a bit unusual since they were one of two brothers and two sisters in the Pullen family married to two brothers and two sisters in the Willett family. My father had two brothers and one sister. Bill, the oldest, and his wife Doris had two sons, Peter and John. Frank, the youngest, married Lorna and they had two sons and two daughters; Geoffrey, David, Ann, and Sherry. Gladys, who never married, was his sister.

Both my mother and father were enthusiastic tennis players. They met at the Purley Tennis Club in Surrey and were married on March 26, 1926.

At the time I was born, my family lived in Hayes, Kent where my parents had a clothing shop called Woollens in the High Street. We lived above the shop.

I have saved the best for last. I first met Anita Margaret Herb, the love of my life, in the summer of 1963. She was born on January 11, 1938 in Bridgeport, Connecticut and we were married on June 6, 1964 at St. Ann's Catholic Church in Devon, Connecticut. Our first daughter Wendy Sharon Margaret was born at Lenox Hill hospital in New York City on June 26, 1965 and our second daughter, Diana Mary was born at the St. Vincentius Hospital in Paramaribo, Suriname, South America on January 26, 1968. Dear Anita passed away on Wednesday, August 27, 2014 at the Cornerstone Hospice Home in The Villages, Florida just eleven weeks after our 50th wedding anniversary.

Anita set the example and the tone for our whole family. Wendy graduated from the University of Georgia with a bachelor's degree in business in 1987 and went on to earn her master's degree in business at Emory University in Atlanta, which she achieved in just one year. Two years later, Diana followed in Wendy's footsteps graduating from the University of Georgia with a bachelor's degree in business. She went on to get a master's in business from DePaul University in Chicago.

A work-related transfer took them both to Chicago in 1990 where they met their husbands-to-be. Wendy married Brian "Buc" Richter in November 1994 and Diana married Robert "Rob" Harvey in August 1999.

In January 1996, Wendy and Buc were blessed with the arrival of beautiful twin girls, Hailey and Melissa. Soon after, they adopted Becky who had been Diana's *little sister* for several years during her participation in the Big Brothers/Big Sisters program. Their family was complete with the arrival of Erin in October 1998

In January 2002, Diana and Rob gave us our first grandson, Ryan, and in April 2005, Sean arrived to keep Ryan company. In August 2007, Becky gave us our first great-grandchild, Marisa.

On June 6, 2014, Anita and I celebrated our 50th wedding anniversary. Although Anita had already been diagnosed with pancreatic cancer, all 13 members of our immediate family celebrated the occasion at a beautiful house on Fox Lake in northern Illinois over the Fourth of July weekend. It was a spectacular ten days filled with happy memories. Eight weeks later our good Lord took Anita to heaven.

Appendix II
Supporting Items

Age 5
On the beach during summer
holiday at Middleton on the
south coast

Age 14
On the fence at my
grandparents' home in
Worthing, Sussex

*Led by our Principal, Doug Lee, our WTC class attends
an Italian wine tasting at the Café Royal*

*Awaiting guests with other service staff
La Regence banquet room Hotel Plaza Athénée*

HOTEL
PLAZA-ATHÉNÉE
SOCIÉTÉ ANONYME
AU CAPITAL DE 60.000.000 FRS

23 à 27, AVENUE MONTAIGNE, PARIS

R.C. SEINE N°960.008 B

N° D'ENTREPRISE INSEE. 771.75.108.0078

U.R.S.S. A.F. 4?, AVENUE SIMON BOLIVAR
N° 771.75.108.0078 M

1122

CERTIFICAT

Je soussigné Directeur de l'Hôtel Plaza-Athénée, certifie que M. **Gullen** Léonard a été employé dans cette maison en qualité de commis stagiaire Relais et Restaurant du 9 décembre 1958 au 4 décembre 1959. Il a quitté à cette date libre de tout engagement. a rempli les fonctions de demi chef de rang pendant les 3 derniers mois de son stage et dans cet emploi il nous a donné toute satisfaction.

Fait à Paris, le 5 décembre 1959

Le Directeur Général

Certificat of Completion
Employment at Plaza Athénée
December 9, 1958-December 4, 1959

READING & BATES EXPLORATION CO.
500 CAPITAL NATIONAL BANK BUILDING
HOUSTON, TEXAS 77002

August 26, 1966

Morris R. DeWoskin & Co.
105 West Madison Street
Chicago 2, Illinois

Gentlemen:

I have just returned from my second trip to Surinam, utilizing the fine
accommodations at the Hotel Torarica. Needless to say, I was quite
pleased with the fine food, service, and maintenance of the facilities.

Special mention is quite appropriate for the excellent manager, Mr. Bill
Pullen. His attention to the details of hotel management can best be
described as most professional.

In June of this year, at my request, he arranged a cocktail party for local
Surinam officials which was handled in a most capable manner. Two weeks
ago we brought into Paramaribo harbor our catamaran drilling ship,
"E. W. THORNTON", prior to starting offshore drilling operations. Due
to the local dock facilities it was necessary to leave the ship at anchor in
the harbor.

Mr. Pullen was requested to arrange a large cocktail party on the ship
under most difficult conditions. The attendance approached 300 persons,
including the governor of Surinam. Due to the physical arrangement of
the ship, the party consumed the spaces on two different decks, in several
different spaces. The orderly manner in which foodstuffs, drinks,
personnel and equipment was transported to the ship by boat, the delicious
hors d'oeuvres, and the efficient serving of refreshments was far above
the normal.

I feel you have a most capable dedicated young man in Mr. Pullen and I
take this opportunity to convey my observations to you for your information.

Yours very truly

D. G. Bokenkamp

D. G. Bokenkamp
Operations Manager

*Letter from the Operations Manager of the Reading and Bates
Exploration Company to our Chairman following the reception
on board the E.W. Thornton*

MORRIS R. DeWOSKIN & CO.
HOTEL BROKERS
105 W. MADISON STREET
CHICAGO-60602

August 29, 1966

Mr. D. G. Bokenkamp
Operations Manager
Reading & Bates Exploration Co.
500 Capital National Bank Building
Houston, Texas 77002

Dear Mr. Bokenkamp:

Thank you very much for your fine letter about our
Mr. Pullen, at the Surinam Torarica Hotel-Casino.
We certainly like to hear these nice comments about
our personnel and are most grateful to you.

We know that Mr. Pullen has difficulty in doing a
big job because of the small hotel he has, but he
has evidenced that he is able to take care of all situations in a wonderful manner.

We are most happy to have him in our Organization.

Cordially yours,

MORRIS R. DE WOSKIN

MRD/b

cc: Mr. Carl Devoe
    Mr. Nathan Schwartz
    Mr. L. J. Pullen

Letter from Morris DeWoskin
Chairman of the Board
Executive House Hotel

*President Johnson
speaking at Zanderij
Airport*

THE WHITE HOUSE
WASHINGTON

April 17, 1967

Dear Bill:

There are many ways you could have reacted
to our sudden invasion of your hotel; and we
could not have been critical if you had acted
other than you did. However, the fact is that
you and your staff were superb. You swiftly
adjusted to our presence and throughout our
stay you were helpful, friendly, imaginative,
and accommodating.

*Letter from
Sherman Markman
Assistant to President
Johnson*

We are all grateful for all that you did for us.
It was a grand stay in a well run hotel. Under
most difficult circumstances you were
magnificent.

Thank you.

Yours truly,

Sherwin J. Markman
Assistant to the President

Mr. William Pullen
General Manager
Hotel Torarica
Paramaribo, Surinam

376

DCAU-E   20 April 1967

Mr. Carl Devoe
President, Executive House
71 East Wacker Drive
Chicago, Illinois

Dear Mr. Devoe:

    In preparation for the recent visit of the President of the United States to Surinam, my organization utilized the facilities of the Surinam Torarica Hotel.

    I would like to take this opportunity to express my appreciation for the courteous service and fine cooperation your hotel extended to my people.

    More specifically, I would like to commend Mr. William Pullen. Mr. Pullen went out of his way many times to insure that our specific needs were met. His personal assistance to my men in Surinam made their stay a more comfortable one.

    I would also like to commend Marijke Schneiders, Ewald Hinds, Evelyn Ngiafoek, Beverley Nobrega, and Marlene Garsia. The competence and strong personal interest shown by Mr. Pullen and his staff have contributed considerably to the accomplishment of our complex mission for the President.

    My sincere thanks for your cooperation and courteous service.

                    Sincerely,

                    JACK A. ALBRIGHT
                    Colonel,   USA
                    Commanding

*Letter from Col. Jack Albright, White House Staff
to Carl Devoe, Executive House President
following President Johnson's visit*

Introducing Bushnegro fire dancers

Some of my collection of "good bottle"

Wayne Newton

February 19, 1969

Dear Mr. Pullen:

Words could not express our gratitude and sincere thanks for your kindness. It's so nice to be able to pick up a telephone and ask a favor of a man whom you have never met. Our stay in Scottsdale both times has been just great thanks to you and your employees. You could not have been more gracious on every level.

Please sir, if I may return the favor at any time, do not fail to call upon me. Next time in Scottsdale, I hope I will have the pleasure of meeting you in person. Until then, may I again just say thank you.

Sincerely,

Mr. William Pullen
Executive House
North Scottsdale Road
Scottsdale, Arizona 85252

Letter from singer Wayne Newton
following his visit to Scottsdale

*With Ann-Margret and her
husband Roger Smith
during her engagement at
Playboy
1971*

January 27, 1972

Four Seasons
Geneva Lake Area Chamber of Commerce

Phone:
414 248-4416

Enjoy
Where You
See This
Sail

Administration and
Information Center
100 Lake Street
Lake Geneva, Wisconsin
53147

Mr. William Pullen
General Manager
Playboy Club - Hotel
Hwy. 50 East
Lake Geneva, Wisc. 53147

Dear Bill,

The Executive Committee of the Geneva Lake Area Chamber of Commerce wishes to write you a formal letter expressing our regret that you are leaving the Playboy Club - Hotel and our community.

The Chamber of Commerce has received your total cooperation in the two years you were general manager here in Lake Geneva and we are truly grateful for it. The tremendous public relations which you have created both with the Chamber of Commerce and with the entire community are easily recognized by all and it has only been under your guidance during the last two years that the community has finally recognized what tremendous gains are received by all by having the Playboy Club - Hotel located in the Geneva Lake area.

If the Geneva Lake Area Chamber of Commerce can ever be of service to you in any way, Bill, please do not hesitate to let us know.

It has been a real and sincere pleasure working with you and we are sure that your leaving is the loss of the Geneva Lake Area. Once again, Bill, we would like to wish to both you and your family our best and sincere wishes and we hope that your future is a great one.

Unanimously Approved This 27th Day of January, 1972,

George Hibbard, President

cc: Hugh Hefner
cc: Arnold Morton

Dave Thompson, Vice President

Dan Derrick, Treasurer

Robert B. Gouch, Executive Vice Pres.

RBC:rh

*Letter from Lake Geneva Chamber of Commerce
upon my departure from Playboy*

Bunnies big and small!
Sonny and Cher with Chastity at Playboy
1971

*With Anita, Wendy and Diana
in Lake Geneva, Wisconsin*

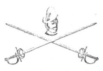

conquistadores del cielo

April 24, 1972

Mr. Henry V. Berry
President
Carefree Developers, Inc.
Box 708
Carefree, Arizona

Dear Mr. Berry:

As you may know, our Club held its Spring Fiesta at The Carefree Inn, attended by 71 members and 78 guests. You may be interested in the enclosed copy of our agenda.

The purpose of this letter is to express our profound thanks and appreciation to Mr. Pullen and his excellent staff on their outstanding support, service and friendly cooperation. Over the years our Club has visited many fine resort hotels in the United States and abroad. The quality of service we enjoyed at Carefree is unmatched in our experience. Every commitment made by the hotel was met or exceeded, which could be done only by a great deal of attention and hard work.

You have good reason to be proud of Mr. Pullen and his staff. Would you please convey to him, Peter Zillich, Neva Davis, and the others our deep appreciation.

Cordially,

J. B. Montgomery

JBM:pb

MEMO from *Henry V. Berry*

May 2, 1972

To Board of Directors:

Just thought you might like to know the type of letters we've been getting recently.

It's not to say we haven't gotten a few of the others, but Bill seems to be doing an outstanding job and I thought you would like to know.

HANK

Letter from General J.B. Montgomery
President of the Conquistadores del Cielo
following prestigious event at
Carefree Inn
with
note from Henry Berry to
Board of Directors

RAY-O-VAC DIVISION
ESB INCORPORATED

210 E. WASHINGTON AVENUE
MADISON, WISCONSIN 53701
TELEPHONE: 608-252-7331

April 26, 1972

Mr. Bill Pullen
The Carefree Inn
Mule Train Road
P.O. Box 758
Carefree, Arizona 85331

Dear Bill:

We are back from Hawaii and it appears things have settled back to normal. Normal at Ray-O-Vac, however, is still a very fast pace as I'm sure you'll now agree.

I didn't want to wait any longer to thank you, Nancy, Pete, Neva, Dave, and the entire staff at The Carefree Inn for the outstanding job they did in hosting our National Sales Meeting. The comments from Ed Dwyer, our Board Chairman, all the way down through the organization were 100% favorable on all facets of your operation.

Being a seasoned hotel man I'm sure you fully realize how important the operation, food, beverage, and services of a hotel contributes to the overall success of a National Meeting. To us, it's as important as the agenda itself.

All comments on our meeting indicated this was the "Best Ever". Your and your people's contributions must then be classified as the best also. --

Since our meeting in Madison in February you certainly have pulled The Carefree Inn together. It's always been a fine place, but you and your staff have added the first class, that something extra, to the operation. It was great for all of us to work with you and your people.

You told us you'd handle it and you sure did. Your efforts made our jobs that much easier.

Please extend my thanks to Hank Berry for bringing Hugh Downs to the meeting and also for setting up the fine luncheon at the Boulders.

Letter from Pete Stebbins,
Merchandising Manager
for Ray-O-Vac,
following their meeting
at Carefree Inn

Pullen
1972

Please send me both Hank's and Mr. Downs' addresses as we have a gift we'd like to send to them.

Bill, please keep in touch. I hope we'll be able to plan a trip your way within the not too distant future.

Again, please extend my thanks to all of your fine people.

Kindest personal regards,

P. W. Stebbins
Merchandising Manager

PWS:jv
cc: R. B. Cook

385

The Coca-Cola Company
1977 TECHNICAL CONFERENCE

TECHNICAL DIVISION

PRODUCT QUALITY THROUGH TECHNOLOGY

P.O. DRAWER 1734, ATLANTA, GEORGIA, 30301

April 4, 1977

Mr. William Pullen
General Manager
Sandpiper Bay
Port St. Lucie, Florida 33452

Dear Bill:

On behalf of The Coca-Cola Company, I would like to express our gratitude to you and your staff for the excellent support given to make our recent worldwide Technical Conference one of our finest meetings. From the maids, bellmen, and set-up crews to the cooks, bartenders and your management team, I received the immediate response and constant assistance so critical to making a meeting of our size successful.

While risking the possibility of omitting someone, I would like to especially thank Ken Benjamin, Al Gorlick, Bill Mullen, Don Hopkins, Bert Dickhut, Millie Carmack, Pat Van Duzer, Marcia Sawick, Hank Lidner and your accounting team. I recognize that these people were doing more than their "regular job."

I believe the 1977 Technical Conference will remain a meaningful, pleasant and fun-filled experience to our people from around the world. Your staff contributed greatly to this experience. We hope to return to Sandpiper Bay in 1980.

Cordially yours,

Gregory J. DeLucca
Operations Engineering

GJD/jj

cc: Mr. K. A. Benjamin
     Mr. R. C. Goizueta

*Letter from Coca Cola following their worldwide
Technical Conference at Sandpiper Bay*

To Pullen
Wm Pullen 4/9/79

PHILIP MORRIS INDUSTRIAL
4200 NORTH HOLTON STREET P.O. BOX 294 MILWAUKEE, WISCONSIN 53201 TELEPHONE (414) 332-3600

Robert J. Moore
DIRECTOR-COMMUNICATIONS

April 2, 1979

Mr. William R. Avella
President
General Development Corp.
1111 S. Bayshore Drive
Miami, Florida 33131

To: Frank Widmann
Express my thanks and
Appreciation for a super job
to Bill & Ken.
Bill Avella 4/6/79
xc. e.e. County

Dear Mr. Avella:

If I were the Chief Executive Officer of General
Development, I would like to be personally aware of the
quality of service rendered to guests at my properties.
The purpose of this letter is to communicate the manner
in which some 65 representatives of our company, including
wives, were handled at Sandpiper Bay during a 5-day meeting
last week.

In a word, Mr. Avella, the quality of service was
outstanding. We have held functions at other fine properties
including The Lodge at Pebble Beach, The Stanford Court
and the Fairmont in San Francisco and Carefree in Arizona
and Sandpiper surpassed them all. The level of service
was exceeded only by the quality of the food and the
excellence of the property.

A vote of thanks goes to your excellent General
Manager, Mr. William Pullen, and your absolutely superb
Director of Sales and Marketing, Mr. Ken Benjamin.
No request was too minuscule to merit less than their
100% attention.

We were most pleased with our stay at Sandpiper
and we shall pass the word throughout the Philip Morris
organization.

If I were you, Mr. Avella, I would be proud to have
two gentlemen of the caliber of Messrs. Pullen and
Benjamin on my team.

Sincerely,

Robert J. Moore

RJM:kh

CHEMICALS   PAPER   PACKAGING

Letter from Philip Morris
following their meeting at Sandpiper Bay

Travel Weekly
ONE PARK AVENUE · NEW YORK, N.Y. 10016
(212) 725-3688 · Cable: Calacour · Telex: 12-5478

IRWIN ROBINSON
Chairman

January 16, 1980

Mr. Bill Pullen, Ken Benjamin
and Marilyn Wagener
Sandpiper Bay
Port St. Lucie, Florida 33452

Dear (Bill) Ken and Marilyn:

I want to add my congratulations to those already expressed by
our Travel Weekly tournament registrants on the warm hospitality
and fine service we experienced during our recent visit to Sandpiper Bay.

It was, in every respect, a notable team performance. The
service was gracious, the people friendly, and the facilities
excellent. I don't know of a better formula for fulfilling your
guests' expectations.

Many thanks to all of you. My earnest hope is that you have
sown the seeds for some worthwhile future business.

With warmest personal regards.

Sincerely,

Published twice a week by the Public Transportation & Travel Division, Ziff-Davis Publishing Co.

*Letter from Irwin "Robbie" Robinson
Chairman of Travel Weekly
following the Travel Weekly Golf Tournament*

It Started at The Savoy

Travel Weekly
THE NATIONAL NEWSPAPER OF THE TRAVEL INDUSTRY

Volume 39 · Number 14   Thursday, February 21, 1980   Two issues weekly

Textbook Example of How to Turn a Property Around

Sandpiper Bay in Port St. Lucie Enjoys Pattern of Growth With Concerted Drive

By JOEL A. GLASS
and JOLYN VARGISH

PORT ST. LUCIE, Fla. — In a most unobtrusive manner, marketing and operations history was quietly made last year at Sandpiper Bay, as the resort at Port St. Lucie ended 1979 in the black and occupancy levels soared to record new highs in what has become an almost textbook example of a successful resort turnaround.

Sandpiper, a 1,000-acre, 273-room General Development Corp. property 45 miles north of West Palm Beach, emerged in 1979 from a history clouded by identity problems, low occupancy and unprofitability and reaped the first fruits of a concerted marketing and administrative effort.

In an exclusive interview with Travel Weekly, L. William Pullen, vice president and general manager of Sandpiper Bay, proudly noted that annual occupancy at the resort has soared from a miserly 44% in 1976 to a healthy 71% last year — a sharp percentage jump of 61%.

Along with the impressive improvement in occupancy, he said, the property's balance sheet also has emerged from its years-long bath in red ink.

"Four years ago," noted Pullen, "Sandpiper was losing in excess of $1 million annually." But in 1978, the resort hit the break-even point and last year became, Pullen said, "the first really profitable year" for the

property as its balance sheet reflected some $250,000 in gross profits.

Pullen said that he also is optimistic about the outlook for 1980 and conceded that the projected 72% annual occupancy for the year, representing growth of only about 1% over 1979, is "conservative," adding that, "I think we can do better."

"1980 looks very strong," he continued. "We already have over $500,000 more in group business on the books than we had at this time a year ago. Only about 20% of that figure is attributable to rate hikes."

The month of January, he added, was expected to close out with an occupancy of 77.5%, compared with 63.8% for the same month a year ago — an increase of 13.7 occupancy points, or nearly 22%.

Pointing out that the uncertain economy could throw a

Pullen

wrench into his expectations of continued improvement at Sandpiper Bay, Pullen said:

"The economy can be a problem with groups and could result in the loss of some business. On the other hand, sometimes a bad economy creates business by creating a need for meetings."

Pullen also said that a gasoline shortage, like the one experienced in Florida early last summer, also could cut into the resort's off-season social business — much of which comes from South Florida — as it did in 1979.

But, he said, Sandpiper Bay is prepared should that situation recur this year, pointing to the fact that one of the resort's storage tanks has been convert-

A view of Sandpiper Bay resort, with the marina on the left, the guest room building in the center and the Brass Sandpiper on the right.

ed to hold unleaded gas.

In the event of another gas crunch, Pullen said, the property would develop and promote a weekend tour package with a $10 coupon for fuel as a key ingredient.

Pullen, who is proud of the record he and his staff have achieved at Sandpiper during the last few years, attributed the turnaround to a number of factors, including:

• The timing of the resort's name change, from the St. Lucie Hilton in 1975 when the Hilton franchise was dropped, to Sandpiper Bay, engendering the development of a whole new identity for the property.

• The continuity of the resort's management team, which

*Front page feature story in Travel Weekly
on successful growth of Sandpiper Bay business*

City Investing Company
767 Fifth Avenue, New York 10022
212-759-5300

GEO. T. SCHARFFENBERGER · CHAIRMAN AND CHIEF EXECUTIVE OFFICER

May 20, 1980

MAY 2 6 1980

Mr. L. William Pullen
Assistant Vice President and
    General Manager
Sandpiper Bay
Port St. Lucie, Florida 33452

Dear Bill:

   A word to tell you how much I appreciated the
fine manner in which our bankers and GDV meetings were
handled at Sandpiper Bay.

   As you well know, we do have many meetings in
the course of the year and these last two, in your hands,
were about the best we have ever had.

   Again, thank you.

                           Cordially,

                           Geo.

cc: Robert F. Ehrling

To
Bill Pullen
   It is obvious from everyone's comments
that you and your people did a superb
job. Many thanks for your excellent
performance and how well it made
General Development look

                           Bob.

Letter from George Scharffenberger
Chairman of City Investing Company
following their meeting at
Sandpiper Bay

390

It Started at The Savoy

Sandpiper Bay Homeowners Association, Inc.

2961 Morningside

November 23, 1982

Mr. William Pullen
1932 Erwin Road
Port St. Lucie, Florida   33452

Dear Bill:

The Board of Directors of the Sandpiper Bay Homeowners Association is writing this letter--but we feel sure
it represents what all 1200 of our members feel--sadness
at losing the very best General Manager here at Sandpiper
Bay we have been priviledged to know.

Your fairness in dealing with a very difficult
situation--Homeowner needs and Hotel Guests' needs-- is
to be highly complimented. We know your duty to the hotel
plus your very acute awareness of all the homeowners who
live here and consider it "their" place, must have put
you in tight situations many, many times. What has always
astonished us has been your ability to smile and be
gracious to everybody at all times.

We shall all miss you, Bill. We wish all the
best for you and Anita and your family in whatever you do.
Most of all, we hope you can stay in the area so we may
keep in friendly contact.

Good Luck!

Sincerely

Irene T. Chapman

For all the Homeowners

cc: Mr. M. Hundley

_Letter from Sandpiper Bay Homeowners Association
when they heard Sandpiper Bay had been sold_

391

SANDPIPER BAY

The resort at Port St. Lucie

December 14, 1983

Dear Bill,

There were so many things I wanted to say to you
before you left. However, never got the courage as
I knew the tears would ruin the whole scene. So, I'll
take the cowardly way out and write!

You mentioned in your letter to the employees in
Sand Scripts that your "years at Sandpiper Bay have
been among the happiest and most rewarding in your
career thanks to everyones friendship and support."
I'll put the shoe on the other foot and say that my
four years at Sandpiper Bay have been the happiest
and most rewarding in my career...thanks mostly to
you! Although I didn't report to you "according to
the organizational charts"...fortunately, (for me),
it seemed in most of my projects, I was dealing
directly with you. So, I thank you, first, for
giving me the opportunity of joining the staff of
Sandpiper Bay. For being fair, honest, for your
patience and for all the learning and valuable
experience I was able to absorb under your guidance.
And, for being a super friend!

You are one-in-a-million, Bill, and Sandpiper Bay
will never be the same without you here. I, along
with so many employees, am grateful for having known
and worked with you.

Bill and I extend every good wish for the holidays
to you, Anita and the girls and we just know that
1983 will bring nothing but the best to all of
you!

Fondly,

[signature]

Port St. Lucie, Florida 33452 Phone: (305) 334 4400

Letter from Jan Shelly
Sandpiper Director of Public Relations

392

Mobil Oil Corporation

3225 GALLOWS ROAD
FAIRFAX, VIRGINIA 22037-0001

T. C. DeLOACH
VICE PRESIDENT — MARKETING
MARKETING AND REFINING DIVISION — , S

January 4, 1989

Mr. William Pullen
General Manager
Indian River Plantation
555 N.E. Ocean Boulevard
Hutchinson Island, FL 34996

Dear Mr. Pullen:

Congratulations! It gives me great pleasure to tell you that the
Indian River Plantation has won the prestigious Mobil Travel Guide
Four-Star Award for 1989. You and your fine staff are to be
applauded for achieving Four-Star excellence.

The Mobil Travel Guide Four-Star Award means "Outstanding -- worth
a special trip," which puts the Indian River Plantation in a special
group. Only 42 dining and lodging places share this distinction in
the state of Florida for 1989. In total, just 383 Four-Star Awards
are bestowed on hotels, motor hotels, motels, inns, resorts, and
restaurants nationwide, out of more than 21,000 listed in the Mobil
Travel Guide.

The Indian River Plantation won the 1989 Four-Star Award entirely
on merit. Each year, independent inspectors and researchers
across the country carefully review and evaluate thousands of fine
establishments against the Mobil Travel Guide's strict criteria to
determine the "outstanding" places.

The national announcement of the Four-Star winners will be made
January 23. Please wait until January 23 to publicize your Award.
To tie in with this publicity, next week you should receive your
Four-Star publicity kit, followed in a few weeks by your Four-Star
plaque.

Your dedication to service, quality, hospitality and consistent
overall excellence makes the Indian River Plantation among the
outstanding properties in America. We are proud to honor you with
the 1989 Mobil Travel Guide Four-Star Award.

Sincerely,

J. C. DeLoach

T. C. DeLoach

RECEIVED
JAN - 6 1989

Letter from Mobil Oil Corporation
announcing that Indian River Plantation
had been awarded their 4-Star Rating
after the first year of operations

*Cover of Palm Springs Life
when the 1990
North American SKAL
Congress was hosted by
the Palm Springs Chapter*

October 20, 1992

Mr. L. William Pullen, CHA
Holiday Inn Oceanside
3793 N. E. Ocean Boulevard
Jensen Beach, Florida 34957

Dear Mr. Pullen:

From our correspondence I had been curious
about the abbreviation "CHA" following your
name.

Being cognizant of the meaning of CPA, M.D.,
etc., this designation was unfamiliar to me.

An inquiry to the Vice President of Florida
International University today provided enlight-
enment that it means Certified Hotel Administrator and that it is earned on the basis of
knowledge, training, and experience in administration, public relations, and all facets
of hospitality management.

This explains the extraordinary courtesies extended to Mrs. Whaley and myself on our recent
visit. The welcoming phone call while off duty
along with the gift of wine and the accompanying
note were greatly appreciated.

You wear the title well!

Very truly yours,

M. E. Whaley

1147 N. E. 112th Street
Miami, Florida 33161

*A guest's letter in reference to the
designation "CHA"*

LAW OFFICES OF

HIPPENMEYER, REILLY & MOODIE, S.C.

720 CLINTON STREET

WILLIAM F. REILLY
ROBERT B. MOODIE
MARK G. BLUM
PAUL F. REILLY

SHAWN N. REILLY

OF COUNSEL
HAROLD J. WOLLENZIEN

P.O. BOX 766
WAUKESHA, WISCONSIN 53187-0766
TELEPHONE (414) 549-8181
FACSIMILE (414) 549-8191

RICHARD S. HIPPENMEYER
(1911-1979)

MUKWONAGO OFFICE
2040 ROCHESTER STREET
MUKWONAGO, WISCONSIN 53149
TELEPHONE (414) 363-5050
FACSIMILE (414) 363-5051

March 15, 1994

Mr. Bryan Langton, President
Holiday Inn Worldwide
3 Ravinia Dr., Suite 2000
Atlanta, Georgia 30346-1249

Dear Mr. President:

I would imagine that you receive your share of letters complaining about your various establishments. My purpose in writing is to let you know that you truly have a thoroughbred in your stable of hotels.

During the past thirty years I have stayed in many Holiday Inns throughout the continental United States and have always found them, with few exceptions, to have nice, clean rooms that are reasonably priced.

In January of 1993, my wife and I had the opportunity to stay at HOLIDAY INN OCEANSIDE on Jensen Beach, Florida. I was so impressed with the kindness and hospitality shown to us that I was moved to write a letter of thanks, a copy of which is enclosed.

This February, (1994) we again visited Florida and again stayed at HOLIDAY INN OCEANSIDE. I'm happy to report that my observations of last year were reaffirmed.

When I was waiting to check in there were two women in line ahead of me - one middle-aged and the other much older. They were completely distraught and upset. The cause was that they had thought they had reservations at Oceanside when in reality they were booked at a different Holiday Inn some miles away. The clerk behind the desk, whose first name was Tom, was most understanding and helpful. He had no rooms available at Oceanside, but he got on the phone and found them rooms in a comparable hotel in the area and talked that hotel into reducing their nightly tab from $190/night to $100/night. These two women

-2-
Mr. Langton
March 15, 1994

were so happy the older one started crying and the younger wanted
Tom's name and the Oceanside's address so she could send a thank
you note. What a good feeling and great way for us to start our
own stay at Jensen Beach!

Throughout our short stay I saw repeated examples of this kind of
concern shown by the staff. There is excellent rapport between
all of the employees that gives the impression that you are
invited into a great Bed & Breakfast and your hosts are `family'.
I know that this atmosphere doesn't just happen and isn't a mere
coincidence. This time I had the opportunity to meet the
motivator and general manager, a Mr. L. William Pullen. It is
obvious to me that the climate described above has been created
by the examples Mr. Pullen sets in his dealings with his
employees.

There is only one question that I have and that is how has
HOLIDAY INN WORLDWIDE kept Mr. Pullen's genius a secret from the
other large hotels? Probably the answer is he loves his job and
loves working with the staff he employs. (He may also like this
part of Florida). If however, I ever buy a hotel (which is very
unlikely) the man I would first approach to run it would be Mr.
L. William Pullen.

Thanks to HOLIDAY INN WORLDWIDE, Mr. Pullen, and all the staff at
HOLIDAY INN OCEANSIDE, Jensen Beach, Florida for another great
vacation.

Sincerely,

William F. Reilly

WFR/slh
Enc.

bcc: Mr. L. William Pullen

*A guest's letter to Bryan Langton
President of Holiday Inn Worldwide
following their stay at the Holiday Inn Oceanside*

MARK ADAM FOLEY
18th District, Florida

Congress of the United States
House of Representatives
Washington, DC 20515–0916

January 31, 1995

Mr. William Pullen
Holiday Inn-Oceanside
3793 N.E. Ocean Blvd.
Jensen Beach, Florida 34957

Dear Bill:

Congratulations on being chosen as the Business Man of the Year
by your colleagues at the Jensen Beach Chamber of Commerce.

You bring compassion, kindness, determination and patience to
the business environment in which you work. I know the respect
that your peers have for you because they have shared that
with me.

Again, Bill, congratulations on your recent award.

Sincerely,

Mark Foley
Member of Congress

MF:js

*Letter from Congressman Mark Foley
Following my being named
1994 Jensen Beach Business Man-of-the-Year
by the Chamber of Commerce*

Florida Governor's Council
on Physical Fitness and Sports

February 2, 1999

Bill Pullen, CHA
Holiday Inn Oceanside
3793 NE Ocean Boulevard
Jensen Beach, FL 34957

Dear Bill:

You did an outstanding job of pulling together the leaders throughout three counties in order to create the Treasure Coast Sports Commission. This organization is now in a position to generate financial support or better yet, to receive financial support from the many entities throughout the community. There will be many sporting events that can be attracted to Treasure Coast area, but more importantly, there will be many opportunities for your citizens to participate. You have been the person behind this, that has made it all possible.

It was a pleasure for me to play a small role in seeing this organization develop. I have watched each of the sports commission's grow throughout Florida and know that it has provided a wonderful opportunity for individuals to be a part of an organization that is doing great things. I look forward to seeing the Treasure Coast Sports Commission grow and the Water Sports Festival be one of its major events.

Please feel free to call on me at any time and I will be happy to provide what ever assistance possible.

Sincerely,

Jimmy Carnes
Executive Director

1408 Northwest 6th Street, Suite A Gainesville, Florida 32601
Telephone (352) 955-2120 Suncom 625-2120 FAX (352) 373-8879

Letter from Jimmy Carnes
Florida Governor's Council on Physical Fitness and Sports
as we were developing the
tri-county Treasure Coast Sports Commission

MARK FOLEY
16TH DISTRICT, FLORIDA
DEPUTY MAJORITY WHIP

WAYS AND MEANS
COMMITTEE
SUBCOMMITTEE ON OVERSIGHT
SUBCOMMITTEE ON SELECT REVENUE
MEASURES

Congress of the United States
House of Representatives
Washington, DC 20515
May 8, 2002

REPLY TO:
104 CANNON BUILDING
WASHINGTON, DC 20515-0916
(202) 225-5792
FAX: (202) 225-3132

E-MAIL: mark.foley@mail.house.gov
WEBSITE: http://www.house.gov/foley

Florida Shore & Beach Preservation Association
2952 Wellington Circle
Tallahassee, FL 32309

Re: William "Bill" Pullen
2002 Member of the Year Award

Dear Sirs:

This letter is being written to support the nomination of Bill Pullen for the 2002 Member of the Year Award.

Bill has been a very active member of the Martin County Chapter of the Florida Beach & Shore Preservation Association. In fact, Bill has been the driving force and the glue which have held the local organization together.

Bill is a highly respected member of the business community. His word is his bond. Bill has a quiet manner about him and a rod of steel within his body frame. He can be counted on to do what he says he will do and always goes above and beyond the call of duty.

Bill has worked tirelessly on behalf of the organization to communicate to residents along a four-mile stretch of beachfront property about the complexities of beach renourishment and sources of government funding. He leads by example and never complains about doing a task.

The Holiday Inn graciously offers their facilities for a meeting location for the organization. Bill organizes the meeting room and is generous with his food and drink amenities.

When anyone in Martin County thinks of the FSPBA the name of Bill Pullen is synonymous with the organization. Bill is an asset to your organization and I hope you will recognize him with the 2002 Member of the Year Award.

With best wishes, I am,

Sincerely,

Ann L. Decker, District Manager
Congressman Mark Foley

PALM BEACH GARDENS
4440 PGA BLVD., SUITE 406
PALM BEACH GARDENS, FL 33410
(561) 627-6192
FAX: (561) 626-4749

PORT ST. LUCIE
COUNTY ANNEX BUILDING
250 NW COUNTRY CLUB DRIVE
PORT ST. LUCIE, FL 34986
(561) 878-3181
FAX: (561) 871-0651

HIGHLANDS COUNTY
SEBRING CITY HALL
(By Appointment Only)
(863) 471-1913

*Letter by Ann Decker, District Manager for
Congressman Mark Foley
nominating me for
2002 FSBPA Member of the Year Award*

FLORIDA SHORE & BEACH
PRESERVATION ASSOCIATION

A League of Cities and Counties on Beach and Coastal issues

2952 Wellington Circle
Tallahassee, Florida 32309
(850) 906-9227
(850) 906-9228 FAX
www.fsbpa.com

August 23, 2002

Mr. William Pullen
General Manager
Holiday Inns of Martin County
3793 N.E. Ocean Boulevard
Jensen Beach, FL 34957

Dear Mr. Pullen:

I am pleased to advise you that you have been named to receive FSBPA's **2002 Member of the Year Award**, for your tireless work on behalf of the Martin County Chapter of the FSBPA and Martin County beaches.

Ann Decker, District Manager for Congressman Mark Foley, nominated you for this award.

The award will be presented Thursday evening, September 26 at FSBPA's annual Awards Banquet at South Seas Plantation on Captiva Island. Please let me know as soon as possible if you will be able to accept the award in person.

Again, Congratulations. I hope to see you in Captiva.

Sincerely,

David L. Tait
Executive Director

printed on recycled paper

Letter from David L. Tait
Executive Director
Florida Shore & Beach Preservation Association
on my being named 2002 Member of the Year

INDIAN RIVER
PLANTATION
Marriott
RESORT
FLORIDA

RECEIVED
MAY -7 1999

May 5, 1999

Mr. L. William Pullen, CHA
Director of Operations
Holiday Inn Oceanside
3793 Northeast Ocean Boulevard
Jensen Beach, Florida 34957

Dear Bill:

On behalf of our entire team here at Indian River Plantation Marriott Resort we would like to congratulate you on being selected as the 1999 Treasure Coast Tourism and Hospitality Leader of the Year.

There is no one who puts more of themself into our industry than you. Your tireless dedication to organizations like: the Martin County Hotel Motel Association, H.I.T.D.C. and Treasure Coast Sports Commission is second to none. Each of these organizations, and especially our industry as a whole is lucky to have you.

Bill again congratulations! We all look forward to working with you in the future in making Martin County and especially Hutchinson Island the best it can be.

Sincerely,

Timothy J. Digby
General Manager

TJD:sh

 555 N.E. Ocean Boulevard • Stuart, Florida 34996 • (561) 225-3700 • FAX (561) 225-0003

Letter from fellow hotelier Tim Digby,
GM of Indian River Plantation,
after I was recognized with the
1999 Treasure Coast Tourism and Hospitality
Leader of the Year Award

*With J. Walter Duncan, Jr., my boss who acted as the
managing partner for the two Holiday Inn properties
in Stuart and Jensen Beach*

APOSTOLIC CARMEL
Tel.No.695045

The Provincial House,
Carmel Convent,
88, Ananda Rajakaruna Mawatha,
Colombo-10.
SRI LANKA.

14. 7. 2004.

Dear Mr. Pullen,

As you have expressed your willingness to help us with another worthy Project, I am presenting to you the Apostolic Carmel School, Maharagama.

Please find enclosed:
1. A Description of the Project.
2. A Statement of the Results of the School in the Ord.Level Exam.

What we would like you to help us to do is to build up a Fund, the Interest from which could be utilised to pay the Teachers' Salaries and the Water, Electricity and Phone Bills, each month.

The Teachers' Salaries come up to Rs.57,000.00 a month and the Water, Electricity and Phone Expenses to Rs.5,700.00 a month.

The School is being helped by other Organisations abroad, but these donations are not regular and hardly enough to cover the costs. The last two years it has been a great struggle for us to pay the teachers, and at present we are considering whether we should close down this School.

If you could help us by getting donors, as you did for the Joe Neary Fund, we will certainly be able to continue this School for our needy children.

Thank you dear Mr. Pullen and all the donors who have been so generous towards us. We appreciate your interest in and concern for our Projects.

God bless you and your Mission.

Yours sincerely in Christ,

(Sr. M. Sunitha A.C.)
Provincial Superior.

The Provincial Superior
Apostolic Carmel
88, Ananda Rajakaruna Mawatha,
Colombo 10. - Sri Lanka.

Letter from Provincial Superior Sister Sunitha, A.C., requesting support from the Joe Neary Memorial Foundation for a small school in Maharagama

Ode to Grill Bar

The Grill Bar, here in The Savoy, is the place where every boy
should start his training in the trade (although at first he's hardly paid).
Where one fine day he may become a 'Hofflin', 'Haynes' or 'Nelligan'.
The work is fairly hard at first, especially if you have a thirst,
but there are times when you should see us doing what we call a 'Dias'.
Sitting, talking, reading too, watching everyone else do
the mise en place – hey, dig that French – but Jean Coulon is not a wench.
Though Jean and Jean are spelt the same, we now know it's a French boy's name.
And then there's Chris – a girl's name too – but there's one job he cannot do
and that's to get the beers all right, although he counts them half the night.
Then from Johannesburg comes Phil. He's only here until
just after Easter when he sails for Canada and new females.
He does the football pools each week and tries so earnestly to seek
a winning perm at any cost but, so far, he has only lost.
The no. 2 here on the staff's a bloke called Bill, but please don't laugh
'cos McEvoy is not a toff and if to you he says "Piss off!"
you know that you have made a friend who always gets you in the 'end'.
For, if your back is ever turned- and this I have already learned –
he will attack with his right hand and say to you "How do you stand
for five or ten or fifteen bob?". I think he's happy in his job.
His home's away across the sea in Ireland – what a place to be –
where savages and creatures too are only fit for London Zoo.
But, Bill's escaped, we understand, he's not bad for an Irishman.
We also see, just now and then, a fellow called Mick Nelligan.
He is in charge here, so I'm told, but even though he's fairly old
he doesn't seem to have a clue at really ever what to do.
With vintage wines with sediments he spoils the very rudiments.
A '37 wine then taken should, he thinks, be stirred or shaken.
When he arrives at 10 o'clock he first of all checks half the stock
and then he tries to be polite. "Were you busy here last night?"
The tune he whistles every day just proves he's always bright and gay
but he's not settled 'til he's had a little climb upon his ladder.
Then last of all there's barman Len who's sensible just now and then.
He's here to learn just what he can on how all cocktails first began
and how the different drinks were taken and then either stirred or shaken.
But now we think he's got the gist of all the main ones on the list
yet, even now, however hard he tries he can't make a Bacardi
without it being far too red, just like tomato juice instead.
There's one more thing he should not ought and that's to drink the vintage port!
Well, that's about the lot for now. If there's anything you don't know how,
ask Mike or Jean or Chris or Phil or see if either Len or Bill
can tell you how or why or when, but never ask Mick Nelligan.

Ode to Greg

In honor of Sergeant Bill Gregory
Ramillies Barracks, Aldershot (1955)

Way back in 1934, the British soldier was no more
than just a little man in khaki dress doing his utmost to impress
his officers...of whom it can be said
spent less time on the battlefield than in bed.

About this time in history, there came a chap called Gregory,
who, by the way, I think we know was then a junior NCO.
He knew he couldn't get the sack, because this comical lance jack
had cast away all work and strife and, like a mug, signed on for life.

He was a man of stature small, very thin and not so tall
and walked around with his one stripe telling the new chaps all his tripe.
These new young lads were keen and bold and very eager to be told
just how to march and turn and halt. They never made a single fault.

The CSM, not of his choice, had then a very high-pitched voice
but Gregory went just one better, yelling orders to the letter
and with his shout he tried to prove "Around me in a half circle – MOVE!"
was the best way to show his rookies, who were very slow
just how to do the 'slope' and 'order'.

But, as we have said before, this is 1934
and in these days of musket drill, Greg really put them through the mill.
He used to throw his weight around and on the "Order Muskets" found
that as the butt plate hit the ground, it made a very dreadful sound.
But Greg soon had that sorted out and ever since there is no doubt
the movement's good without that clatter, 'cos now the banging noise don't matter.

One day while lecturing to his squad, he saw a chappie give a nod,
for with arms folded on his chest, the little lad was doing his best
and trying very hard to keep himself from going off to sleep.
Greg saw that he was uninterested, so once more his voice he tested.
"You'd better get a heave on Mister or else you'll be like my sister.
She did that quite unmolested, now she's finished up flat chested."

In later years Greg (friends called him 'Bill') got very hot on teaching drill.
He picked some blokes for "guard mounting", but none of them knew anything
so first he showed them how to hold a rifle correctly on the shoulder
which, in case you don't know where, is the space below left ear.
In this a hollow can be seen and in it goes the magazine.

It Started at The Savoy

This tale goes back to days of old and down the ages, it's been told
how God made Adam big and strong, not too short and not too long.
He was a very perfect gent for in his shoulder was a dent.
The reason for it he couldn't stifle, God knew one day he'd hold a rifle.

Though Greg has never been to war, his knowledge is quite far from poor.
He knows a lot of men and guns, and now he takes the OR1s
He takes the drilling on the square and though he sometimes makes us swear,
He says we're meant to be the cream and therefore held in high esteem.
Although he's trying to make us tough, he still says we're not good enough.
He's always looking for improvements in all the complicated movements.
If anyone is wrong or slow, he always takes great pains to show
exactly how it should be done, because the lad's an OR1
But then if someone's still behind, Greg very likely is inclined
to spout some phraseology, although it is quite meanlessly,
"The trouble with you is kiddo, too much of the five-fingered widow!"

With rifles too, it can be seen, Greg is also very keen
and it comes as no surprise, when he looks at you with squinted eyes.
"Hit the rifle good and hard! I've still to find two blokes for guard.
Your rifle does a loop-the-loop. I make more noise by drinking soup!"

Now, one day Greg was C.O.S. and spent all evening in the mess
While we were working very hard bulling kit up for the guard.
But still we hear at 10:15, "Get those lights out M13!"

The hours passed and came the morn and enter Greg with usual scorn
and seeing naught but rows of heads said, "Get sorted out! Stand by your beds!"
With bullshit too, he's on the ball, he will take no excuse at all
If belt and gaiters are not good and boots especially always should
be burnt and bulled up really well so that Gregory cannot tell you off for being mankey.
The pimples all should be removed and in Selection it was proved
the only really thorough way was to burn them every day.
Then, if all the bumps weren't out, on parade old Greg would shout...
"You'll burn those boots 'til they're in ruins. There's more wrinkles in 'em than a box of
pruins!"

Still, in his horrid little way, he brightens every dreary day
And what e're the future holds in store, though there's much skiving in the Corps,
It would never be the A.C.C. without Sergeant Gregory.

The End

Places of Employment in the United States

Florida

Colony Hotel, Palm Beach

Sandpiper Bay Resort, Port St. Lucie

Frances Langford's Outrigger Resort, Jensen Beach

Indian River Plantation, Stuart

Holiday Inn Oceanside, Jensen Beach

Holiday Inn, Downtown Stuart

New York

Delmonico Hotel, New York City

Forum of the XII Caesars, Rockefeller Center, New York City

New York World's Fair, Flushing Meadow

Connecticut

Mermaid Tavern and Stratford Motor Inn, Stratford

Arizona

Camelback Inn, Scottsdale

Executive House Hotel, Scottsdale

Valley Ho Hotel/Casa Blanca Inn/Scottsdale Ramada Inn/

Scottsdale Country Club/Safari Hotel, Scottsdale

The Carefree Inn, Carefree

Wisconsin

Playboy Club Hotel, Lake Geneva

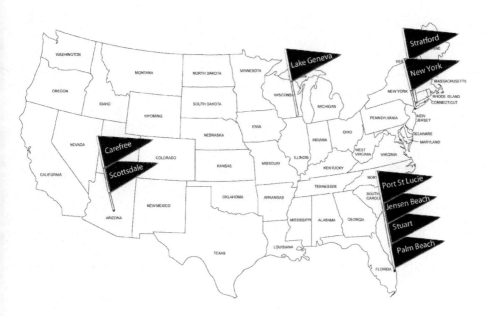

It Started at The Savoy

Made in the USA
Middletown, DE
07 April 2021